Business Diagnostics
4th Edition

THE ULTIMATE RESOURCE GUIDE TO
EVALUATE AND GROW YOUR BUSINESS

Richard Mimick
Michael Thompson
Terry Rachwalski

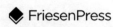
Suite 300 - 990 Fort St
Victoria, BC, V8V 3K2
Canada

www.friesenpress.com

Copyright © 2021 by Richard Mimick, Michael Thompson, Terry Rachwalski
First Edition — 2000
Fourth Edition — 2021

All rights reserved. No part of this publication may be reproduced in any form, or by any means, electronic or mechanical, including photocopying, recording, or any information browsing, storage, or retrieval system, without permission in writing from FriesenPress.

Considerable care has been taken to trace ownership of copyright materials contained in this text with the appropriate written permissions obtained and/or citations made. The authors will gladly accept any information that will enable them to rectify any missing reference or credit in subsequent editions.

This publication is designed to provide accurate and current information with regard to the subject matter. It is sold on the understanding that neither the publisher nor the authors are engaged in rendering financial, accounting, strategic or other professional services by way of this text. If financial, legal or strategic assistance is required, the services of a competent professional should be obtained.

ISBN
978-1-03-910400-6 (Hardcover)
978-1-03-910399-3 (Paperback)
978-1-03-910401-3 (eBook)

1. BUSINESS & ECONOMICS, MANAGEMENT

Distributed to the trade by The Ingram Book Company

PRAISE FOR *BUSINESS DIAGNOSTICS*

A major challenge to most business managers, especially those operating in the fast-paced world of high technology, is to find the time to learn good management practices while on the job; most people simply do not have the luxury of taking time off for formal training. Business Diagnostics addresses this critical need by packaging the essentials into a manageable text.

Denzil Doyle, Officer of the Order of Canada

Chairman, DoyleTech Corporation

Author - *Making Technology Happen*

Business Diagnostics highlights the importance of digital, content, and social media marketing. It is a go-to reference guide for businesspeople who need to do an evaluation of their operations.

Chris Burdge and Paul Holmes, Co-Founders of Social Media Camp, Canada's largest social media conference.

If you are the CEO of a small- to medium-sized company and want a pragmatic framework for sizing up the health of your business, then I suggest you look at Rich and Mike's gem of a book, Business Diagnostics. Track with the case study, use their novel size-up grids, and you will have the pulse on your corporate health and a sound framework for revitalizing your business.

T. John Drew

Former Chair, TEC (The Executive Committee), Victoria, B.C

Business Diagnostics introduces a powerful system on how to plan and grow your business. Today, more than ever in the highly competitive global marketplace that impacts all businesses, this book is mandatory reading. It is also an essential reference guide for executives and managers in all types of firms from SMEs to large corporations along with business students aspiring to managerial and entrepreneurial success.

Frank Bouree, CEO and Principal

Chemistry Consulting Group

Business Diagnostics is like a one-stop shop for diagnosing and finding the remedy to take your business from good to great and great to excellent! It takes the guessing out of where you need to take your business next!

Debrah Wirtzfeld MD MBA

Royal College of Physicians and Surgeons Canada

Business Diagnostics is an essential resource for businesses providing easy to navigate tools. The book offers applied and pragmatic solutions for businesses to navigate internal and external evaluations in addition to insight on the business planning and fundraising.

This is a well thought-out resource that I often refer to when planning 'what's next'.

Shannon Hood-Niefer, PhD, MBA

Vice President, Innovation and Technology

Saskatchewan FIDC

ABOUT THE AUTHORS

Rich Mimick

Rich Mimick is a founder and principal of PPM Professional Practice Management, Inc., a management consulting and executive development firm based in Victoria, BC. He commenced his consulting career with Andersen Consulting, now Accenture.

His academic appointments include Director and Professor at the world ranked Ivey Business School, Director of Royal Roads University Business Programs, and Director of University of Victoria's Executive Programs. He recently retired as Director, Business, Management and Technology programs, Division of Continuing Studies, University of Victoria.

Rich has designed, developed and delivered consulting engagements and executive programs for Canadian, American, European and Asian clients.

His areas of expertise are strategic management, finance and marketing strategy. He has received international recognition for his outstanding teaching abilities and is known for his exceptional ability to turn complex topics into understandable practical learning.

Rich also provides consulting assistance in strategy and finance to various companies. He is a director and advisory Board member of growth-oriented companies and a past director of VIATeC, the Vancouver Island Advanced Technology Centre.

Mike Thompson

Mike Thompson has recently retired as Associate Professor, Management Consulting with the Faculty of Management at Royal Roads University.

Prior to this appointment, he held senior management positions within commercial banking sectors in the U.K, Ontario, and British Columbia. His academic credentials include an Honours Degree in Economics from the University of Manchester and a Diploma in Land Economics from the University of British Columbia. Professional certifications include Fellow of Institute of Canadian Bankers (FICB) and Fellow Certified Management Consultant (FCMC).

He is a former Trustee representing CMC Canada within the International Council for Management Consulting Institutes (ICMCI). In 2013, he was awarded the prestigious ICMCI Academic Fellow designation in recognition of his commitment to the field of Management Consulting education.

In October 2020, he received the Lifetime Achievement Award from the Certified Management Consultants Association of B.C.

He also holds a visiting professor appointment at the Graduate School of Business, Grenoble, France.

TERRY RACHWALSKI

Terry Rachwalski is President of Front Porch Perspectives, a Canadian management consulting firm providing business development and go-to-market plans for technology firms. Terry specializes in developing sales and marketing strategy and action plans for new product launches.

She has worked extensively providing industry, market and competitive analyses along with digital reviews, social media launches and integrated marketing, advertising and public relations campaigns in Canada, the United States, Europe and Central America.

Prior to opening her management consulting company, Terry worked as an executive with multiple Canadian and international technology firms in progressive management, sales, marketing and operational roles. She is an award-winning Certified Management Consultant and holds an MBA from Royal Roads University, a certificate in Enterprise Development from Camosun College and a Diploma in Marketing from BCIT.

She is Associate Faculty at Royal Roads University School of Business in the MBA program running the problem-based learning section of the live consulting cases during the rigorous capstone project. She developed the CAPE model to assist clients determine whether web products can be monetized. In 2016, she joined Alberta Innovates Entrepreneurial Investments business unit to strengthen the province's innovation ecosystem with a series of interconnected programs offering coaching, community. This position is responsible for Alberta's investment fund supporting promising technology and accelerating high growth, high potential technology enterprise.

Contents

Preface And Acknowledgements ... Ix
Introduction ... 1

Section 1: The External Size Up ... 5
Chapter 1: The Business Environment ... 7
Chapter 2: Industry and: Competitive Conditions ... 17

Section 2: The Internal Size Up ... 27
Chapter 3: The Financial Evaluation ... 29
Chapter 4: Sales and : Marketing Strategy ... 49
Chapter 5:: The Operations Review ... 73
Chapter 6: Human Resources Management ... 89
Chapter 7: The Technology Assessment ... 103

Section 3: The Company Life Cycle and Related Funding Initiatives ... 115
Chapter 8: New Business Opportunities and Strategies ... 117
Chapter 9: Managing Growth ... 133
Chapter 10: Sources of Equity Funding ... 151
Chapter 11: Sources of Debt Financing ... 165
Chapter 12: Survival Strategies ... 181

Section 4: Strategic Planning ... 189
Chapter 13: Strategic and Business Planning ... 191

Section 5: Case Study ... 205

Appendix 1 : External/Internal Size Up & : Strategy Review ... 235
Appendix 2 : Current Company Valuation ... 249
Appendix 3: Enterprise Review Summary ... 253
Appendix 4: Preliminary Estimate Of Future Value From An Investor's Perspective ... 259

PREFACE AND ACKNOWLEDGEMENTS

Business Diagnostics was born out of a need to quickly and simply summarize business concepts for adult learners in fast-track business courses and a desire to help business owners. From that original concept drawn up over a couple of pints by Rich Mimick and Mike Thompson, *Business Diagnostics* has been used with hundreds of businesses, with over 30 live MBA cases, and has sold thousands of copies.

As we sat down to reimagine the fourth edition, we were in the middle of a pandemic with no end in sight. While the book has been popular, we sought to provide additional value, introduce new concepts and insights gleaned since the last edition was launched, and make *Business Diagnostics* available online for all those learners and business owners forced to adapt to a quickly changing world.

The Business Diagnostics Framework has been introduced to our live MBA cases at Royal Roads University, management consulting classes at the University of Victoria, and, more recently, it has informed Terry Rachwalski's leading-edge work at Alberta Innovates. Given the ever-changing global and national business environment, we have enhanced our framework as part of a broader Business Growth Road Map. Accordingly, this fourth edition links the Business Diagnostics Framework to the intersecting elements of business scale-up and growth.

As authors, our most prized moments occur when readers say, "this is the one business text I refer to the most and continue to use." That was our goal—to create a heavily thumbed, much used and prized desktop business reference guide. Today, our new goal is to extend our reach in providing a unique and essential online reference that will help businesspeople worldwide.

Whether you are a business student struggling to reference dozens of lengthy textbooks, a management team assessing prospects for scaling-up, or the owner of an existing business needing to size up your growth opportunities, *Business Diagnostics* provides a simple system through which to evaluate and grow your business.

Special thanks and acknowledgment are given to our respective spouses, Claudia, Trish, and Maurice for their patience and cheerful encouragement, and we remember the late Kathy, always in our hearts.

Richard Mimick, Michael Thompson, Terry Rachwalski. Victoria, B.C.

INTRODUCTION

The authors have designed *Business Diagnostics* as valuable reference content that can be easily read over a weekend or a few weekday evenings. The book is grounded in the Business Diagnostics Framework and each of the sections is stand-alone, providing a reference for each of the primary areas of business: strategy, finance, operations, human resources, marketing/sales, IT/technology plus an overview of scale-up and growth tactics, and how-to checklists for valuation and business planning.

Business Diagnostics has been written to overcome a significant challenge facing business owners and business students, specifically the time constraints in acquiring business management skills.

- Business owners have limited time or inclination to attend extended business school courses. Likewise, accessing topical information on enhancing corporate performance (books, magazines, and websites) can be sporadic and time-consuming, and the information may be out of context with the bigger picture.
- Business students take multiple courses over a short period of time, then are challenged to find the information in all the textbooks they own both in school and when they enter the workforce.

Business Diagnostics fourth edition has two primary audiences in mind:

1. Business owners–are now facing significant and daunting challenges as they navigate the perilous threats arising from the Covid pandemic. It is our view that today's business owner must take steps to build strategic resiliency—a critical first step is to complete a set of diagnostic checks to assess the relative health of the organization. By following the size-up process outlined in this book, the reader will be able to identify the key strengths and weaknesses of the business and then develop the necessary action plans to rebound and grow the enterprise.
2. Business students–the text provides a concise set of practical diagnostic tools to complement generic course materials. At the same time, the material will provide a fast track to understanding the fundamentals and challenges in running and growing a company.

This text has been used in the MBA program at Royal Roads University for 15 years and students consistently say, "*Of all the textbooks I bought, this is the one I refer to the most and continue to use.*" We trust the fourth edition and the online version will be as valuable.

Business Diagnostics provides practical insights into the following key areas:

Sections 1 and 2 provide step-by-step instructions on how to size up a business operation, and to assess its relative strengths and weaknesses.

- The External size up examines the business environment (political, economic, societal, and technological factors) along with prevailing industry conditions.

- The Internal size up then drills down into the individual company's performance, evaluating its relative health from different viewpoints–financial, marketing, operations, human resources, and technology.

Section 3 explains company life cycles and how the various sources of funding (equity and debt) can be accessed. Within company life cycles, Chapter 9 has been expanded with new content on scale-up and growth and includes the Business Growth Road Map, which builds on the Business Diagnostics Framework. Survival and turnaround strategies are also evaluated. Recognizing potential danger signals is increasingly important given today's rapidly changing business environment.

Section 4 provides tips and insights on the effective completion of strategic business plans.

Section 5 consists of a short case study of a fictitious company called Marston Control Devices Ltd. You can size up Marston Control Devices Ltd. using the Business Diagnostics Framework techniques covered in earlier sections to assess the company's health and prospects by completing optional size-up worksheets as part of the evaluation process. Try to apply the Business Growth Road Map to Marston.

Marston Control Devices Ltd. is also seeking investment capital. You have the opportunity to expand your size-up skills by completing a preliminary company valuation and reviewing the capital raising process by way of a tactical Enterprise Review Summary.

We have included an answer key that is based on the size-up templates for classroom use or to check your skills.

These five sections are interrelated and are summarized in the Business Diagnostics Framework graphic.

In the appendices, we provide the author's suggested size-up summaries, company valuations, and sample Enterprise Review Summary to round out the learning process.

The fourth edition of *Business Diagnostics* contains some updated materials and insights based upon the authors' teaching and consulting experiences since the original edition was published. Be sure to refer back to our website for more advice, tools, and templates at www.ceobusinessdiagnostics.com.

Business Diagnostics Overview

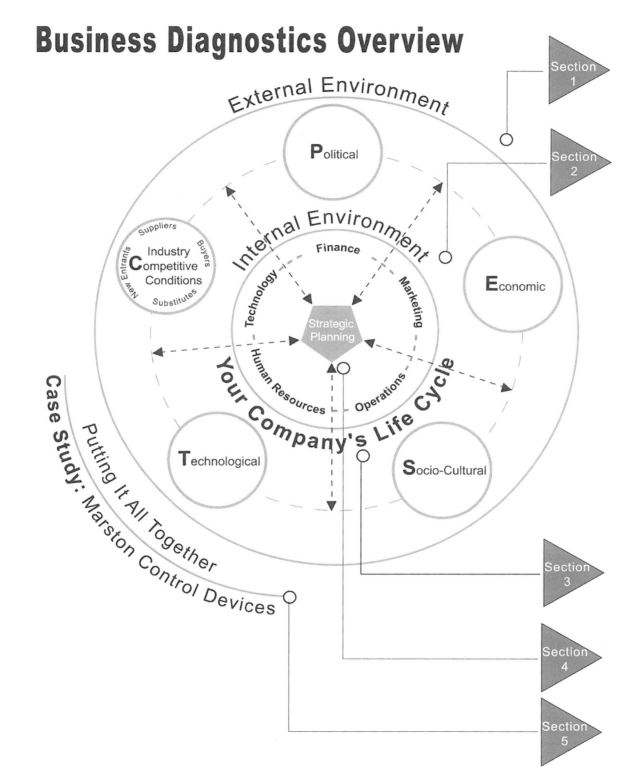

Figure 1. Business Diagnostics Framework

Section 1
The External Size Up

Business Diagnostics Overview

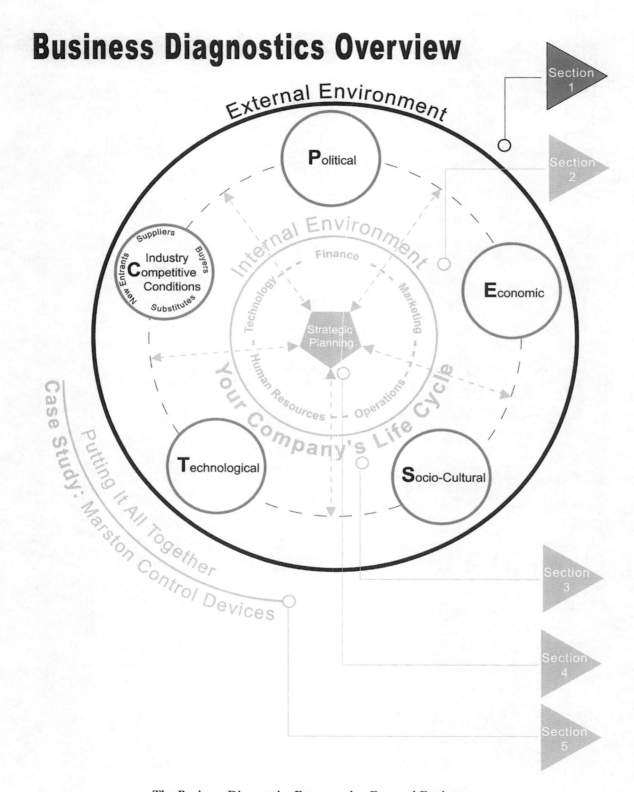

The Business Diagnostics Framework – External Environment

Chapter 1
The Business Environment

Overview

The first key element of the Business Diagnostics Framework, outlined in the introduction, is to do an external scan or size up of the company by looking at the big picture. The prevailing business environment, recent trends, and related industry conditions need to be critically reviewed by company management.

This chapter covers the outer ring of the Business Diagnostics Framework, which is a scan of the business environment you operate in. Think of it as an outer atmosphere that, while distinct from day-to-day company operations, exerts a significant impact on the company's prospects and performance.

A useful tool to assess the business environment is a PEST-C analysis, an easy-to- remember tool that encompasses the following five key areas:

- Political-Legal factors
- Economic forces
- Socio – cultural trends
- Technological considerations
- Industry and competitive conditions

Chapters 1 and 2 review the PEST-C elements, providing commentary and checklists of issues to consider. While some of these issues are industry specific (i.e., they relate to the industry within which a company operates or plans to operate), the focus remains on the big picture.

The PEST-C structure and the impact on an individual company is illustrated in Figure 3. For background, we start with the Chapter 1 PEST review before moving on to Chapter 2, the C part of the PEST-C, which describes how to analyze industry competitive conditions. In practice, since business people are likely familiar with the industry they operate in, these two reviews can be done concurrently. This practice can be helpful since information discovered in the PEST can be applied to industry competitive conditions, and vice versa, to connect data and provide insight.

PEST-C Additions and Alternatives.

There are a variety of ways to extend the PEST-C tool. Some analysts prefer to use a PEST-EL tool by adding specific environmental and legal sections or moving the letters around to get various iterations like SLEPT or STEEPLE. This is a decision based on the individual facts of the company you are analyzing. The PEST-C tool is typically sufficiently robust to encompass the intent of the other tools.

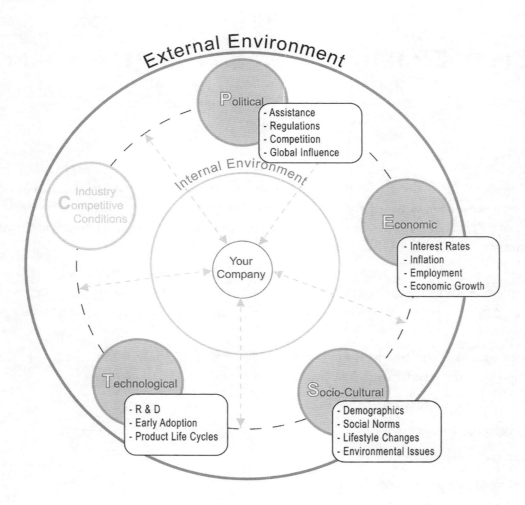

Figure 3. PEST-C – An Overview

POLITICAL-LEGAL FACTORS

The predominant political-legal factors are government influence and legal/regulatory issues that range from forces exerted by global governmental entities to federal to provincial/state and municipal entities or a combination of all four.

You should be aware that governments could exert influence in any of the following ways:
- Assist you
- Regulate you
- Compete with you
- Exert global influence that could affect you

Consider your company and the industry in which it operates and then review the following list to determine the extent to which government activities influence your business environment. It is also worthwhile to assess the extent of business-friendly policies implemented by your federal, provincial/state, or municipal governments.

- Is new legislation pending that may change policy approaches? What is driving proposed legislative changes?
- Will the political climate change in the near term? Are there pending elections that might affect your business or your industry? What are the potential impacts on your business?
- Are there global or societal trends that could lead to changes in government policy or how government acts or reacts internationally that could impact your business?

Government Assistance to Business.

In your review, you can research whether government support is available for any of the following aspects of your business:

- Industrial research
- Technological innovation
- Commercialization
- Marketing or management advice
- Productivity advancements
- Export opportunities
- Financing
- Employment programs

Be mindful that if grants or subsidies are available for you, they are also available to your competitors. What are your obligations or the conditions of the grant? How much time will it take you to complete the required paperwork and complete reporting requirements compared to the benefit of the grant funds?

Legal Regulation of Business.

Within your external scan, review and consider how the following regulatory mechanisms might impact your business:

- Taxation will reduce your return on investment and may increase or decrease your competitive advantage if your company faces lower or higher tax rates than your competition.

- Health and safety regulations or workplace regulations differ greatly in different jurisdictions.

- Environmental policies and controls may have incentives, fees, or penalties, or they might create potential project delays.

- Competition regulations can prohibit or regulate certain market practices.

- Consumer protection laws are created to discourage and penalize unfair business practices.

- Various securities laws and governance requirements protect investors and can have heavy compliance requirements.

- Intellectual property laws protect intangible assets via trademarks, patents, copyrights, and industrial design.

Government Competition with Business

Are there any government competitors operating in your industry that you should consider? Consider government-owned assets, industrial companies, and agencies. Government- or state-owned enterprises can be unpredictable competitors with deep pockets. Alternatively, privatization of government agencies can intensify competitive pressures by altering traditional buying and selling practices.

Further, how governments choose to design, build, manage, and fund infrastructure projects can often impact a business' ability to compete. For example, a government's move to use Public, Private Partnerships, also known as P3s, may make it more difficult for smaller construction companies to bid on infrastructure projects, work with different funding models, and absorb risk.

Government competition isn't always easy to spot. Consider how your business will interact or respond to existing or new government competition.

Government Global Influence

Governments can work together in multinational cooperation, or they can exert influence globally in ways that could affect your business. Consider how global governmental influences might affect your business.

- Significant political events like emerging political movements, terrorism, regional wars and conflicts, and trade sanctions can quickly change geo-political landscapes and government actions and policies.

- Instability from pandemics and other health crises can create a patchwork of governmental interventions that affect supply chains, production, and travel.

- Emerging global markets and competitors or declining market powers can cause disruption.

- Transnational bureaucracies and agencies can be created or dismantled and layer on regulations that may affect your business.

ECONOMIC FORCES

The state of the economy has an obvious impact on your business, yet many business owners are confused by the overwhelming weight of economic data and information available to them. There are over one hundred economic indicators published on a regular basis by financial and economic analysts and government agencies. This section clarifies key indicators by summarizing six areas of macroeconomic activity that will impact the business owner.

Key Macroeconomic Indicators.

Six areas of macroeconomic activity that will impact the business owner follow.

- Economic growth
- Price levels
- Interest rates
- Employment
- Government policy
- Global economic influences

Economic Growth.

The primary indicator of economic growth is Gross Domestic Product (GDP), which measures a country's economic output. This indicator is a consumption measure. It combines consumer and government spending, private investments, and subtracts imports from exports.

Real GDP recognizes that the effect of inflation on price levels has been removed, thereby providing a more accurate fix on actual economic growth. Typically, governments strive for sustainable economic growth, which means they don't want to grow too quickly because such growth can create inflation or too slowly because doing so can lead to high unemployment and recession.

Different economic agencies have different definitions though typically, two consecutive quarters (each of three months) of decline in GDP growth are generally considered to indicate the onset of a recession.

Price Levels.

The prevailing level of price inflation has a crucial effect on consumer confidence along with business revenue and earnings performance. The primary indicator is the Consumer Price Index (CPI), which is the traditional yardstick for tracking inflation.

The CPI measures the relative price increases of a basket of goods and services. The index's accuracy has been questioned for its susceptibility to interest rate swings, short-term erratic price fluctuations, and the extent to which energy and food costs have been included.

Inflation can be broadly segmented as follows:

Demand Pull: Prices are pulled up by strong consumer and business demand for goods and services.

Cost Push: Prices are pushed up by increased raw material and labour costs.

Interest Rates.

Interest rates have a key influence on economic activity. Both short- and long-term rates need to be considered.

Short-term (one to twelve months) interest rates are set by government banking entities like the Bank of Canada and/ or the U.S Federal Reserve Bank. They exert a significant impact on consumer credit and business borrowings.

Long-term (one to twenty years) rates follow corporate and government bond markets. These rates have a major impact on consumer big-ticket purchases and business expansion/capital expenditure decisions.

The relationship between short-term and long-term interest rates has historically been defined by a positive yield curve with short-term rates lower than long-term rates since investors typically require a greater reward to lock in investments for a longer time period.

An inverted yield curve occurs when short-term rates are higher than long-term rates and is often considered to be a precursor to a recession. Figure 4 provides a graphical representation of positive and negative yield curves.

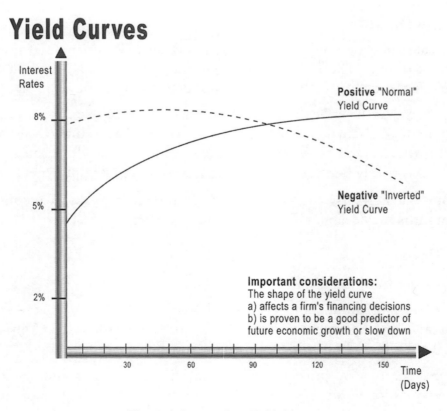

Figure 4. Interest Rate Yield Curves

Interest rates can have a significant impact on a company's financial performance and strategies. For example, in a rising interest rate environment, the company's ability to repay debt will be impaired since with higher interest costs, less principal will be paid back.

Even if an early-stage company has been funded by equity, as opposed to debt financing, increasing interest rates will tend to exert a dampening effect on overall economic growth prospects.

Employment.

The primary indicator of labour market health is the percentage of the available workforce that is unemployed. This will vary over time and in different countries. There are significant differences in the kinds of employment experienced by workers and the resulting impact on the economy. The following are examples of unemployment categories:

- Frictional unemployment: Workers are temporarily unemployed.
- Cyclical unemployment: Workers are without jobs due to downturns in business cycles (i.e. shipbuilding and the auto sector).
- Structural unemployment: People are out of work for long periods of time due to lack of skills (e.g. pursuing higher education) or fundamental changes in economic resources (e.g., energy, fisheries, and forestry).

Government Policy.

Governments change and with that change can come slight or drastic changes in policies, which can affect your business. Consider how these changes in the following areas might affect your business:

- The current levels of direct and indirect taxes and/or fees compared to competitors' countries.
- The potential for transfer payment cutbacks (federal to provincial/state to local governments).
- The level of government spending, which is impacted by current fiscal budget performance.
- The level of budget deficits, surpluses, and debt can cause considerable concern when the debt is held offshore.

Global Economic Influences.

While businesses tend to consider their regional and local government actions, global influences can have profound influence on your business. Consider these key areas in your assessment:

- The relative value of your currency versus that of your trading partner's jurisdiction has a major impact on exporters and importers. While short-term fluctuations are difficult to anticipate, longer-term trends can often be identified and hedged against by forward exchange rate contracts that are available through your bank.

- Trade agreements can upset your market and cause positive or negative ripples. Free trade areas versus economies that remain protected by tariffs and quotas are key considerations.

- Monopolistic multinational companies with enormous buying power and economies of scale can disrupt business quickly.

- Governments can impose preferential buy-at-home policies on departments and agencies to ensure local companies have opportunities.

- Economic shocks in resource-based economies can cause government and banking reactions that can upset business operations.

Socio-Cultural Trends

While some societal and cultural trends take time to unfold, others have sheer force, momentum, and speed of change that have significant implications for business owners. Consider the following items:

- The current world population is nearing eight billion with China and India accounting for approximately 35% of the total with unprecedented economic growth. What global population trends could affect you?

- Different countries have vastly different age profiles. How will this and other demographics affect your marketplace?

- Behavioural, lifestyle, and psychological factors are rapidly impacting purchasing patterns. What psychographic patterns will be important for your business?

- Purchasing decisions can be influenced by heritage and ethnic communities. How can your business adapt to changing influences?

- Social change is rapid in some areas and slow to be accepted in others. How will social structure changes affect your business? Consider how some of the following issues affect your business:
    - Online consumerism versus the buy-local and hand-crafted movements
    - Diverse family configurations
    - Desire to work to make a difference, not just an income
    - Remote work, co-working spaces, particularly in the post-pandemic world
    - Short-term work assignments, contracting, and the gig economy
    - Employee mobility
    - Prevalence of smartphones and social media
    - Workforce gender, equity, diversity, and inclusion
    - Housing costs in urban areas
    - Environmentalism and climate change

- Early/post retirement issues

TECHNOLOGICAL CONSIDERATIONS

It is crucial to follow current technology trends both outside and within your industry segments. Technology is being developed so quickly that it is difficult to keep up and watch for new competitors.

Moore's Law states that while prices keep constant, the processing power of microchips doubles every 18 months, with the result that our mobile devices have more memory and are faster than many personal computers were only a few years ago. Yet, with the advent of more processing power, battery life has not seen any major shifts. With more computing power and the Internet of Things (IoT) pushing sensors into more parts of our lives, energy harvesting, new computing architecture, and artificial intelligence are mainstream. Any business can be disrupted by new technology or technology that enables new business models, so it is critical that you monitor emerging technologies and how different technologies can be used together to create new products or processes. For example, fiber optics collided with laser technology to form the backbone of telecommunications and the Internet.

What are the technology developments and big disruptions that could affect your industry and your business? Understanding technology trends can help you create new product and market opportunities.

You can keep up with potential technology disruptions by taking the following actions:

- Reading technology blogs and magazines
- Following futurists
- Watching for industry technology updates

Technology can be used in your products or in your operations. As part of your continuing PEST analysis, be sure to monitor and record technology that needs to be on your watch list and consider opportunities to make technology moves before your competition.

Early adopters of new technologies often derive greater market share and improved returns on their capital investment. Businesses that use iterative and sustainable innovation processes that solve client problems tend to create more successful products, have improved productivity, and more often, are more profitable.

What are the technology issues that could impact your business? Technology can be used internally for productivity, but it can also drive product development and growth. The following are technology items to consider:

Operations

- How will your company exploit digital transformation and stay current on trends?
- What software and hardware do you need to increase productivity?

- How can your operations use technology to increase logistics performance, delivery, and transportation optimization?
- What other opportunities exist for process improvements and cost savings?
- How can you facilitate remote work?
- Can your company exploit technology opportunities to keep current in your industry and market as a part of your day-to-day operation?

Sales and Marketing

- How can you automate your marketing and sales functions and funnel?
- Can you use technology for repeatable go-to-market strategies and tactics?
- Can you anticipate customer needs using technology and increase sales forecasting accuracy?
- How will your customers find your business online?
- How will you improve the customer journey to keep your customers happy?
- How will you improve your customer experience to reduce churn?
- Can you use technology to acquire and retain customers and increase referrals?
- Can technology increase your repeat sales and upselling?

Product Development and Go-to-Market

- What are the Research and Development (R&D) requirements for your industry? How does your company compare with your competitors?
- How can technology help with product development and iteration?
- How might you use technology to validate whether consumers will buy your product?
- Can you monitor the results of your minimally viable product releases?
- Can you monitor results of shorter, faster product life cycles?

Finance

- What technology tools will increase monitoring and reporting on financial measures?
- Are there new tools to reduce friction in financing your company?

Human Resources

- What tools can help you hire and train employees and contractors?
- How can you assist in aligning each employee to their departmental and organizational goals?
- Are there employee engagement and retention tools you could use?

Chapter 2
Industry and Competitive Conditions

Overview

The next scan that is required to review the external business environment is an in-depth assessment of the industry segment in which your company operates followed by an analysis of the competitive conditions that exist. This is the C part of the PEST-C analysis, which is the outer ring of the Business Diagnostics Framework. Industry trends and risks have a fundamental impact on a firm's performance and strategy. It is important to remember that using the PEST-C tools and researching industry and competitive conditions are not done only one time. The concept of the Business Growth Road Map that is outlined in Chapter 9 and using the Business Diagnostics Framework is that you should be doing this research on a regular basis to zoom in and out of the process, impact, and measurement, always scanning for new ways to improve your business, find a new market niche, or grow your business.

Creating a document of your key findings will help you keep track of your industry over time and help you see recurring themes so you can better understand the industry and the opportunities and threats to your business. This type of document will also help you identify trends to take action on.

This section provides high-level industry evaluation tools and is followed by a more localized assessment of industry competitive conditions and the key factors for success in the industry. We also address the importance of defining your competitive advantages and determining how you measure up to competitors in your industry segment.

Rounding out this process is a review of the industry assessment models that are detailed in the *Blue Ocean Strategy* by W. Chan Kim and Renee Mauborgne.

Industry Evaluation

An industry evaluation examines the characteristics and trends found in your industry sector. The following assessment process is suggested:

- Complete an industry description. This concise summary identifies the industry's market size and growth. Other factors to consider include the industry geographic scope, number of direct and indirect competitors, the pace of technological change, innovation, and the number and size of buyers and sellers.
- Assess typical capital requirements. Is the industry fixed asset or working capital intensive? Or both?

Ask yourself the following questions:

- How profitable are companies in the industry?
- How quickly does this industry change?
- Which of the PEST factors are most relevant and important? Determine how vulnerable your industry is to the external PEST factors that were covered in the first chapter:
  - Macroeconomic conditions
  - Political, legal, or regulatory issues
  - Social or demographic influences
  - Environmental concerns and /technological trends

Consider the life-cycle stage of the industry and the segment you operate in. By examining the product, service, and market life-cycle stages, you can pinpoint the present age of your industry segment. What opportunities or threats does the assessment present? Industries typically go through the following stages:

  - Early stage
  - Growth
  - Consolidating/shake-out
  - Maturity
  - Decline

- Conduct an industry business system analysis. This analysis identifies the supply and distribution channels used in the industry segment and assesses which are the most efficient.
- Assess the driving forces in your industry. These are factors that may exert major future change in your industry segment. These driving forces can be assessed to determine either a positive (+) or negative (-) influence on the industry. The following examples show some of the driving forces:
  - Globalization or nationalization of industry segments
  - Significant change in buyer's tastes and needs

- Changes in societal attitudes
- Changes in pricing models
- Significant changes in business models
- New methods of marketing or distributing products
- Entry, exit, or merger of major firms
- Fundamental changes in government regulatory policies
- New technologies that open up new values and benefits

INDUSTRY COMPETITIVE CONDITIONS

Having completed the industry evaluation, the next step is to assess the competitive environment. The key question to answer is whether this is an attractive industry that we want to operate within, given the relative intensity of competition.

There are multiple tools and frameworks that can be used to make sense of the information found. The tool itself is less important than the analysis of the information you find. We encourage you to explore different tools and ways to display the information in a way that helps you improve your analysis.

One way to analyze an industry is to group industry information into categories and determine what are the most important Key success factors (KSFs) in this industry.

Key success factors (KSFs) are special skills and resources that must be possessed to gain a competitive advantage in a particular industry segment. All firms in the particular industry sector must pay close attention to them: KSFs are competitive factors that determine whether industry participants will be financially and strategically successful. They can also offer a differentiator if you discover that a KSF is not actually needed. For example, quality expectations may be different for different market segments and buying personas. Industry key success factors include the following examples:

- Cost structure
- Quality expectations
- Unique technology requirements along with intellectual property protection
- Specialized manufacturing processes
- Proximity to materials, skilled employees, and markets
- Effective and efficient distribution channels
- Highly skilled workforce
- Ability to navigate regulatory approval processes
- Favourable image and reputation with clients

As an example, the wine industry has the following desired KSFs:

- Efficient, high-quality winemaking capacity
- Grape supply and comprehensive distribution network
- Creative promotion tactics to differentiate in an overcrowded marketplace

In the wine industry, to compete successfully, a company must possess all three of these KSFs, but to have competitive advantage, it must execute these KSFs distinctively better than competitors.

Another effective way to assess competitive forces within an industry segment is to use Michael Porter's Five Forces model. This model provides a framework that allows the analysis of the primary competitive forces prevalent within an industry segment. Figure 5 illustrates the relationship between various companies that operate within a specific industry segment, which, in turn, is impacted by various competitive forces.

The Five Forces are listed below along with some reflective questions that allow you to gauge the relative intensity of the forces.

1. **Threat of new entrants**
   - What are the barriers to entry into this industry?
   - Are there large amounts of capital or knowledge required to enter?
   - Do existing players have the ability for competitive retaliation via pricing or new product strategies?
   - Is it difficult to obtain the necessary skilled personnel or materials?
   - Is it difficult to get regulatory approvals?

2. **Bargaining power of customers**
   - How much power do buyers have?
   - Will customers face significant switching costs (inconvenience) to other sellers?
   - Do your customers recognize your product as unique?
   - Are there multiple other sellers available to customers?

3. **Bargaining power of suppliers**
   - How much power do suppliers have?
   - Are material/labour inputs standard, or are they unique and differentiated?
   - Do purchases and direct labour within the Cost of Goods Sold (COGS), have a significant impact on overall costs?
   - Is there potential to switch between suppliers quickly and cheaply?
   - Are there other potential suppliers or alternative inputs?

4. **Threat of substitute products**
   - How do customers solve the problem now?
   - Are customers unlikely or unable to switch to substitute products offered by firms in other industries or different types of products?

- Will customers incur costs when switching to substitutes?

5. **Intensity of rivalry among existing competitors**
- What competitive response can be expected?
- Is the industry segment growing rapidly, thereby accommodating new competitors?
- Is competition local, national, global, or online?

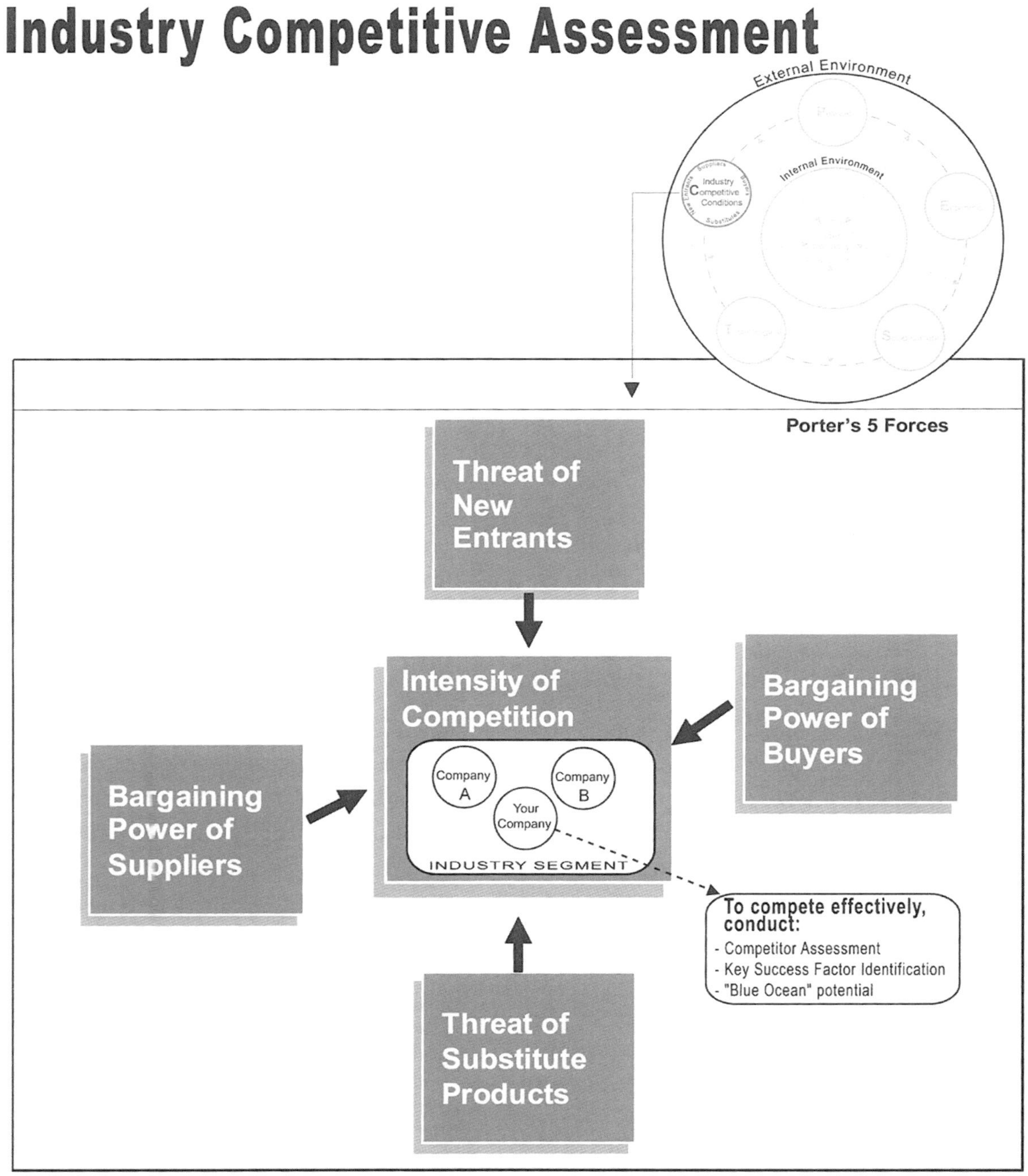

Industry Competitive Assessment

Figure 5. Industry Competitive Assessment

To assess the level of competition in your industry segment, you can create a simple table like the one in Figure 6 to rank each of the forces as low, medium, or high risk. For example, if it is unlikely that there will be new entrants to the market, circle low to indicate that this factor is favourable.

	Favorable	Neutral	Unfavorable
Threat of New Entrants	Low	Medium	High
Bargaining Power of Customers	Low	Medium	High
Bargaining Power of Suppliers	Low	Medium	High
Threat of Substitutes	Low	Medium	High
Intensity of Rivalry between Competitors	Low	Medium	High

Figure 6. Evaluation of Industry Competitive Conditions

Using Figure 6 will give you a visual indication of what forces are in your favour and where risk needs to be mitigated.

- If you determine that the threat of new entrants is low, this would be considered a favourable influence, allowing your firm to survive and prosper in its particular industry segment.

- Likewise, if you determine that the bargaining power of suppliers is high, this would be considered an unfavourable influence and should lead you to consider strategies to overcome their bargaining power and influence. One solution might be to reduce supplier power by adopting a business-to-business (B2B) consortia-purchasing model or to actively seek different parts, inputs, or resources that could reduce the power of suppliers.

After understanding the competitive forces individually, it is useful to consider the impact of all Five Forces of competition collectively. In general, the stronger the collective impact of the five competitive forces, the harder it is for rival companies in this industry to be profitable. A classic example is the restaurant industry where the Five Forces are generally unfavourable and many operators struggle to maintain a profitable performance. The key point here is that the more your company's strategy insulates you from competitive pressures, the more effective it will be.

An addition to Porter's Five Forces, called the sixth force concept—from Brandenburger and Nalebuff—describes complementers or co-opetition. These products or companies can be put together or partner to make a better total product offering. This is common in technology partnerships where a company may license various parts and components to create a single product.

Competitor Assessment

After reviewing your industry's competitive environment, the next step is to complete an assessment of the identified competition. A useful process is to determine what factors or influences have contributed to the competitive strength of your industry peers. Consider the following questions:

- Do your competitors have better economies of scale?
- Are they more productive and efficient?
- Do they have sufficient financial resources to not only meet working capital requirements, but to deter new entrants?
- What are their human resource capabilities and availability of their workforce?
- Do they have any government regulatory protection?
- Do they have superior distribution channels?
- Do they have a stronger brand image or marketing that differentiates them?
- How often do they introduce new products or innovations?
- How effective is their customer service?
- Have they communicated a defined future strategic objective?

To gain an accurate fix on competition and industry segment trends, consider the following useful intelligence sources:

- Ask Your employees. They will likely have current knowledge about your competition and how they measure up in your industry segment.
- Ask your customers how you measure up against your competitors.
- Determine how active competitors are at trade and industry exhibitions and congresses. Who are the key influencers? What topics do they present in poster sessions, papers, or speeches?
- Review conference notes and proceedings for clues to new technology, research, or discoveries from your competition.
- Review industry associations, journals, and magazines.
- Check commercial databases, research services, consulting group reports, and analyst updates.
- Research and compare competitors' online presence and websites. Use online tools to check if they have run any online advertising campaigns and how their website ranks against other sites in the same industry or industry category.
- How active are your competitors on social media? What networks are they on? Are they effectively telling their story online? How influential are they?
- Does your competition have a sophisticated and effective online or industry presence?

COMPETITIVE ADVANTAGE

Any product has to solve a problem for a customer who is willing to pay enough for the product that you will make a profit. The starting point for your competitive advantage is the value proposition for your customer. This is a clearly worded statement of what value your customers will get from your product, the benefit to them, and why they should buy from you. A value proposition is one of the tools to help you better understand your customer and the value you bring them with your product or service. Many companies agonize over their value proposition. While it is important, it isn't the wording that matters so much as the identifiable and validated problem you are solving.

To grow and prosper in your industry segment, it is crucial to create and maintain a strong, sustainable, competitive advantage over your competitors. Another way to assess your competitors and your relative competitive advantage is to review your industry's key success factors (KSFs) that were discussed in the Industry Competitive Conditions section and compare your results to your competition.

Simple Multi-Attribute Rating Technique (SMART Model).

One useful tool for comparing your company against the competition is a Simple, Multi-Attribute Rating Technique (SMART model). Typically, a SMART model has key success factors, determined from your industry research, listed on the left and your various competitors listed on the top. Based on your research, decide what the key success factors are and assign a weight or relative importance to each criterion.

As an example, take the three key success factors for the wine industry: quality, distribution network, and promotion. Assign weights to each factor. In this example, we have assigned the following weights based on our considerable experience buying wine.

Key Success Factor	Weight
Quality	30%
Distribution Network	20%
Promotion	50%

Next, assess your company and competitors on their performance in each of the factors out of a total of ten. You can use one hundred if you need more granularity though a total of ten works for this example. As indicated in the following table, you take each score, and multiply it by the assigned weight.

Key Success Factor	Weight	My Business		Competitor 1		Competitor 2	
Quality	30%	8	2.4	8	2.4	4	1.2
Distribution Network	20%	5	1	8	1.6	5	1
Promotion	50%	4	2	8	4	8	4
Total score			5.4		8		6.2

Key Success Factor example

In this example, competitor one is the clear industry leader in all three KSFs with a total score of eight. However, you can see that while competitor two has terrible quality, their sophisticated promotion makes them a threat. This means we can increase our competitiveness if we increase our promotion.

Some might argue that the weightings are arbitrary and can skew results. This is true; however, the tool can be refined over time and creates a visual indicator to compare your results against your competition to see which KSFs need to be improved. Your focus is to be distinctively, quantifiably, better than your competitors on one or two of the KSFs that make a difference to your customers and your business operation.

COMPETITIVE MAP

Once you have gathered information on your competitors, you can use different techniques and tools to help you visualize your relative strength and advantages. One tool is to create a competitive map, which is also known as a competitive strategy canvas, that consists of a horizontal and vertical axis to graphically illustrate where your opportunity to operate with fewer competitors is found.

You can map your competitors based on different criteria and axes determined by your research. You may want to create several competitive maps with different criteria to test out different scenarios.

For example, the horizontal axis could capture the range of factors that an industry competes on and invests in. Within the wine industry, the competitive map would track factors like the need for a refined packaging image, the aging and quality of the wine, and the prestige of the wine vineyard. The vertical axis could capture the price categories across the competing factors that are detailed on the horizontal axis.

An alternative is to do a perceptual map that uses factors based on user perceptions of the product rather than key success factors. Perceptions might include perceived value for dollar or prestige.

Potential for a Blue Ocean Strategy

Your goal is to increase your success and reduce becoming mired in competitive challenges. Another framework to help you map your success path is based on the book *Blue Ocean Strategy: How to Create Uncontested Market Space and Make the Competition Irrelevant* (Kim and Mauborgne, 2004).

The central message is that leading companies will succeed, not by battling competitors, but by creating blue oceans of uncontested market space that is ripe for growth. This is in dramatic contrast to many of today's overcrowded industries where head-on competition results in nothing more than a bloody, red ocean of rivals fighting over a shrinking profit pool.

The Blue Ocean Strategy consists of the following six principles:

1. Reconstruct market boundaries—Break from the competition and the accepted boundaries that define how you can compete.

2. Focus on the big picture—Move from a smorgasbord of tactics to the preparation of a strategy canvas that unlocks the creativity of people within the organization.

3. Reach beyond existing demand—Instead of concentrating only on existing customers, you need to explore non-customers and an expanded view of value for the client. An example is how Callaway Golf found a new target market for its golf clubs by looking to who were looking for a large club head to improve their golf game. Instead of marketing to great golfers, they created the Big Bertha club for those golfers who needed a more forgiving club. Callaway has continued to iterate the club and its marketing over the subsequent years.

4. Get the strategic sequence right—Ask the following questions:

- Is there exceptional buyer utility in your business idea?
- Is your price easily accessible to the majority of buyers?
- Can you attain your cost targets?
- What are the adoption hurdles in implementing your business idea?

5. Overcome organizational hurdles—Be sure to understand the need to win employees trust and commitment when developing your strategy, so you don't fall back into the status quo.

6. Build execution into strategy—Minimize the management risk of distrust and non-cooperation.

The test to determine if you can implement an effective Blue Ocean Strategy is captured by the following three characteristics:

- Is there focus? – Southwest Airlines emphasizes their wheels-up strategy, understanding that their revenue was only realized when the wheels on the plane are up. Friendly service, speed, and frequent point-to-point departures are add-ons to the wheels-up strategy.

- Is there divergence? – Is there something that you can do that diverges from the rest of the industry or competitors? Southwest pioneered point-to-point travel between less expensive mid-size city airports versus the industry norm of operating through a hub-and-spoke system in expensive major airports.

- Can the strategy be summed up with a simple pitch? Consider the compelling tagline. While marketing taglines change, one of Southwest Airlines' slogans has been "Low fares. Nothing to hide. That's TransFarency," which is directly related to their wheels-up focus.

Section 2
The Internal Size Up

Chapter 3
The Financial Evaluation

Chapter 3 deals with the financial health of your company—a crucial component to your survival and success. The purpose is to give you a refresher or new insights into your corporate finances. While you may want to delegate finance operations to an accountant, business leaders need to have a fundamental understanding of their finances and the language of finance. We look at six key areas, starting with break-even analysis and completing the chapter with a discussion of capital budgeting.

1. **Break-Even Analysis**

   We provide a concise explanation of the relationship between revenue and fixed/variable costs.

2. **Financial Statements**

   This section provides an overview of the balance sheet, income statement, and statement of cash flows along with a brief summary of the available types of financial statement presentations.

3. **Financial Ratio Analysis**

   The six key indicators of your corporate financial health are presented. We also demystify ratio analysis and show you how to build an effective diagnostic toolbox.

4. **Managing Cash Drivers**

   We provide some useful tips to manage your working capital and outline the concepts of cash cycles.

5. **Financial Projections**

   This section is an overview of proforma balance sheet, income and cash flow statements that forecast your anticipated financial performance in the future.

6. **Capital Investment Analysis**

    This section gives an overview of long-term investment decision making.

BREAK-EVEN ANALYSIS

A break-even analysis is used to understand the relationship between revenue and fixed/variable costs. All organizations incur various costs in order to operate. Break-even analysis is a managerial technique that separates costs into fixed and variable components. At a certain level of activity, revenues are equal to the total costs, fixed plus variable. At that level of activity, the organization is at its break-even point. It has covered all its costs but has not made a profit or surplus. Generally, costs can be broken down into two categories, fixed costs and variable costs.

> **Fixed costs** are costs that, in total, remain much the same over some relevant range of activity levels. For example, office rent will stay the same over the year no matter what level of service is provided. Additional examples of fixed costs include salaries, as distinct from hourly wages, property taxes, depreciation expenses, and lease costs.
>
> **Variable costs** are costs that vary with activity volume changes. These costs can generally be expressed as cost per unit or as a percentage of revenue.

Example: It takes a certain number of dollars worth of materials (paper, ink, labour wages) to produce a book. If the variable cost of producing a book is $10, a print run of 100 books would incur variable costs of $1,000 while a run of 1,000 books would incur variable costs of $10,000.

Some costs can be semivariable, or semifixed.

Example: If a retail outlet in a shopping mall pays $1,000 per month rent plus 5% of monthly gross sales, the $1,000 is fixed, and 5% of each month's sales amount paid is variable. Electricity costs and salary plus commission-style compensation plans are other examples of semivariable costs.

Figure 8 provides a graphical view of break-even analysis and indicates the break-even point. The total fixed costs are fixed over a range of activity volume (units), as indicated by the horizontal line. In addition, each unit sold incurs a variable cost. As volume increases, the total variable costs increase. The break-even point is where total revenues equal total costs and is indicated by the point where the revenue line intersects with the total cost line.

Point A at the bottom of the graph shows the volume level in activity units required to be sold in order to break even. Point B indicates the dollar amount of revenues required to break even. If the number of units sold exceeds the volume at the break-even point, a profit or surplus is generated. Alternatively, if the number of units fails to meet the break-even volume, a loss or deficit occurs.

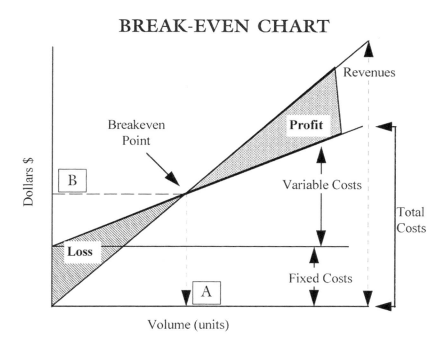

Figure 8. Break-Even Chart

Contribution Margin Analysis.

Understanding the break-even point is an input to understanding contribution margin. Contribution margin is the amount left over from a unit sale after its variable cost is covered. This remaining contribution then goes to cover fixed costs. Therefore, selling price (SP) minus unit variable cost (UVC) equals the unit contribution margin (UCM).

Example: If a book is sold for $100 and has a variable cost of $60, the difference of $40 is the unit contribution margin (UCM) that is available to cover total fixed costs.

If total fixed costs are $10,000, it will take $10,000 divided by the $40 UCM or 250 books to break even. Each and every book sold contributes $40 towards fixed costs. If more than 250 books are sold, each book sold over the 250 break-even volume contributes $40 to profit (surplus). Thus, if 300 books are sold, the organization has a profit (surplus) of $2,000 ($40 UCM x 50 units over the break-even point). Understanding this concept allows us to change any of the items and assess the impact.

For example, if we thought that variable costs would rise to $65 and we wanted to earn a profit (surplus) of $4,000, we can easily calculate the impact:

Selling price or SP	$100
Minus unit variable cost or UVC	65
Equals unit contribution margin or UCM	$35

- Fixed costs + desired profit = $14,000 ($10,000 + $4,000).
- $14,000/$35 = 400 books need to be sold to meet our objective.
- This translates into $40,000 in revenues (400 books x $100 selling price).

Another approach is on a percentage basis. If the unit contribution margin (UCM) is 35% of the selling price, by dividing the amount required to be covered ($14,000) by .35, we arrive at the required $40,000 figure.

Key points to remember:

- The lower the break-even point, the less vulnerable the firm is to unexpected cost increases.
- The more costs that can be made variable (i.e., occur only once a sale is made), the better.
- Strive to keep the contribution (gross profit) margin high and the break-even point low.
- Minimize fixed costs.

Financial Statements

Financial statements are essential tools that are used to analyze and assess your business performance.

- Lenders require them to expedite loan applications.
- Company owners need them to track financial performance and to determine their financial health.
- Suppliers often want to review them in order to grant credit and to ensure that new clients can pay them.
- Clients may check them to reassure themselves that their key suppliers will be around for a while.

The following three separate, yet closely interrelated, financial statements, will be reviewed:

- **The balance sheet** provides a snapshot of a company's financial position at a set point in time.
- **The income statement**, also known as a profit and loss or P&L Statement, reveals the company's revenue, expenses, and profit performance over a specific period of time.
- **The cash flow statement** indicates how much and by what means cash was generated by the company over a specific time and how it was used.

The Balance Sheet.

The balance sheet lists and totals the assets, liabilities, and owners' equity at the end of an operating period (i.e. December 31st, 2016 in the examples). The relationship between assets and liabilities is shown by the following formula.

ASSETS – LIABILITIES = OWNERS' EQUITY

Assets consist of cash and items you can easily convert into cash, like securities and Accounts Receivable, and include items like inventory, equipment, or machinery that you need to make products and provide services. Assets on the balance sheet are usually listed in order of how quickly each can be converted into cash or liquidity.

Liabilities are amounts owed by the company and are usually classified as current liabilities, which are due within one year, or long-term liabilities, which are listed according to how soon each liability has to be repaid.

Owners' or shareholders' equity reflect the funds contributed to the company for ownership interest as well as the accumulation of profits or losses derived in the past (retained earnings).

Figure 9 shows an example of a balance sheet.

ABC Company
Balance Sheet
As of December 31, 2016
(thousands of dollars)

Assets		2015		2016	Change
Current Assets:					
Cash		$ 4,000		$ 1,800	-$ 2,200
Marketable securities		$ 2,000		$ 2,000	
Accounts receivable		$ 4,000		$ 5,000	$ 1,000
Inventory		$ 4,000		$ 4,600	$ 600
Prepaid expenses		$ 200		$ 200	
Total Current Assets		$ 14,200		$ 13,600	-$ 600
Property, Plant, And Equipment					
Historical cost	$ 10,000		$ 12,000		
Less accumulated depreciation	$ 6,000	$ 4,000	$ 6,400	$ 5,600	$ 1,600
Other Assets					
Investment in subsidiary		$ 800		$ 800	
Total Assets		$ 19,000		$ 20,000	$ 1,000
Liabilities & Owners' Equity					
Current Liabilities:					
Accounts payable		$ 600		$ 1,000	$ 400
Accrued expenses		$ 2,600		$ 2,400	-$ 200
Current portion of long-term debt		$ 400		$ 400	
Total Current Liabilities		$ 3,600		$ 3,800	$ 200
Long-term Debt		$ 4,000		$ 3,600	-$ 400
Total Liabilities		$ 7,600		$ 7,400	
Shareholders' Equity:					
Capital Stock	$ 4,000		$ 4,000		
Retained Earnings	$ 7,400	$ 11,400	$ 8,600	$ 12,600	$ 1,200
Total Liabilities & Shareholders Equity		$ 19,000		$ 20,000	$ 1,000

Figure 9. Balance Sheet

Income Statement (Profit or Loss).

- The income statement indicates how much money the company made or lost over a reporting period.

- The statement shows revenues that were generated from selling goods and/or services with the Cost of Goods Sold (COGS), operating expenses, financing costs, and taxes deducted to arrive at a net income figure.

Profit, earnings, and income are terms that are often interchanged and for the purposes of this chapter, essentially have the same meaning. Figure 10 shows the key components of an income statement:

```
ABC Company
Income Statement
For the year ending December 31, 2016
(thousands of dollars)

Net Sales                                    $ 20,000
Cost of goods sold                           $ 14,000
Gross Profit                                 $  6,000

Operating Expenses:
  Selling              $ 1,200
  Administrative       $ 2,000
  Depreciation         $   400              $  3,600

Income from operations                       $  2,400
Interest expense                             $    400
Income before taxes                          $  2,000
Income tax expense                           $    800

Net Income                                   $  1,200
```

Figure 10. Income Statement

The Cash Flow Statement.

The cash flow statement is also known as a statement of changes in financial position. Remember that revenue is not necessarily received when it is earned, and expenses are not always paid when they are incurred, so it is important to chart the inflow or outflow of cash experienced by the company. The following statement shows the flows of cash, both sources and uses of cash, within a company for an operating period of one year. Make note of how the cash flows relate with the changes to the balance sheet and to the income statement as outlined previously.

```
                    ABC Company
                 Statement of Cash Flow
          For the year ending December 31, 2016
                   (thousands of dollars)

Cash flow from Operations:
    Net income                              $     1,200
    Depreciation (non cash item)            $       400
                                            $     1,600
    Changes in:
        Accounts receivable                 $    (1,000)
        Inventory                           $      (600)
        Accounts payable                    $       400
        Accrued expenses                    $      (200)

Net cash provided by Operations             $       200

Cash flows from investing activities:
    Purchase of capital assets              $    (2,000)

Net Cash from financing activities:
    Repayment of long-term debt                    (400)

Net cash provided (used)                    $    (2,200)
```

Figure 11. Cash Flow Statement

Types of Financial Statements

While financial statements provide critical information to company owners, the basis of presentation and the source of the information deserve careful consideration.

- Basis of presentation

    Company owners need to ensure that their financial statements are prepared in accordance with the laws and rules in the jurisdiction in which they operate. Fundamental principles and rules from the International Financial Reporting Standards (IFRS) and under Generally Accepted Accounting Principles (GAAP) ensure that financial data is consistently presented, allowing meaningful comparison between time periods.

    The key principle of full disclosure compels management to ensure that all liabilities and material facts are presented.

- The source and integrity of the information

    In Canada, you will encounter three types of financial statements that provide different levels of comfort to their readers.

    a. Notice to reader

The Notice to reader financial statement is essentially a compilation of the company owners' financial records with no verifications or with only limited investigation completed by the external accountant.

b. Review engagement

The Review Engagement financial statement provides greater comfort by reflecting certain tests and verifications that are completed by the accountant and accompanied by detailed explanatory notes. The resulting financial statements are the most common form of presentation and are usually acceptable to most investors, bankers, or suppliers.

c. Audited financial statements:

These are the most expensive and comprehensive financial statements and are normally completed by large private firms, public companies, and government institutions.

In the United States, the formats are generally the same though referred to as review, compiled, and audited statements.

Financial Ratio Analysis

Ratio analysis allows measurement of comparative performance over selected time periods. For example, by comparing the current ratio over time, positive or negative trends can be identified and acted on. It is important to ensure that the same time periods and time of year are used, for example, compare the same twelve-month period or fiscal period.

To effectively assess a company's relative financial health, we present six key indicators that you should consider:

- Profitability and cash flow
- Liquidity
- Stability
- Debt service
- Efficiency
- Growth

These key indicators are presented along with brief explanations. The financial ratios or financial diagnostic tests which are pertinent to each category are also provided.

Profitability and Cash Flow

1. Gross profit

- Indicates the total profit margin available to cover operating expenses.

- Reflects product line pricing decisions and/or the impact of purchases/materials on price levels. This is an indicator of the gross margin performance.
- The formula is: ((Sales − Cost of Goods Sold) ÷ Sales) x 100 = (%)

2. Net profit or the bottom line

- Shows after tax profits per $ of sales (%).
- Below expected standard performance points to weak sales performance, relatively high costs, or both.
- Also stated as net income or earnings.
- The formula is: (Profit after Taxes × 100) ÷ Sales = (%)

3. Return on equity

- Measures the rate of return on a shareholders' investment in the company.
- Compares whether the return compensates for risk in relation to other investments such as government bond returns.
- The formula is: (Profit after Taxes × 100) ÷ Total Shareholders Equity = (%)

4. EBITDA

- EBITDA is an acronym for Earnings before interest, taxes, depreciation, and amortization.
- It indicates the effective cash flow that a company generates on an annual basis.
- There is a more complex and sophisticated step that uses a free cash flow measurement. This calculates the company's annual cash flows by including changes in Accounts Receivable, inventory, and Accounts Payable (which are working capital items). The use and application of more advanced indictors is beyond the scope of this text.

Liquidity

Liquidity is defined as the ability to meet short-term obligations, and it measures the relationship between current assets and current liabilities. Working capital is the total liquidity available to run day-to-day business operations.

Working Capital

- Reveals the balance between liquid assets and claims of short-term creditors.
- Is derived by deducting current liabilities from current assets.
- The current ratio formula is: Current Assets ÷ Current Liabilities
- A current ratio over 1.5:1 is normally a positive indicator, although the nature and relative liquidity of the current assets need to be considered.
- The quick ratio demonstrates a firm's ability to pay off short-term obligations without reliance on the need to sell inventory.
- The Quick Ratio formula is: (Current Assets - Inventory) ÷ Current Liabilities

Stability

Stability refers to the relationship between debt and equity. Businesses typically need more money to grow, and they can get that capital from their shareholders or by leveraging debt. Depending on the industry, this simple measure will help lenders and investors understand how the business is capitalized.

1. **Debt to Equity Ratio**
   - Measures the relationship between debt and equity.
   - Indicates the extent of funds that are provided by creditors (debt) and company owners (equity).
   - Leverage varies from industry to industry—under 2.5:1 is normally a reasonable comfort zone.
   - The Debt to Equity formula is: Total Liabilities ÷ Total Equity

   Note: Intangible assets such as patents, goodwill, and so on should be deducted from the equity number.

2. **Total Debt/EBITDA Ratio**
   - Measures the relationship between debt and cash flow to indicate the time frame over which debt is retired from cash flow.
   - The formula is: Total Liabilities ÷ EBITDA

Note: The EBITDA number is often trimmed back by deducting annual capital expenditures (abbreviated as *capex*) that reoccur on a regular basis. This provides a more accurate indication of cash generation for the year period.

Debt Service

Debt service refers to the ability of a company to pay interest and principal on its debt obligations, and it is a key indicator of financial health.

1. **Interest Coverage**
   - Demonstrates the extent that annual cash flow covers debt interest obligations.
   - The formula is: EBITDA ÷ Annual Interest

2. **Debt Service Coverage**
   - Reveals the extent that annual cash flows cover annual required debt payments (principal and interest).
   - The formula is: EBITDA ÷ Annual Principal and Interest payments

Note: Annual capital expenditures can also be deducted from the EBITDA number to derive a more accurate cash generation figure.

Efficiency

Efficiency formulas measure the effective management of working capital items such as Accounts Receivable, Inventory, Accounts Payable.

1. **Accounts Receivable Collection**

- Measures the average time (number of days) it takes the business to collect sales made on credit terms.
- A weak ratio, such as more than 60 days, points to poor collection procedures, slow billing, or poor credit judgment.
- The formula is: (Accounts Receivable x 365) ÷ Sales

2. **Inventory Turnover**

- Indicates whether the firm has excessive or inadequate inventories.
- Industry comparisons are required to accurately assess the numbers.
- Slow inventory turnover may point to company policy of accepting too many quantity discounts from suppliers or slow-moving product lines.
- The formula is: Cost of Goods Sold ÷ Average Inventory

3. **Accounts Payable Settlement**

- Indicates the average time, indicated by the number of days, taken to settle accounts with creditors and suppliers and could be an indication of poor cash management.
- Consider negotiating extended payment terms, early payment discounts, or looking for alternative credit sources.
- The formula is: (Accounts Payable x 365) ÷ Annual Purchases

Growth

Growth indicators are typically stated as year-over-year percentages in financial terms. They measure the extent and pace of expansion and are usually calculated for sales, net profits, assets, debt, and equity.

To assess a company's growth strategy, the following issues must be considered:

- What future sales volumes are anticipated as the company expands its product lines and markets?
- What levels of profitability and cash generation are forecast, and are they sustainable?
- What level of bank operating credit is required? Are there seasonal financing needs?
- What level of long-term debt is required to finance future capital expenditures, and will the company be able to service and repay its increased debt load?
- What are the working capital implications of a particular growth strategy, and will higher levels of staff, marketing, Accounts Receivable, and/or inventories result (uses of cash)?

- Can extended payment terms be negotiated with suppliers (sources of cash)?
- Can the company raise additional equity? If equity is raised, is there a market for minority shares; what percentage ownership stake would be sold and at what price?
- Does the company have assets (i.e. real estate) that could be sold or refinanced to raise additional funds?

Some Concluding Comments About Financial Ratios

Performance in relation to competitor firms can be assessed by obtaining industry comparable data from national or international risk management firms or commercial financial data firms like Dun & Bradstreet. If, for example, Company A has a current ratio of 1.2 (weaker) in fiscal 2019 and the industry comparable ratio for the same year is 1.8, we know that Company A is performing below the industry standard.

Managing Cash Drivers

Effective management of short-term assets like cash, Accounts Receivable, and inventories, along with short-term sources of financing like Accounts Payable and bank operating lines of credit are important components of the internal financial evaluation. Cash drivers are those management strategies that result in accelerated generation and accumulation of cash resources as part the working capital cycle.

Before detailing the three primary cash drivers, a key distinction needs to be made between net income or profit or earnings and net cash flow.

- Net income equals the difference between revenues and expenses.
- Net cash flow equals the difference between cash inflows and outflows.

These will invariably be different, reflecting the uneven timing of cash disbursements and the accounting treatment of them and the uneven timing of sales revenues and cash receipts due to delays in account receivable collection.

Due to these timing differences, a company may achieve a strong net profit performance (paper profit) and yet experience a serious cash flow shortfall due to negative cash flows. This section illustrates how a company can improve its net cash flow performance by employing selective cash driver strategies.

There are three primary methods to manage your working capital and cash cycles.

- Improved Accounts Receivable collection
- Defined Accounts Payable settlement
- Optimized Inventory turnover

Improved Accounts Receivable Collection

1. **Practice Astute Credit Management**

Establish credit limits for each customer category, and use banks or agencies for credit reports. Where appropriate, charge interest on overdue accounts, and consider modifying your business model so that recurring revenue and online payments become standard as opposed to extending credit, which may lead to prolonged repayment or repayment delays.

2. **Effective Invoicing**

   Where recurring revenue models are not appropriate, ensure that invoices are submitted on the same day that goods are shipped, and issue statements monthly. Work on your client relationships so you can negotiate upfront payments for custom orders.

3. **Careful Monitoring**

   Age your receivables by current, 30-, 60-, and over 90-day categories, and place overdue accounts on prepayment or Cash on Delivery (COD). Monitor and contact overdue accounts on a regular basis.

4. **Prompt Collection**

   Establish a formal credit-granting, management, and collection policy, including litigation procedures. Wherever possible, negotiate personal guarantees for new and overdue accounts.

Defined Accounts Payable Settlement

Working closely with your suppliers, you can carefully define your payment terms with them.

1. Age your payables into current, 30-, 60-day and over 90-day categories.

2. Extend terms with key suppliers, especially to mirror seasonal cash needs. However, if attractive early payment discounts are offered, take advantage of them as long as you are not overstocking with inventory.

3. Establish a method to prioritize and manage expenses, operating requirements, and payments.

Optimize Inventory Turnover

Inventory is needed to generate profit, and yet it is a huge demand on cash and credit resources. Timing of your Cost of Goods Sold and what inventory you need on hand is a necessary business efficiency that can determine your success.

1. Where possible, negotiate just-in-time or demand-driven supply. This will require close partnering with suppliers that goes beyond contracts. When things go awry, personal relationships matter.

2. Return or sell off outdated or obsolete merchandise.

3. Determine the number of times your major product lines turn each year. How does this compare to industry averages? The faster the inventory turnover, the greater the cash flow.

4. Be sure to monitor and implement shrinkage control processes to guard against theft and goods mysteriously going missing.
5. Ensure reorder policies are in place, based on past inventory levels and target turn-over numbers.
6. Be sure to understand the costs of carrying inventory such as interest, handling, and storage costs. Implement methods to reduce these costs.
7. Build a resilient supply chain with alternative sources of supply (i.e., can you negotiate improved delivery terms)?
8. Determine which 20% of your customers contribute to 80% of your sales, and ensure your inventory management is designed to meet their needs first.

Figure 12 illustrates the interrelationship between the primary cash drivers: Inventory Turnover, Accounts Receivable collection, and Accounts Payable settlement.

Reduced days in inventory (A) and Accounts Receivable (B) allied with lengthened days in Accounts Payable (C) indicates the relative success of the company's cash driver strategies.

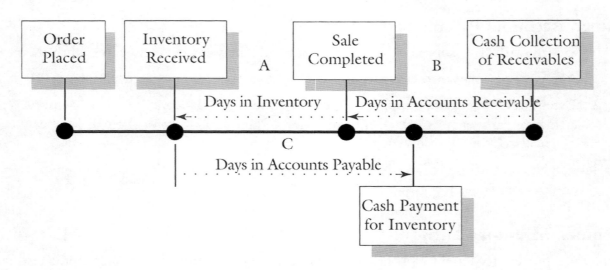

Figure 12. Cash Driver Relationships

Source: Adapted from *Short-Term Financial Management* by Maness & Zietlow. Copyright ©1997, The Dryden Press, reproduced with permission of the publisher.

Other Cash Driver Opportunities

Cash availability or liquidity is necessary to manage working capital, expand products or markets, and can keep your business solvent in a downturn. If you have identified a good opportunity for growth, you need to consider other methods to generate cash, rather than immediately looking to sell equity or get a loan.

1. Increases in property values (appraisal values versus net book value on the balance sheet) may allow refinancing and generate surplus cash (working capital) to finance expansion.
2. Consider leasing out under-utilized assets to third parties.
3. Borrow short term for short-term needs and borrow long term for longer-term needs. Match the amortization of the loan with the expected useful life of the asset.

FINANCIAL PROJECTIONS

Historical financial information allows the diagnoses of financial health and performance. An equally important element of the evaluation process is the completion of financial forecasts, in essence, the creation of a financial road map that enables company management to foresee where they are going. This process is particularly important if you are seeking increased bank financing or additional sources of equity.

The following section details the following key documents and tools that comprise a comprehensive financial forecast:

- Pro Forma cash flow budget
- Pro Forma (Projected) income statement
- Pro Forma balance sheet
- Financial modeling

Pro Forma Cash Flow Budget

A budget is how you intend to spend money in the future, based on your strategy and operational tactics. The cash flow budget process, also known as pro forma working capital, highlights the importance of timing differences in cash receipts and disbursements. The cash flow budget is an effective early warning system, especially when negative variances between actual and forecast month-end cash positions emerge. It also indicates to a bank or investor that you understand the operations and cash drivers for your business. Month by month presentation is crucial because it enables you to react quickly to shortfalls or significant variances.

Gathering the cash-in and cash-out data allows the completion of a twelve-month cash flow forecast, which determines the cash position on a monthly basis and resultant short-term borrowing or investment requirements. The cash flow budget will flow into the pro forma income statement and balance sheet and vice versa.

The cash flow budget should project up to three years out with the first year calculated on a monthly basis. In your budget, you should consider the cash-in and cash-out items noted in the following sections.

Cash-In Items

- Convert revenue forecasts into cash receipts by month for the projected income statement.

- Review historical or assumed Accounts Receivable to determine payment term assumptions. (i.e., historically, if 20% of your receivables were paid in 90 days, in your forecast, this means that 20% of invoiced January sales will not be received in cash until April.)
- Other cash receipts would include:
  - Supplier rebates
  - New bank loans
  - Cash injections from new shareholders

Cash-Out Items:

- Include overhead expenses like fixed costs such as rent, salaries, heat, and power
- Include cash outlays for purchases like inventory, operating expenses, and for direct labour.
- Consider intermittent expenses such as loan payments, capital expenditures, dividends, and tax payments.

Other Cash Flow Budget Considerations

- Coordinate the dates of your projections in alignment with the proforma income statement and balance sheet.
- Clearly document assumptions.
- Contrast to actual performance, thereby highlighting the impact of your cash driver performance.

Pro Forma Income Statement

Pro forma income statements demonstrate that you understand your costs and potential profits and can show the relationship between them. It is understood that for a pre-revenue start-up business, until there is revenue and a track record of sales, these pro forma tools are not as useful as for a company with a track record. Every start-up wants to show the typical rapid takeoff or hockey stick growth.

Industry data on market size and growth can reveal how your marketplace is changing as opposed to relying on your own internal numbers. Many analysts will do a sensitivity analysis, providing low, medium, and high forecasts, depending on market share penetration rates (see the section on sensitivity analysis). Particularly, in the case of start-ups, it is important to inject realism based on customer discovery and product/market validation work into your revenue assumptions.

Nonetheless, in a steady-state, existing company, the ability to build an income model will build the understanding of your company and allow more sophisticated analyses. A pro forma income statement should include the following information:

- Cover three to five years into the future.
- Have complete quarterly income projections for the first two years, and project annually for the next two years, depending on the cash flow budget projections.

- Base projected revenues on historical and anticipated sales performance with details on your assumptions such as seasonality.
- Derive revenue forecasts from either of the following:
  - Serviceable, obtainable, market size multiplied by estimated growth rate
  - Percentage growth, based on historical performance (i.e. 10% sales growth over the next three years, etc.)
- Forecast Cost of Goods Sold (COGS) based on prevailing industry gross profit margins unless there is a compelling and validated business model or efficiency disruption.

Other Pro Forma Income Statement Considerations

- Sales, general and administration (SGA) expenses represent company overhead. If revenues are forecast to grow beyond a fixed or relevant range, use an SGA to Revenue ratio to ensure support costs grow in tandem with revenues.
- Interest expense should be based on forecast levels of long-term financing.
- Taxes and depreciation forecasts should be based on prevailing tax rates and depreciation allowances at the time the pro forma income statement is built.

Pro Forma Balance Sheet

While the pro forma income statement models show projected revenue and costs, the pro forma balance sheet projects how your assets will be managed. It is intended to demonstrate how you might finance your business and treat equity. This is particularly important if you choose to grow through mergers or acquisitions. It is crucial to document any assumptions that are derived from strategy decisions, operational tactics, or financial ratios.

A pro forma balance sheet should consider the following items:

- Use three years as the time horizon outlook. It should be derived from historic ratio analysis and the pro forma income statement.
- Estimate Accounts Receivable, inventory, and Accounts Payable from historic ratios and forecast revenues/costs/purchases.
- Reflect any fixed assets and any future significant capital expenditures required in the future.
- Indicate any new, intended sources of capital or equity and treatment of ongoing retained earnings from forecast net profits (after dividend payout).
- Use either cash or bank operating debt as a balancing item.

Financial Modeling

It is understood that many CEOs may not use these financial modeling tools themselves. As companies grow, employing a chief financial officer to manage cash and analytics is essential. However, it is also true that most successful CEOs understand how the models work and the assumptions made. Unfortunately, many CEOs wait until a crisis hits to better understand and increase their forecasting abilities, which inhibits their ability to model growth and do scenario planning for growth and economic downturns.

Financial analysis software is used extensively by CEOs to focus on their financial growth potential and by commercial banks to understand their clients' ability to generate sustainable cash flow to repay the bank and other creditor debt.

A major benefit of these financial software tools is speed, rather than building endless Excel spreadsheets. Financial analysis tools can be used to analyze how well a company can service debt and create scenarios to model different strategies.

Besides Excel, there are a number of excellent off-the-shelf financial management software packages. They use historical accounting data to evaluate and analyze past performance and to develop strategy for business operations' future financial and growth performance. The purpose is to do scenario planning using key drivers from the income statement and balance sheet to determine what impact they will have on working capital and operating results.

Operating strategies can be modelled from two perspectives:

- **The what-if perspective:** If sales increased by 15%, what would be the impact on other related financial variables?
- **The target-based perspective**: If a net cash income target of $100K was set, investigate which cash drivers/variables would combine to achieve the desired results.

For example, you might model scenarios to achieve one of the following:

- Test the impact of new business models.
- Model best/expected/worst case revenue and costs for new products and services.
- Test the impact of sales growth and operational costs.
- Test price sensitivity and debt service requirements.
- Reduce days in Accounts Receivable or inventory.
- Reduce Cost of Goods Sold (COGS) or operating costs.

Capital Investment Analysis

Capital budgeting allows a company owner to make financial decisions about long-term investments. The following list provides some examples of capital budgeting decisions.

- Replacement of a company's fleet of vehicles with new models.
- Development of a new product line that will require extensive R&D and commercialization.
- Purchase of a land parcel and the construction of a new commercial building.
- Purchase of manufacturing and/or computer equipment.

The key question in any capital investment is, "Do the future benefits from the investment exceed the costs of making the investment?" We present three different techniques, Accounting Return on Investment, Pay-Back Period, and Discounted Cash Flow, that can be used to determine the future benefits. Each one answers a specific question.

1. Accounting Return on Investment

Question: What average dollar profits are generated per average investment dollar?

Calculation: Average annual after-tax profit per year ÷ Average book value of investment = %

Example:

New equipment costs $20,000 and is depreciated over four years to the final year with a zero salvage value. Average net book value is $10,000.

Expected after-tax profits:	Year	After-tax profit
	1	$2,000
	2	$4,000
	3	$5,000
	4	$6,000

Average expected profits over a four-year period = $4,250

Accounting return on investment = $4,250 ÷ $10,000 = 42.5%

Shortcomings of the Accounting Return on Investment technique include the following items:

- It is based on accounting profits rather than actual cash flows.
- It ignores the time value of money.
- The company owners' minimum acceptable return (hurdle rate) needs to be established in order to determine acceptance or rejection of the project.

2. Pay Back Period

Question: How long will it take to recover the original investment?

Calculation: New equipment costs $45,000 with an expected life of 10 years and is depreciated on a straight-line basis at $4,500 per year.

Expected After-Tax Cash Flows:

Year	After-Tax Profit	Depreciation	After-Tax Cash Flow
1 to 2	$3,000	+ $4,500	= $7,500

Year	After-Tax Profit	Depreciation	After-Tax Cash Flow
3 to 6	$6,000	+ $4,500	= $10,500
7 to 10	$7,500	+ $4,500	= $11,000

The pay-back period will be approximately 4.9 years and is derived by allocating the cumulative annual cash flows against the original $45,000 investment.

Strength of the Pay-Back Period Technique

- This technique gives an indication of risk – the longer the pay-back period, the greater the risk.

Weaknesses of the Pay-Back Period Technique

- The technique does not consider the time value of money.
- The technique does not consider the financial impact of cash flows received after the pay-back period.

3. Discounted Cash Flow

Question: How does the present value of future benefits that arise from the investment compare with the present-day cost of the investment?

Discount cash flow (DCF) techniques can be complex. Two analytical methods can be used, although we present only the concepts, not the formulas.

Net Present Value (NPV)

Using a predetermined rate of return (discount rate), the original cash outlay is compared to the value of future cash flows, discounted back to the present. The key to the calculation is the required rate of return. If the NPV is positive, the project is acceptable.

Internal Rate of Return (IRR)

The internal rate of return considers the rate of return that is derived where the present value of the cost of the investment equals the present value of future cash flows. The word internal means that it excludes factors like inflation, or financial risks that are outside the company's control.

Chapter 4
Sales and Marketing Strategy

Overview

One of the key elements of the Business Diagnostics Framework is a review of sales and marketing. Whether you are scaling-up and implementing efficient processes or growing into new products and markets, sales and marketing are critical elements. Without customers, you don't have a business. For our purposes, we present marketing concepts first though, in practicality, you have to find your target client and create a process to sell to them.

What is Marketing?

There tends to be much confusion about what marketing is. Many people think that marketing is selling or simply summarize it, using the four Ps of marketing: price, product, promotion, and place (distribution). While these items are encompassed by marketing, there is much more to this critical area of business. Take the time to analyze your marketing strategy and tactics and understand that they will never stay the same. Your customers change, their perceptions and needs change, so your marketing should change too.

While marketing is not sales, its purpose is to drive sales. Think of marketing and sales as two sides of the same coin. Later in this chapter, we will cover the sales process and the role of sales.

Our definition of marketing is a set of market-related activities that analyze the marketplace, develop market-driven strategy, and execute tactics that make a discernible difference to sales. These activities allow a company to provide targeted customers with a portfolio of products and services that add customer value and meet unfulfilled customer needs.

Our marketing diagnosis is divided into the following sections:

- Stage 1   Preliminary Analysis
- Stage 2   Portfolio Assessment
- Stage 3   Market Strategy Execution

The initial marketing diagnosis framework is summarized in the Figure 13.

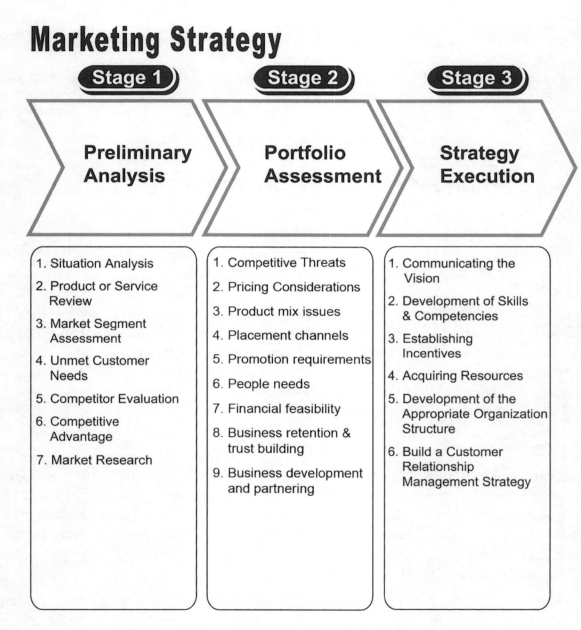

Figure 13. Marketing Diagnosis Framework

Stage 1
Preliminary Analysis

Completion of a careful preliminary analysis is the first stage in diagnosing your business's marketing and crafting a comprehensive marketing strategy. There are seven steps to this process:

1. Situation analysis
2. Product and/or services review
3. Market segment assessment
4. Addressing unmet customer needs
5. Competitor evaluation
6. Competitive advantage
7. Market research

Situation Analysis

Any marketing or sales review should have a brief documentation process that delves into a number of areas. Following the Business Diagnostics Framework, you will have completed an external scan of the industry you operate in and understand the gaps, trends, and opportunities in that industry. A sales and marketing scan is part of the overall internal assessment of your company. You will want to include the following areas in your analysis:

- A brief history of the organization for context.
- Industry and competitive analysis.
- Analysis of external opportunities and threats.
- Internal environment (strengths and weaknesses).

Part of a robust situation analysis for any company includes consideration of the aspirations of both the company and its founders. We like the SOARR model. It considers the following areas:

- Strengths and capabilities.
- Opportunities.
- Aspirations of the company and the founders.
- Results and risk expectations.

Like all good marketing analyses, the purpose is to gather insights that will improve sales and marketing outcomes and provide information for an informed review. There are a variety of tools and frameworks that can help you gather your thoughts, and we encourage you to explore different techniques.

Including the aspirations and expectations of the founders and their appetite for risk and reward can be a source of inspiration for marketers and also moderate the strategy. For example, if your company is a lifestyle business with moderate aspirations for growth and a risk-intolerant founder, the sales and marketing strategy and tactics will look very different than a high-growth business-to-consumer brand. While we add the SOARR model as part of the sales and marketing analysis, it can be a separate analysis as it affects all the elements of the external and internal scan.

If you are a start-up with a new product, the more effort you put into customer discovery and validating whether the product you offer is a fit for the market, the less risk you take on. This fact also holds true for existing businesses that are looking to offer new products and services. You still need to do your homework to ensure the market size and potential return on investment is sufficient to warrant your investment of time and money, though the bigger risk is building something no one will buy. Before you market, make sure you have validated that the pain you are solving will make a customer open their wallet.

Product and/or Services Review

A product and/or services review can be high level or in depth depending on the size and complexity of the business. It will involve careful consideration of each product and service, including the business model for each product if it is in any way different from the overall business.

Here is a list of some considerations.

1. Create a list of current products/services, including pricing and profitability.
2. If you can, estimate your possible market share per market segment.
3. List the features, advantages, and benefits of each product.
4. Write your value proposition statement for each product or service. What makes your product valuable for your customers? What pain does your product solve for your clients, and why is it important and different from others?
5. Consider how each product or service relates to the others. Are some products enablers that help your clients bridge to more profitable items?
6. List the potential for follow-on products or revenue sources and the conditions under which these follow-on products could exist.
7. Consider what triggers a buying decision for your client.
8. List product adoption behaviors and needs. What might inhibit a client from switching to your product?
9. List how many prospects you will need in the sales funnel to convert to a sale for each product?
10. What repeat client touch points (customer service) or repeat sales can be anticipated?
11. What is the client maintenance requirement for each product or service?

A useful tool for a product and services review is Alex Osterwalder's Business Model Canvas. This tool has been modified by various different authors like Ash Maurya, who created the Lean Canvas tool. Whichever tool you choose to use, each offers different ways to analyze the information and gather insights and ideas.

Market Segment Assessment

Any market analysis or sales plan needs to first determine if the market is big enough to meet your aspirations and mitigate your investment risk. Building on the information gathered in your external industry scan, you need to be able to describe your market segment or various market segments in size (dollars and units) and estimated growth rates. You then need to provide more information, so you can determine which market segment is the most attractive and most available to you, based on your validated client need (the pain you solve). Segment criteria can include the following categories:

- Geographical considerations
- Industry gaps and trends
- Demographics
- Psychographics

Psychographics are particularly important as they consider the psychology behind a buying decision and are particularly important in values-and-lifestyles- (VALs) - based buying decisions. For example, the psychology behind a buyer who will pay top dollar to stay at a pricey sustainable tourism resort is quite different than those consumers who choose to stay at a cabana on the beach. The need for a bed-on-the-beach product might be similar, but the experience is different. The entire client experience and product is driven by the marketing segment definition and the psychology behind the buying trigger.

A market segment can be defined as groups of customers and potential customers who have similar pains, needs, and desires that are distinct from other segments and can be collected as a group by adopting unique, targeted, marketing strategies. Start your segmentation broadly by identifying the total potential market and then start narrowing it down realistically.

For example, let's consider the motorcycle market in the United States. There are roughly 81.5 million persons between the ages of 45 and 64 in the United States. However, the market available to you is less than half that if you assume the product is only marketed to men. From your total available market, narrow the market down to the total available and the total qualified market. Let's presume you have tested your market and determined that, due to your unique value proposition, your total available market is men over the age of 45, qualified by those who drive or wish to drive motorcycles. You then need to consider why they want a motorcycle, what type of motorcycle they will buy, and what the buying trigger is for that motorcycle.

Finally, you want to define your target market with a statement that will drive your marketing efforts and will help visualize who you are marketing and ultimately selling to. Each of the qualifiers in the target market statement should have been validated in some way. An example of a target market statement might be:

> *We are marketing to men aged 45 to 64 in the Southern United States with incomes over $100k who desire a retro-look vintage motorcycle to advance their desire to recapture the feeling of freedom and youth.*

The market assessment may help determine if this is, in fact, the first segment you should target. Another target might be women over the age of 45 in a different geographic market with a different buying trigger and psychographic profile. You can see that bad assumptions can make for bad marketing. Determining your target market has to be done by linking to the pain you are solving with lots of testing and iterations to remove any guesswork.

It might take several attempts to truly find each target audience. Once you have nailed down the audience, many companies will do a mood board with images that helps them visualize who they are marketing to and to keep the customer in mind at all times. There are multiple online tools to help you build a mood board.

Market segmentation isn't done just once. It is an iterative process that considers a number of items:

- Future trends for each segment and customer needs and wants in each segment.
- Changing business, distribution, or purchasing models that emerge from external and industry scans.
- Secondary and tertiary segments that may change to primary segments, based on changing needs.

To further build out your marketing plan, consider the following questions:

- How or where do segment customers research and learn about your products, and how do they purchase?
- Who is the alternative decision maker? For example, your market may be men, but do their partners make or influence the decision?
- Who are the influencers in this industry? Is the influencer a magazine, a person, a celebrity, or an online network? Where do you find them? Can they be leveraged as a third-party endorser of your product?
- What is the profit potential of each segment? If there is a smaller but more lucrative segment, it may make more sense to target that segment. Or, if there is a smaller segment that is more easily accessible to you and is easier to sell into, that might make more sense. Don't just chase the largest segment—you want the segment that is available to you, qualified and profitable.

Unmet Customer Needs?

The world of business is really about solving problems. An unmet need may be obvious or may need to be uncovered. Marketing and product development seem to be different fields and yet they are both grounded in understanding what the real problem is. Marketing is about finding and building awareness and driving actions from the target customer, and it is about uncovering potential new offerings. In order to identify unmet customers' needs, consider the following questions:

- When your clients buy from you, what are they really buying? Are they buying a pen or a method to collect their thoughts?

- What new needs could be derived from your development of new technology, processes, or equipment?
- Is there a way to create a simpler or more accessible product by moving it online, making it mobile, or otherwise making it digital?
- Can you remove the friction in the transaction to make it easier for the client and perhaps develop a new product from that efficiency?
- Are there any new regulations such as those around environmental or health concerns that could create new opportunities?
- Are there any gaps and trends coming from your continual external scanning work that could create new opportunities?
- Are there any opportunities for creating value-added products and services or migrating into higher margin products or into a different part of the value chain?
- Successful companies must know and satisfy customer needs!

Competitor Evaluation

When analyzing competitors from a marketing perspective, you need to consider the following broad issues:

- What is the estimated market share of competitors, categorized by your primary product/service offering categories? List the competitors in order of their relative current impact, features, geographical areas served, and business models.
- Endeavour to assess competitor financial resources, product quality, service, and pricing strategies. Your competitor analysis can be made into a chart or bubble graph for presentations and for inclusion in your business plan.
- Review the competition's technology base (intellectual property protection), channels of distribution, and other attributes that are important in your industry.

More sophisticated companies use ongoing competitive intelligence (CI) as a proactive and structured approach to gather information about competitors' market-related activities. In building a defined CI strategy, the identification, monitoring, and measuring of specific information is a key process. Such information would include current pricing initiatives, trade shows and conferences, recruitment drives, online databases, magazines, and product catalogs. A key ethical consideration is to gather information that is publicly available rather than engaging in clandestine, undercover activities.

Another key element to an effective CI strategy is properly early warning system via structured internal communications with marketing and sales so competitor activities are monitored on a regular basis. Using a service like Google Alerts is helpful to monitor your competitors and industry. Also follow competitor's blogs, and social media accounts. An effective CI process enables the company to more effectively gauge its relative competitive advantage.

Competitive Advantage

A critical step in the preliminary analysis is to ask yourself if you have a sustainable competitive advantage? That is, what measurable advantage do you have that would be difficult for your competitors to offer and that customers are willing to pay for over a period of time (sustainable)?

You probably have a competitive advantage if you meet the following criteria:

- Competitors find it difficult to imitate your products or services.
- You have access to a diverse set of market segments.
- You contribute in a significant way to customers' perceived value of the offered product or service.

Sustainable competitive advantages are generally derived through factors like significant advancements that allow you to lower costs, to add dramatically to quality or useability in a manner that the customer will pay for and that can't be quickly adapted by others.

Added value and specific advantages such as a geographic monopoly, management strength, franchise strength, or brand image have to be very strong to be considered a sustainable competitive advantage.

Market Research

There are two critical types of market research.

- Customer discovery and product/market fit validation
- Market/industry assessment research

Customer Discovery and Product/Market Fit Validation

In many cases, you will have to do both types of market research, though to varying degrees, depending on your required speed to market and capital intensity of your product. If you are entering a market with a long development time and high capital intensity like a new pharmaceutical, you will need to do in-depth market and industry assessment and continually update the information as the product is developed. If you have an idea for a web application for consumers, speed to market may be the critical driver, so your market research needs would be different and conducted using different methods.

When speed to market is the primary driver, you want to first determine if anyone else is doing the same thing and then determine your unique value proposition. Finding the competition is not that difficult but determining your unique value proposition is.

With speed to market, you need to test your premise directly with potential clients. The concept of testing with clients is to stay focussed on their problem, so you can uncover what really matters to them. Too often, we fall in love with our idea and tend to validate only what we think is true, rather than looking for the negative feedback. The other pitfall is that we often ask people we trust who might not want to hurt our feelings. Many product launches have failed because of denial and the inability to uncover the true client need. A great resource for developing customer validation questions and product tests is a book called *The Mom Test* by Rob Fitzpatrick.

Client discovery is an iterative process as is product validation. Eric Reis' book, *The Lean Startup*, outlines a build-measure-learn feedback methodology and discusses how to use minimally viable product tests to gather market data while still developing the product. The key take-away is that the start-up or new product concept should be based on data and validation, not just the passion of the founder or developer. This technique is valid for start-ups but also for established companies that want to increase their product launch success.

It is not unusual to have a product idea radically change once there is real use data. Companies can pivot to preserve their original concept or pause based on client and market data.

It is common for companies to use online tools to run surveys and gather marketing intelligence from social networks. A test might be to see how many people will respond to product mock-up videos by entering their email address to receive product updates.

The customer discovery and product tests need to be valid. Just because 100 people on Twitter say they like a product with the hashtag #justtakemymoney, it doesn't mean they will actually buy it.

The term *traction* is used to describe the proof that a product is validated. There are different traction metrics depending on who you talk to and their point of view. The traction metrics will also change based on where you are in your go-to-market journey. Some founders will point to their Instagram followers and social engagement, which is one indicator, though the only one that really matters is whether people convert from engagement to the purchase funnel. The most important metrics are how many people buy and how often they buy. Then can you can measure how much it costs to acquire each customer and whether they will refer others. Marketing metrics are critical to keep you on track.

Market research, whether you use lean start-up or more formal methodology, can also be used to inform product design and development.

Market/Industry Assessment Research

A key component in identifying unmet customer needs is undertaking a market research process, which involves completing the following steps:

1. Define the marketing issues and the objectives of the research project. What do you want to get out of the project? What problem are you trying to solve?
2. Develop a research plan:
- What types of resources and data are available?
- What are the expected outcomes?
- What research methodology will be used? Secondary or primary research or both?
- What secondary research materials are available? (Statistics Canada, industry associations, or commercial marketing research from external research firms.)
- How much primary research and talking to clients is required; will you interview or survey?
- How will research participants be identified and contacted as part of the primary research process?

- How much will the research cost, and how long will it take?

    Note: It is important that small business owners do the majority of the analysis themselves or work closely with their team in order to draw specific conclusions about existing or potential products and services. The small business owner needs to understand the fundamental data, so relying too heavily on consultants and staff can be risky. If this is your business and your risk, you need to understand the data well. Secondary literature sources can be used to create a background document that will inform any primary research that needs to happen.

3. Collect unbiased data. It is critical to ensure that the data collected is unbiased to maintain its validity. Care must be taken to exclude interviewer bias or questionable answers.
4. Analyze the data. After data is collected, a wide variety of statistical and summary techniques can be used to interpret it. These techniques should have been identified in the research plan.
5. Draw conclusions. These will lead to the identification of specific customer wants and needs, and they will assist in pinpointing target segments. Such conclusions must be logically derived from the research findings.

The five steps for market research apply with digital data collection too; the data set collection needs to be identified, collected, analyzed, and used to draw conclusions. The difference is that using web techniques, social media, and lean product techniques can reduce the time to market and, potentially, increase product success with better input data.

Stage 2 Portfolio Assessment

The preliminary analysis stage is followed by the portfolio assessment stage during which growth initiatives are charted for each discrete product or service. While many businesses have only one product, as they grow, the product and service offering will expand. We have developed a Nine-step Portfolio Assessment tool. The Portfolio Assessment Tool assists in monitoring—to ensure products and services remain relevant and support the brand.

For example, consider an upscale resort that is based on the Canadian west coast, on Vancouver Island, and offers a selection of service offerings to discrete market segments, which can be classified as follows:

For this particular business, there are four separate service offerings, each with two discrete market segments. Thus, there will be eight separate product/market portfolios that need to be assessed through the following portfolio assessment process.

We recommend that for each product/service offered (or to be offered), a market positioning statement be developed. Each statement should leverage the brand image in the minds of customers and other related stakeholders.

An example of a market positioning statement is, "To connect our weekend getaway clients with a sense of place; to enhance their experience, our food services will highlight locally grown and freshly prepared west coast cuisine."

PRODUCT OFFERING	MARKET SEGMENT
1. Accommodation and food services	a) Business traveler b) Weekend get a ways
2. Meetings	a) Business sector b) Government sector
3. Weddings	a) Local b) Out of province
4. Tours	a) Golf b) Ecotourism

Figure 14. Resort Product Offerings and Market Segments

Nine-Step Portfolio Assessment Tool

As seen in Figure 14, the portfolio assessment has nine steps. Much of the information may have already been gathered in your external and marketing scan.

1. **Competitive Threats**

   For each portfolio item, consider the following questions:

   - Can you assess the market share of competitors? Have there been any market share changes over the past few years? Why did the changes occur?

   - Is there potential for competitive actions and reactions to any new product or service introductions? How might competitors react?

   - At what stage is the market segment on the product/service life cycle?

2. **Pricing Considerations**

   A price should be set that communicates value to your targeted customers. To help think through pricing, consider that the price people will pay is a function of the following judgments:

   - How much they care about the pain you are solving for them.

   - How aware they are of the product and its value to them.

   - What they experience.

In pricing your product offerings, complete the following assessment process:

- What is the value and who is willing to pay for that value? What can you add to your experience that will increase the value to the client? For example, some eco-lodges are able to charge a much higher room rate than a hotel because they offer an experience targeted to those who value their offering.

- What is the overall objective? Is it to build market share, maximize revenues, or maximize profits? Do you aspire to achieve product quality leadership if that will lead to more sales or profit?

- What are the product costs at different volumes? What is the average gross margin?
- How do your prices compare to competitors' prices?
- Have you considered the potential for volume/segment discounts?
- What will be the impact of transportation costs, handling, and insurance?

3. **Product/Service Mix Issues**

    You will need to consider the following for your line up of products or services:

- Have you designed and developed products and services so that the targeted customers can easily identify, understand, and determine the value that is delivered to them?
- Are you generating at least one new product/service development ahead of the marketplace?
- Is the product easy to use? Does it have a clear description and concept to deliver supporting customer service(s) or training as needed?
- Is there a need for some form of visual representation (photos, videos, drawings, infographics, etc.)?
- Are there support or warranty implications (what is covered, timing, who will support, etc.)?
- What are the packaging and display requirements and designs, if any?

4. **Placement Channels**

    Placement is the analysis of the distribution channels, in essence the best way to deliver your products or services. Consider the following:

- How do you plan to distribute your products and services? How do your competitors distribute their products and services?
- Do you need to create your own online store, or can you use an online marketplace?
- Are there other potential distribution channel options? Is there an opportunity to outsource product fulfillment? Fulfillment is how a product order is taken, delivered, and possibly, returned. There are third-party fulfillment companies that handle these aspects of operations for companies.
- What parts of the value chain can you optimize?
- How and where does your company add value? Are there opportunities to outsource operations that do not add value?
- How and where do your competitors add value?
- Can you partner with appropriate suppliers or distributors to increase value?

5. **Promotion Requirements**

    Promotion includes advertising, direct marketing, digital marketing, content marketing, social media, sales promotions, and public relations for both your firm and product offerings. Answering the following questions will help you develop effective promotional game plan:

- Do you advertise and promote your product and services in places that your target audiences frequent and in a manner consistent with the feelings and perceptions that your products and services create?
- What is the current amount of the promotion budget? What is the cost for customer acquisition versus the lifetime value of that client?
- What major message theme(s) is required for integrated marketing communications and your desired brand positioning?
- Are you running campaigns that you are able to change and adapt to sales needs?
- Is personal selling required? How many salespeople are required? What training, incentives, and compensation are needed?
- Are there website development issues and digital initiatives to consider? Has your website been optimized for search engine marketing?
- Is your content being refreshed on a regular basis?
- Do you have outbound marketing tools like email and newsletters to keep customers up-to-date on new specials, promotions, and so on using an opt-in email list?
- Do you have inbound marketing tools like content marketing and influencer marketing to pique client interest, build awareness, and drive clicks and conversions on your webpage? Are you able to activate prospects to move along the journey to become clients, and can you activate existing clients to buy more or other products?
- Are there any privacy policy implications (a need to clearly state how customer information will be administered)?

6. **People Needs**

    Human resources are critical to acquire, service, cross sell, and retain clients. Be prepared to address the following questions:

    - What are the staffing requirements to position and then sell the product?
    - What level of service is required for the market segment?
    - Are there training and compensation issues to address?
    - Will teams be set up by product function and /or market segment?

7. **Financial Feasibility**

    Will there be a reasonable return on investment for existing products and/or services:

    - What are the forecast revenues and contributions for the next fiscal year?
    - Has a sensitivity analysis been performed for –best, expected, and worst cases?

For new products/services:

- What are the variable and fixed start-up costs and the projected break-even point?

- What is the burn rate of funds that are devoted to the project? When will they run out?

8. **Business Retention and Trust Building**

    It is important to note the importance of existing clients:

- Ensure there is a clear *client retention* focus to guard the back door.
- Explore ways to cross sell or up sell products/services or sell higher value or higher profit products.
- Explore loyalty and reward programs. Many online services exist.
- Continuously build trust and request client testimonials and referrals.

9. **Business Development and Partnering**

    Business development is strategic and specific to building partners and market expansions for long-term growth and profitability. Partners could be technology partners, sales or distribution partners, or marketing partners. Business development also identifies large opportunities in any of the business functional areas.

    Sales has a specific responsibility for revenues and client interactions. There may be instances where the salesperson also does marketing and business development, though we believe that, in many cases, these are separate functions. As with marketing, the functions need to work closely together. Understanding the differences between sales, marketing, and business development can help you assign relative weights to the different functions in terms of your priorities. If you need revenue now, sales might be your priority. If you need to ensure your sales funnel is full, marketing might be your priority. If you need to build new markets and partners, business development may be your priority.

    Consider the following business development initiatives to review :

- What industry trends need to be followed to ensure long-term profitability?
- Which industry associations could be helpful to build connections and for knowledge sharing?
- In order to monitor long-term trends, what trade, industry, or engineering groups or developments does your business development team need to be involved with—rather than just joining as a member? For example, engineering firms might choose to be involved in I.E.E.E. engineering working or standards groups. Are there industry standards or regulatory groups that would help you keep on top of changes and network with potential partners?
- Are there opportunities to research and write white papers or articles and to use these to promote your product/service at conferences, trade shows, in the media, and on blogs and/or social media?

Partnering Opportunities

A key element of business development is fostering partnering and alliances to further enhance revenue and earnings performance. Having completed the nine-step portfolio assessment, you should also consider the following questions that deal with partnering opportunities:

- Is there potential for strategic alliances, licensing arrangements, or joint ventures to share the costs of market development or market entry?
- Are there opportunities to work with value-added resellers or different forms of distribution like affiliate networks?
- Are there opportunities to create a value-added network of products? For example, selling transportation and hotel bundles?
- What due diligence steps need to be taken to ensure compatibility with partners?
- Do you have written criteria for vetting partners and a process for developing your partnering networks?

PRODUCT AND MARKET PORTFOLIO ASSESSMENT TEMPLATES

We have developed two useful templates that can be used for the rigorous process of product and market portfolio assessment. Using the first template, list each product with the market positioning statement and market segment. Then, using the second template, for each product offering, complete the Nine-step Portfolio Assessment.

Template #1

Product Offering	Market Positioning Statement	Market Segment
1)		
2)		
3)		

Template #2

9 Step Portfolio Assessment	
Steps	Issues to consider?
1 Competitive threats	
2) Pricing considerations	
3) Product mix issues	
4) Placement channels	
5) Promotion requirements	
6) People needs	
7) Financial feasibility	
8) Business retention & trust building	
9) Business development and partnering	

Figure 15. Templates

Stage 3 Market Strategy Execution

After the market analysis and portfolio positioning process have been completed, the agreed-upon initiatives and tactics must now be executed. A market strategy includes marketing plus all the elements of the portfolio assessment.

A solid market strategy execution or implementation plan requires the following elements:

- Communicate the vision.

    It is important to ensure that company personnel buy into your company's market vision and its products and services. Create a plan to communicate the plan in a manner that engages staff and inspires them to contribute to the vision.

- Establish and measure progress on goals.

    Setting achievable, measurable, market-facing, marketing goals that are aligned with the overall strategy creates a methodology to ensure you are on track and can adjust course when you are off track. The goals have to be operationalized to consider the required resources and activities. Depending on the goal, monitoring might be done weekly, monthly, or quarterly. Some objectives might be short-term ones that lead into longer term goals. Some companies are able to strip down to do only exception reporting, highlighting only the outlier data by reporting what is going well and what needs to be improved. Operational excellence means establishing goals, measuring, and monitoring as part of your standard operating procedures.

- Develop skills and competencies.

    You need to assess which skills your people need to execute the market vision and strategy Do your people have them now? Can the skills be developed? Can you acquire the skills?

    Proper incentives are required to motivate your people to perform the required market-driven tasks and initiatives. Lack of proper incentives will lead to slower execution and change. Incentives can be either financial or not, but they need to reward the behaviours you want.

- Acquire needed resources.

    The execution of a market strategy cannot be successfully accomplished without having the necessary resources to implement the plan. A lack of required resources such as the appropriate people, financing, or strategic partners causes frustration, lack of motivation, and ultimately reduces staff engagement.

- Develop an appropriate organizational structure.

    An appropriate market-oriented structure needs to be set up with clearly defined lines of authority and responsibility in place.

    The structure should be linked to key success factors that have been developed by the various departments and divisions within the firm. These responsibility units will be motivated by specific accomplishment targets that have been agreed upon.

- Build a customer relationship management strategy.

It is critical that a formal system is in place to manage customer relationships. The system should involve the installation of an appropriate I.T. infrastructure, and it should include training and support for employees who are guided by a strategic process to acquire, service, cross sell, and retain clients. Use a customer relationship management software system to track your clients, stakeholders, suppliers, and competition.

- Build out your sales process.

    Sales is related to business development and marketing, but it requires different skills. The reality is that someone who is a great marketer may not be a good salesperson and vice versa.

The Role of Sales

Very often, companies are built on the industry relationships and sheer determination of a founder, and when they need to grow, they don't have the in-house expertise to develop a sophisticated sales and marketing program. Professional sales requires discipline, knowledge, and process—plus the ability to negotiate and know when to close a deal. Marketing is critical, but sales keeps the doors open. There are excellent sales training courses available both online and in face-to-face models. We have provided the following checklist for you to start to assess your sales capacity.

To size up the sales performance in your organization, consider the following questions:

- Are your sales goals achievable? Are your incentives structured to encourage the behaviours you want?

- Beside overall sales revenue, are you monitoring your close rate, customer acquisition costs, and return on campaigns? What works and what doesn't?

- Are you running promotions, incentives, loyalty programs, or other incentive-based programs for clients?

- Do you have a prospect database and a qualification pipeline? Depending on where the prospect is in the sales process, different collateral and interaction with different parties may be required. For example, the initial prospect contact might be in a technical department, but then finance will become involved. How do you handle different buyer types?

- Do you have a formal prospecting system using a sales funnel process? Do you understand how many prospects need to be in your funnel, and can you estimate how many will convert to sales?

- Do you know your close ratio for the number of contacts it takes to close a sale along the sales engagement funnel? When you lose a sale, do you know why? Where does the information go?

- Have you systematized your sales process for repeatable, reliable outcomes? Have you automated the parts of the process that can be automated without sacrificing results?

- Do you provide regular sales training? Do you include different departments that have contact with your clients?

- Do you have a product manager who is responsible for the product life cycle, the performance of the product, and the relationship with other products?
- Do you have product training tools designed for different audiences, based on need? Do you have face-to-face tools, videos, online documents?
- Do your sales people have the collateral they need for prospects, completed sales, and sales follow up?
- Is your sales process linked to your operations and order fulfillment to ensure sales campaigns coincide with your ability to deliver?
- Have you created a formalized feedback system, so information from sales feeds into the company for product, service, and business and marketing intelligence?
- Have you formalized, standardized, and templated your bidding process to make your bid process efficient?

Lastly, we provide a few final thoughts on the role of sales.

You can increase your customer understanding by recording the customer buying process and journey. If your customers buy only every March or on a specific identifiable trigger, be prepared, and pro-active.

Understand the Pareto 80:20 rule–80% of contribution margin comes from 20% of your customers—then you should adjust where you spend your time and effort.

Take the time to read and inform yourself on sales practices. Read the book, *Predictable Revenue: Turn Your Business Into A Sales Machine With The $100 Million Best Practices of Salesforce.com*, by Aaron Ross and Marylou Tyler.

Digital Marketing

The importance of understanding the fundamentals of digital marketing cannot be understated. While as a business owner or manager, you need to understand the fundamentals of marketing and sales, you also need to understand how to optimize your digital presence. While *Business Diagnostics* is designed to be high level rather than delving into the details of tactical and operational functions, digital marketing is so important that more information is necessary.

There are multiple elements of digital marketing with some of them beyond the scope of this chapter. The purpose of this section is to have you understand the fundamentals. At the early stages of bootstrapping your business, you may need to do your own digital marketing, and as you grow, you will need to know what questions to ask and how to manage the work. You need to be aware of the following concepts and ask yourself the accompanying questions.

Website

A key question is – what are you using your website for?

The majority of business owners have a website that describes their business and operations. In terms of website quality and access, they vary from low-cost, *postcard* offerings to highly professional, well-conceived portals. We discuss e-commerce websites and offer a general website assessment tool in Chapter 5.

Consider the following questions:

- When people land on your page, do they immediately know what you do and what you are asking them to do? For example, are you looking for conversions to sign up for a newsletter, to read a blog post, download an article, or buy something? Do you have metrics for each conversion?

- Are you able to make simple changes to your page via the content management system yourself, or are you tied to a web developer/designer who charges for the changes? Do you have the capacity or desire to learn or train a staff member? If not, do you have a contract in place that includes simple changes, adding images, doing the search engine optimization (SEO), and regular maintenance and upgrades. What are the associated costs?

- Do you need to build your own website or is using a website and e-commerce marketplace like Shopify sufficient?

- If you need to build your own website, is your website technology platform (the type of software coding that the site is built with) flexible enough to accommodate changes such as social media integration and e-commerce? Do you understand what your future needs might be? Are you using a custom platform that ties you to a single development company, or is the platform common enough that you can replace your supplier if needed?

- Is your website mobile friendly? Viewing on a mobile or even wearable device is a necessary consideration. Ease of use and navigation with mobile devices, and scaling forms and tools to work with small screens is a necessity.

- Are you aware of recent design trends for sites and mobile sites? Will recent design trends matter for you? How often will you update your site?

- Is your site search engine optimized (SEO)? There are some (albeit rare) situations where SEO is not as critical as advertising or marketing. For example, if you are focused on near-term sales for a one-time gala event, perhaps search engine marketing and social media promotion might be more important than long-term, organic search metrics with SEO. How will your site rank for voice search?

- If your site needs to be found via a search engine search (also known as organic search), do you have a basic understanding of what this means and how to do it? If you have a basic understanding, it is easier to hire someone to do this work for you.

The Three Elements of Digital Marketing

There are three critical elements in your digital marketing plan:

- Search Engine Optimization (SEO)
- Search Engine Marketing (SEM)

- Social Media Optimization (SMO)

A successful digital marketing plan will integrate the three elements as required to increase results.

SEO + SEM+ SMO = ROI (Return on Investment)

Search Engine Optimization

Search Engine Optimization (SEO) is a combination of elements that help the search engines find recent and relevant content, based on organic search terms and phrases. We understand that it is unlikely that you will be coding your own site, but understanding the basics will help you make better decisions.

Why do you need to know about SEO? We have heard too many horror stories about CEOs and marketing managers who hire and pay companies thousands of dollars to build beautiful websites, but no one bothers to do basic SEO. While you don't need to know everything about SEO, your marketing department needs to have a basic understanding, and you need to know what questions to ask. Further, with the rise of social media optimization and content marketing, the interaction between your site and your content is more important than ever.

There are a number of companies that provide SEO training. We like MOZ.com and their SEO basic tools found at www.moz.com/learn/seo are updated, reliable, and credible.

Here are some things to consider when faced with search engine optimization decisions:

- SEO rankings work over time. The rankings won't happen immediately.

- Your domain name matters. If you are a consultant, you want to have consultant in your domain name.

- Use every opportunity on your site to tell the search engines what your site is about. For example, use the page title, headers, descriptions, images, and internal links to your advantage.

- Use keyword planner tools from Google or other providers to find out what search terms and phrases you should use on your site.

- Use your blog to have dynamic content on your website, and keep it up-to-date. Your blog needs to be on your site, not on a separate blog site. Give your blog posts titles that your audience will find intriguing, so they will click and read. Always have an image on your post, and ensure the website is set up so the image will be carried along when you share the post on social media sites.

- Build quality backlinks or sites that link to your site. The higher the value of the backlink, the better value it is for your site ranking. For example, if your industry association has a large and well-trafficked site, a link to your site will be more valuable than if the link exists on a site that is unrelated to your industry.

- Build your social media networks as a method to socialize, and share your content to a wider audience, thereby ensuring more clicks.

- Use different content like videos, infographics, graphs, and images.

- Provide value to your audience with relevant free tools or information to keep them on your site longer and so they return for more valuable content.
- Track your progress! Use Google Analytics or third-party tools to measure your progress.
- If your business relies on organic search, keep up-to-date with changes in SEO. Google changes its algorithm regularly.

Search Engine Marketing

Search engine marketing or SEM refers to online or digital ads (paid search) that promote an action by directing the visitor to a website or a dedicated landing page. The purpose of the advertising can be awareness or sales. The ads are purchased by cost per thousand impressions (CPM) for awareness only or by cost per click (CPC), which is more common because it delivers an outcome—a click. The ads are served up, based on a combination of words that the visitor is searching for. SEM can be expensive and very effective when done well. Typically, large SEM buys are done via a media broker who matches ad content with the media.

To size up your firm's SEM needs, consider the following:

- Do you already advertise in print or broadcast media? What is your buy amount? What are your results?
- What outcome do you want, and what does success look like?
- Do you want to build sales or awareness?
- Do you have a landing page or a dedicated page that the advertising leads to?
- Are you monitoring and measuring the conversions on that page?
- Is the campaign part of a larger promotion or for a specific purpose?
- Does your competition use SEM?
- Is there a well-trafficked industry site that you could advertise on?
- What networks might make sense for you? Are you using influencer, affiliate sites, or specific networks like Google, Linked In, Facebook or Instagram, Youtube, Twitter, Snapchat, or any other social media site?
- Can you leverage social media internal advertising systems, which are highly targeted to serve ads to people who have self-identified their interests?

Social Media Optimization

Entering and committing to social media (SMO) is a difficult decision for many businesses. Many enter without a strategy or plan. They enter just because someone told them they should. Most CEOs have a difficult time understanding that social media and content marketing is really influence marketing. Many business people say that most of their business comes from word-of-mouth marketing that is built on relationships, which are built over time. Contrast that belief with data that says most people do an Internet search to check out a company before they buy.

An extended community of followers, fans, and listeners influence decision makers. Whether online or in person, the goal of influence marketing is to connect with someone who can influence their audience to take a certain action, which increases a marketing campaign's chance of success.

Brands use trickles of support from influencers to create ripples within communities and ultimately to influence a buy decision.

Very few businesses will not benefit from some sort of social media strategy that builds their influencers and online reputation.

To size up your company's social media optimization (SMO), consider the following:

- Do you know what you fear most about social media? Can you identify and acknowledge your fear to find a way to mitigate the risk?
- Do you have a balanced and fair social media policy for employees and specifically for those employees who will be interacting online for the company?
- Do you have a crisis management plan that can leverage social accounts? Do you have a plan for moderators should your feed become negative or filled with trolls? Who is in charge and when?
- Do you know what networks your clients, industry associations, or industry influencers are on?
- Do you know who your industry and product influencers are and how to work with them?
- Do you balance corporate social media with in-house employee influencers? How do you support your in-house social media influencers?
- Do you use a storyboard or manage your content across networks?
- Do you have unique content plans for each social media network?
- Do you integrate your social media with promotions and marketing campaigns?
- Does your content plan balance information and sales?
- Do you attend or send your staff to social media workshops or invest in training?
- Do you have the resources to stick with a social media strategy for the long term?

A Note on Content Marketing

> "Marketing effectively, revolves around those three 'little' requirements: Trust, Authority, Reputation."
>
> - David Amerland

Content marketing was born out of the tenets of relationship selling. If you can provide helpful information that other people trust and share, you build credibility, and people are more likely to believe what you have to say. If a third party who is a trusted advisor then repeats your message, their influence helps build your credibility. Content marketing helps build your online trust, authority, and reputation. And this is something every business needs to size up for themselves on a regular basis.

In his book, *Content Chemistry: The Illustrated Handbook for Content Marketing*, Andy Crestodina of Orbit Media Studios describes content marketing as a process to create and promote useful, relevant information with the goal of attracting and engaging website visitors and then converting those visitors into leads and customers.

Like other operational and functional skills and tasks, you likely don't need to be an expert in content marketing, but if SEO and being found online matter to your business, you need to build a digital presence for your company. The starting point is content marketing knowledge. Size up your efforts by considering the following:

- Have you considered what part of your content is proprietary and what is already public? If something is public, have you considered ways to repurpose that content as part of your digital presence?

- You are likely already an expert in your field and answer questions about your industry. Can you imagine how you might take that expertise and put it online to help your audience see you as an authority?

- Have you or anyone in your company written papers, done research, or given presentations? Can that content be repurposed on your website or shared on social media networks?

- Have you ever given public sales presentations? Can these be recorded via a webinar and posted out on your site to be shared more publicly?

- Do you have training or explainer videos that can become part of your online content?

- Which product images or images that you own are currently in use? Can you use these as part of your content?

Chapter 5:
The Operations Review

Overview

Operations consists of the completion of activities that are necessary to get a task performed. The operations process transforms inputs into outputs. The end result is the successful delivery of a product or service that meets customers' quality requirements and expectations.

A key outcome of this function is the improved productivity of the company, which allows it to compete more effectively and likely, more profitably in its marketplace. Generally, organizations with higher productivity possess a superior competitive advantage. The Aberdeen Group reports that reducing logistics costs by 5% is typically equivalent to a 30% increase in sales turnover.

Operations are not an isolated function. They are closely intertwined with the other functional areas of the business, especially finance, legal, marketing, and human resources.

The manner in which a business conducts its basic operations is an important element in our Business Diagnostics Framework. In order to effectively assess the impact of the Operations function, this chapter is divided into two parts:

Part One provides background information on business structure, different product and service considerations within operations, and internal information technology needs.

Part Two outlines and describes the six stages for operations management: process, quality, facilities, inventory, risk, and project management.

Part One
Legal: Business and Corporate Structures

Before discussing operations management, it is important to discuss the various business structures. Your legal obligations are a fundamental piece of operations and the legal structure you adopt will impact your operations. Here are three basic options, each with advantages and disadvantages:

- Sole proprietorship
- Partnership
- Corporation

Sole Proprietorship

The key feature of a sole proprietorship is that you own the business outright, and your business income is treated as personal income.

Advantages of sole proprietorship:

- Business losses can be offset against your personal taxable income.
- Costs for set up and operation are lower than with the other options.
- There are fewer regulation and reporting requirements than with the other options.

Disadvantages of sole proprietorship:

- Your access to capital for operations and growth will be limited.
- You are personally liable for all business obligations and any related litigation.
- Some government programs are available only to incorporated entities.

Partnerships

In a partnership, each partner shares in profits and losses, based on their percentage interest in the business. The partners' responsibilities and obligations are normally defined in a written partnership agreement.

Advantages of a partnership:

- Workload and capital requirements and obligations are shared among the partners.
- New partners can be added, which can provide more flexibility.
- Partners provide different skill sets, mutual support, and more sources of capital.
- Partners may have separate tax liabilities.

Disadvantages of a partnership:

- Unlimited liability for partnership debts.
- Business and personal assets are at risk for any financial losses suffered.
- One partner can potentially make decisions that bind all the others.
- Dissolution can be difficult and time-consuming.

Note: There are some different structures in different regulatory environments. For example, limited liability partnerships (LLPs) can limit the amount of personal liability. These are generally used in professional service organizations.

Corporations

A corporation is a separate legal entity that is granted authority by either federal or provincial law. A corporation is legally separate from the shareholders.

There is a trend toward Benefit corporations or B Corps. These corporations are formed to improve on the corporate profit motive by including social, economical, and environmental needs and actions. There are different legal implications in different jurisdictions, and there is a certification body separate from legal incorporation.

Advantages of corporations:

- Greater access to sources of capital via share issues (equity) and security agreements (debt).
- Potential for becoming a public corporation for wider equity share issues.
- Expanded estate planning benefits.
- Shareholders are not personally responsible for corporations' debts unless personal guarantees have been signed.
- Stock options can create incentives for employees.
- Potentially enhanced personal and business credibility.

Disadvantages of corporations:

- Higher start-up costs and a more complex regulatory environment.
- Potentially fewer tax writeoffs at commencement of business operations.

Engaging an experienced and skilled commercial lawyer is an essential element to the operations-planning process, especially before any significant business commitments or decisions are made.

Your commercial lawyer can assist in the following areas:

- Business incorporation and partnership agreement structuring.
- Setting up and negotiating commercial property leases.
- Reviewing franchise agreements.
- Resolving employment issues (terminations, severance agreements).
- Initiating overdue receivable collections.
- Drafting buy and sell agreements between shareholders.
- Structuring legal contracts such as joint ventures, co-ownership agreements, licensing agreements, and so on
- Acquisition agreements (buying and selling assets or shares) along with the necessary due diligence.

Products Versus Services

There are differences in how operations are handled between companies that are product-oriented and those that are in-person and service-oriented.

The following list provides some of the important distinctions between the two orientations:

- Service firms have greater direct customer contact. Individuals who provide services normally have more face-to-face contact with customers than those performing manufacturing operations.

- Quality standards may be more difficult to establish and measure in service operations.

- Product manufacturing operations can build or deplete product inventories to meet demand cycles, whereas service providers cannot store up their services. They have to adopt strategies that level out the demand process.

- Productivity is generally easier to measure in production operations.

The notable exception are online service-oriented firms that use business models such as Software as a Service (SaaS) or Product as a Service (PaaS) firms. Online, sharing economy and peer-to-peer services will be driven by data and metrics. Service levels and operational efforts can be tracked and directly linked to customer need and satisfaction.

Internal Information Technology Needs

The impact of information or digital technology on company operations is a huge and rapidly evolving topic. In this section we provide some high-level information about technology and e-commerce as they relate to the operations function.

- A brief summary of information technology needs that impact company operations.
- An overview of e-commerce opportunities and strategies.

Information Technology Applications

Computer technology is widely used to track financial, marketing, and operational activities. Software has become simple to use, is easily integrated into business operations, and is inexpensive. While business meetings and e-commerce have been quickly adopted, many businesses are still nervous about taking the leap into productivity and business intelligence products. The following list provides some of the tools that you might adopt to increase efficiency:

- Customizable cloud-based software is now extensively used for tasks such as human resources, payroll, inventory management, billing, customer relationship management (CRM), and accounting.

- CRM software can be integrated with social media to gather client and industry intelligence. CRM software may also be integrated with online advertising and content management.

- Productivity software to integrate teamwork can generate significant cost savings.

- E-commerce marketplaces or website plug-ins and payment systems make selling online and operating virtually in either business to consumer (B2C) or business to business (B2B) easier to implement now than in previous times.
- Client-facing websites are connected to backend operations to create enterprise data management and intelligence.

What emerging technologies can you integrate into your operations? While a technology scan is part of the external scan in the Business Diagnostics Framework, you need to continually learn which technologies can improve your business and ask whether your competitors will be early adopters and disrupt your market and business.

- Small manufacturers today make extensive use of computer-assisted design (CAD) and computer-assisted manufacturing (CAM), yet few have unlocked the potential of additive manufacturing, also known as additive manufacturing to trial concepts. American futurist Amy Webb describes a world of 'micro-factories' printing parts in a distributed supply chain which is less dependent on overseas suppliers.
- Virtual, mixed, and augmented reality can be used for training and, before investing dollars, for visualizing infrastructure projects via digital twinning.
- Block chain technology can be used to build immutable digital ledgers or to track provenance of goods and data.
- Microsensors and improvements in energy harvesting and in battery-life combine with fast, low-latency wireless data transfer to make remote monitoring easier than ever.
- Artificial intelligence and machine learning can use large data sets to make inferences and add to decision-making capabilities.

We discussed your digital presence in Chapter 4; however, in some cases and most particularly for e-commerce, a website may be part of operations. While websites are typically considered a piece of the marketing puzzle, with the advent of mobile e-commerce, we believe it is appropriate to discuss websites in the context of operations as well.

A key question is: What is the purpose of your website, and how does it fit with your sales operations, order fulfillment, or operations? In order to make informed decisions about websites and mobile e-commerce, we provide the following list with some of the issues to consider:

- Is your website intended as an e-commerce portal or a brochure with a simple layout that provides information or a bit of both? The website functionality could determine whether your site is managed by operations as part of sales fulfillment or marketing. E-commerce sites may have front-end information that is managed by marketing and a data and e-commerce backend that is managed by a different operational group.
- New technology means that websites are less expensive and easier to build and maintain than ever before. Do you have the knowledge, skills, and resources available to build and maintain your site yourself, or do you need to engage a third party? What skills will they need?
- There are multiple options for e-commerce, some of which are web services available for a monthly fee and others that can be integrated into your site.

- If you need a great deal of options or will have a large database, you will need to carefully match your requirements to the developer's skill set. For example, with complex e-commerce sites, developers skilled with specific tools like Magento may be more difficult to find.

KEY AREAS OF OPERATIONS MANAGEMENT

Operations management has a focus on the planning, organizing, and supervising of activities associated with production, manufacturing or the provision of services. The following six facets need to be considered to ensure the organization successfully transforms inputs to outputs in an efficient manner.

- Process management
- Quality management
- Facilities management
- Inventory management
- Risk management
- Project management

The Operations Review Summary

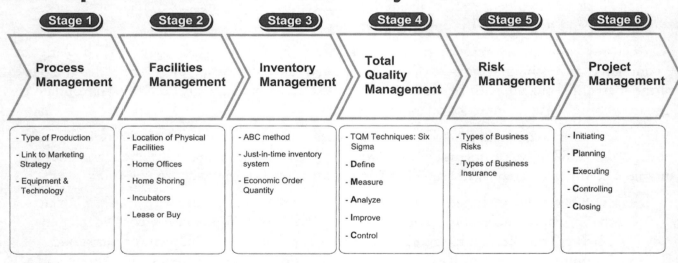

Figure 16. Operations Review Summary

Process Management

What type of production process is employed? Consider the following supply chain and types of manufacturing processes:

- Assembly line: work is broken down into small, repetitive tasks. This process involves long production runs and is usually associated with large manufacturing companies like car assembly plants.

- Batch flow: intermediate type of production that involves more variety and less volume than an assembly line. It has less variety and more volume than job shops. An example would be aa bottling plant with different drink varieties.

- Job shop: has short production runs. One or only a few products are produced before shifting to a different production setup. A job shop involves general purpose equipment and workforce. Each job is usually unique. A couple of examples are machine shops and printing companies.

- Just in time: parts go through each manufacturing step driven by a daily demand or pull schedule, which reduces inventories and speeds up the response time.

Software Delivery Considerations

If you are in software or a digital firm that relies on software to deliver its product or service, you need to consider:

- What is your development operation process? Are you familiar with and do you use agile techniques?

- Are you able to effectively use development sprints and iterative development and testing?

It is important to link your processes to customer demand. Is your production process linked to relate to your marketing and sales campaigns and to manage operations based on demand?

- Are there seasonal or sales swings that affect costs in production? How can these be managed (e.g. suppliers carry safety stock, seasonal labour, use process facilities from partners, outsource parts of product)?

- What types of equipment and manufacturing technologies are being used? Are any changes required or planned in order to remain competitive?

A good introduction into process management is Goldratt's classic 1986 book, *The Goal about the Theory of Constraints.* The book is written as a novel but highlights the various techniques to increase production flow. Goldratt's concepts have been rolled into lean theories, which are used to minimize waste while preserving customer value that the customer will pay for. Lean concepts can be applied to operations and also to management.

Toyota's quality system links three different concepts within lean: muda, mura, and muri. Muda refers to waste. Mura is unevenness, which leads to muri or unsustainable workload burdens.

Other process and production measurements include Six Sigma, which is widely used in logistics, production, and manufacturing. Six Sigma focuses on reducing variation and waste. Different productivity theories use different definitions of waste, although it is commonly understood that defects in parts, overproduction and overprocessing, wait times, under-utilized equipment, staff, parts, and finances, transportation, inventory variance, and motion need to be understood and reduced without impacting customer value.

Having a good understanding of the concepts will help you be efficient and productive while preserving customer value. There are a number of different concepts, tools, resources and institutes for learning more about lean operations. The basics can be found at www.lean.org/whatslean/

Facilities Management

Facilities can be defined as a company's physical settings, support services, and infrastructure that must be utilized to support business processes and strategic objectives. Often, companies overestimate their space needs and, consequently, overpay for space and equipment that is underutilized, or they do not have plans in place for spikes in demand and long-term capacity needs. This issue over space is particularly valid since digital tools have transformed office work, putting into question the need for physical office space when remote work and distributed workspaces have become so prevalent and accepted.

A key question to ask yourself is—how might my business secure optimum benefit from my facilities?

When thinking about facilities management, you might want to consider the following questions:

- What do we really need? How are we monitoring and evaluating our facilities needs?
- What is the capacity of each facility, and how close is current output to that capacity?
- Are the facilities being fully used, or are they underutilized? If they are underutilized, what strategies can you put in place to optimize use that won't jeopardize capacity to produce? For example, could you enter into a short-term lease with a compatible company, and lease equipment in off hours.)
- Are there any plans to increase capacity? What are the associated costs?
- Is production or service delivery planning a difficult task? Is demand difficult to estimate?
- What is the near-term capital expenditure (capex) requirement?
- Is there potential to outsource certain elements of facilities services?

Location of Physical Facilities

If you need a physical, bricks and mortar location to operate your business, location is a key success factor. The location decision for a company owner is an important one and can range from operating a home office to purchasing, leasing, or renting a commercial building. Very often, owners will decide on a location based on their personal needs (proximity to home and services) and later discover that the other factors are more important.

The following five key factors important aspects when determining an appropriate location:

1. **Market Access**

    Proximity and ease of access for customers and your target market should be the primary location consideration. Convenience and access for suppliers is another consideration.

2. **Financial**

    Consider the cost of land and improvements and current property lease costs and terms. Local labour costs and tax structures should play a part in the financial aspects of the location decision.

3. **Resource Availability**

   Access to raw materials and supply chain efficiencies will be part of the location decision. Look for effective transportation links, communications, a qualified labour force, and access to relevant knowledge and management talent.

4. **Business Environment**

   Environmental conditions to explore before making a location decision include local laws and the regulatory structure and potential government support and incentives.

5. **Personal and Employee Preferences**

   Business owners recognize that their businesses run more efficiently and effectively when employee needs are part of the decision-making process. Along with digital transformation, improved quality of life is a key decision factor for employees, and this particular detail needs to be considered when deciding where to locate your office. Housing and cost of living, climate, culture, and proximity to services, home, and climate all form part of decisions for employees and owners.

Remote Work and Home Offices

Small companies often begin operations as home-based businesses. This decision is usually driven by cost considerations because the business is in a vulnerable, early growth stage and needs to preserve cash for costs that contribute to revenue and value.

Business technology has made remote work and the home office scenario easier than ever because of the relatively low cost of office equipment and software that makes video-conferencing simple. Further, some companies allow staff to work from home a number of days a week to ease traffic congestion, balance the need for office space, and in times of pandemic, provide safe physical distancing.

The benefit of remote work is being able to hire the best person for the job, regardless of where they are physically located. Instead of paying to relocate staff, companies have regular face-to-face business-related and culture-building activities. It is not unusual to have staff all over the world who connect and collaborate through morning huddles via short video calls and extensive use of project management software. The rise of virtual companies and virtual teams means that there may not even be a head office.

There are obvious advantages with a home-based business scenario, both for small businesses and for employees, but such arrangements may not work for everyone. Culture, connection, collaboration, and innovative teamwork are all cited as critical success factors that can suffer in a virtual work team world.

The following items are considerations when reviewing your remote work and home offices capabilities.

- Client and company demands can lead to an expectation of being available for work at all times, leading to reduced productivity and burn out.
- Communications issues, which create havoc in an office, can be exacerbated in an online setting. Even with face-to-face video conferencing, subtle office politics, client

and supplier communication, and information can be misinterpreted. These issues could lead to a negative culture, reduced productivity, and longer customer response times, especially if colleagues in separate locations have not created a process to manage communications.

- Distractions from family and pets and difficulty maintaining spatial boundaries between home and work became part of the new normal and cultural conversation during the pandemic. Some technologies companies require remote work employees to have a separate workspace and reliable daycare. How will you manage this new business issue?
- Regulations, bylaws, and taxation can affect remote work and home office decisions. Are there any local, regional, or national policies that can impact your business or employees?

Incubators, Business Accelerators, and Shared Workspace

Other location options for business are business incubators or shared workspaces.

Business incubators provide early-stage entrepreneurs with affordable space, shared administration and office equipment, and access to business workshops, mentorship, and angel or venture capital, perhaps both. Many incubators also provide access to legal and accounting services. With high-profile incubators, the company receives credibility by being associated with the incubator. Many incubators are funded by government agencies, universities and venture capital firms looking for the next killer app.

Incubators are often confused with business accelerators, which are typically intensive, cohort-based and time bound programs that combine business education, practical hands-on homework to advance the business, and access to mentors and investors.

Conversely, shared workspaces may be non-profit or for-profit and offer some similar benefits as incubators, but they tend to focus on peer-to-peer networks rather than formal mentorship.

Facilities: Lease or Buy?

Early-stage companies invariably lease premises and often start their operations by renting space on a short-term (month-to-month) basis before entering into longer term and more formalized lease arrangements that are based on the sustainability of their revenues. It is important to carefully consider the options of leasing or buying facilities.

The Advantages of Leasing Facilities

- Leasing facilities allows you to preserve capital for other uses. While this is somewhat obvious for start-ups, many established companies fail to recognize the significant impact that a property purchase decision will have on their working capital and future potential for growth.

    Example:

    Company X purchases a commercial property for $1 million and obtains $600,000 in long-term financing with loan payments equivalent to lease payments, and the balance of the purchase is funded by $400,000 in cash.

The $400,000 cash outflow reduces the company's working capital resources. These funds could have been used to identify additional markets and then launch a new generation of product lines, providing enhanced revenue and earnings performance.

- Leasing facilities provides greater flexibility because you have the ability to relocate at the end of the lease term and find larger premises if necessary, and you can ignore the fluctuations in local property values, especially decreases in market values. These property values do not affect the value of the company.

The Advantages of Buying Facilities

Just as there are advantages for leasing facilities, buying facilities has some benefits. The following items are some of the opportunities that buying offers:

- The ability exists to modify or customize the property to increase profitability and efficiency.
- There are no contractual relationship to a landlord.
- Those companies that buy their facilities may enjoy property value appreciation as a way to increase the value of their business.
- Surplus space can be leased out to subsidize facilities costs.

It is not uncommon for companies that buy their facilities to make more profit on the real estate transaction than from the product created in the facility. In this case, it may be prudent to separate the real estate holding from the company operations. High-value land assets can attract predatory actors who buy the company to realize a short-term profit from its land rather than investing for the long term in products.

Inventory Management

The effective management of inventories is a critical component of business operations and can often mean the difference between success and failure, especially in smaller retail or wholesale firms where inventories represent a major financial investment. Inventory or warehousing software can be cloud-based, used with smart phones and tablets, and integrated with financial systems. Here are some questions to consider:

- What type of inventory is carried (raw materials, work in process, finished goods)?
- What is the makeup of each type of inventory and how significant is each?
- How are inventories managed with a focus on controlling costs and managing value?

Inventory management techniques include:

- The ABC method involves the classification of inventory into three categories: A, B, and C, based on their respective cost value. Managerial focus is applied to the most expensive and important A items.

- Just-in-time inventory systems focus on reducing storage by putting items into service when they are needed. This process requires close cooperation with suppliers to ensure that they can deliver materials quickly and in a highly predictable manner.

- The economic order quantity process focuses on minimizing high-ordering and high-carrying costs by determining only the amount that can be ordered and stored to reduce costs.

- Demand-driven inventory management combines the concepts of constraints, lean management, and Six Sigma to create demand-driven, material-requirements planning (DDMRP) management systems and software to link customer demand, supplier resources, and company capability to reduce costs and improve delivery times.

Inventory carrying costs can have a significant negative impact on the financial position of a company, so when deciding how to manage your inventory, consider the following:

- Minimize inventory investment by carrying smaller inventories, which result in lower financing, storage, and obsolescence costs.

- Keep work in process on schedule.

- Maximize sales and product selection by keeping sufficient inventory to avoid stock outs and missed sales opportunities.

- Guard against spoilage, product deterioration, shrinkage, and theft.

- Explore what hardware and software technologies can support your inventory management, automate your processes, or both.

Quality Management

Product and service quality are critical success factors to ensure survival in today's highly competitive business environment. There are myriad quality frameworks and tools. We have chosen the Total Quality Management (TQM) concept to demonstrate the steps to creating a comprehensive, holistic approach to provide high-quality products and services that meet customer needs.

When thinking about quality management, the following items provide some key points to consider:

- How are customer expectations managed? It is critical to understand client needs and satisfaction drivers when crafting a TQM strategy within a business.

- How important is production and service delivery quality?

- Quality is a design-in element. That is, sometimes low cost and low quality are what the client wants and needs. For example, beach balls are inexpensive and are typically not expected to last long. In this case, superior quality is not the main driver, but product consistency may be.

- Has a clearly defined organizational culture where there is an unrelenting focus on quality issues been developed? You can use continuous improvement in a constant effort to improve product and service quality and benchmarking to study the leading practices of competing or similar firms.

- Are there any product return policies or warranty implications? Are product failures studied to improve future iterations? (failure mode analysis)
- Is it possible to obtain regional or international recognition of the firm's quality management programs by meeting industry standards or relevant quality standards for your particular industry?

Developing techniques and tools will assist in building a defined quality management program. Consider the following tactics to improve quality:

- Encourage employee participation. You can involve front line employees to identify continuous and quality improvement opportunities. Quality circles involve regular meetings to identify, analyze, and resolve quality-related problems. Creating a non-judgmental, safe space to identify quality issues is a critical element for employee participation.
- Develop inspection standards that define a desired quality level and allowable tolerances.
- Use statistical process control.

One of the best-known quality techniques is Six Sigma, which is being increasingly adopted to improve process quality. Six Sigma offers a structured and distinct method to reduce defects, variation, and waste, which can often account for a significant percentage of sales revenue.

Six Sigma is more than just a process control tool. It is a quality program that improves customer's experience, lowers costs, and builds sticky relationships with customers by eliminating unpleasant surprises and broken promises. The system continues to be used worldwide by leading firms. Motorola Inc., which implemented the technique in the 1980s, is a Six Sigma organization that is striving to achieve just 3.4 defects per million.

To work on an existing process, which needs improvement, Six Sigma uses the DMAIC approach, see Figure 17 below:

- Define the process goals in terms of key critical quality parameters.
- Measure the current process performance in context of goals.
- Analyze the current situation in terms of causes of variations and defects.
- Improve the process by systematically reducing variation and eliminating defects.
- Control the future performance of the process.

The DMAIC Approach

Figure 17. DMAIC Approach

Risk Management

Risk management implements programs that identify risk factors and reduce risk exposure to preserve assets, the earning power, and reputation of the business. The risk management process should include a disaster recovery plan and emergency management for risks like pandemic, fire, flood, and earthquake.

Ask yourself, "what could possibly go wrong?" Your risk mitigation strategy should systematically and regularly address the following areas:

- List risks by category: property, personnel, product, customer, and reputation
- Identify which risks can be controlled and mitigated and which are out of your control.

- Identify which business risks are the highest priority and need to be mitigated immediately.
- Review your business insurance protection regularly.

Insurance

Insurance protection is an integral part of a sound risk management program. Insurance coverage should be limited to major potential losses by determining the size of loss that could be handled without serious financial difficulty, then relating the premium cost to the relative probability of loss. The following is a list of the major types of business insurance to discuss with your insurance professional:

- Product insurance covers damages that result from faulty product. The cost will depend on risk factors inherent in the product. A medical device that could result in harm to the patient will have a higher risk profile compared to say, a clothing retailer.

Commercial property insurance covers damages resulting from fire, storm, theft, and other dangers. Many policies cover all risks and if a specific type of damage is not excluded, it is covered.

- General liability insurance is usually combined with property coverage in a standard business owner's policy and covers legal defense costs if someone is injured on your property or by your product.
- Auto insurance can provide comprehensive coverage for non-collision related losses, collision, liability, accident benefits, and loss of use risk.
- Business interruption insurance covers fixed expenses that would continue if, for example, a fire shut down the business.
- Key person insurance covers the loss of key people, through death or prolonged disability, that can result in reduced profitability to your business.
- Buy-sell insurance is a life insurance policy for each company owner's share of the business. If one of the owners dies, a cash settlement is received by their estate or family in exchange for their business interests.
- Business loan insurance is offered through lenders. They receive insurance proceeds to retire the company loan principal after the death of the business owner.
- Group insurance is tailored to provide a combination of life, health, dental, and disability insurance for the benefit of business employees and their families.
- Credit insurance protects businesses from unexpected bad debts.
- Surety bonds insure against failure of other firms to complete contractual obligations and are frequently used in the construction industry.

Project Management

According to the Project Management Institute (PMI), project management is the application of knowledge, skills, tools, and techniques to a broad range of like activities in order to meet the requirements of a particular project.

Every business—small, medium or large—will encounter the need to utilize project management techniques within its operations. It's helpful to have someone on staff who is skilled at project management. Typical projects could be the development of new products or services, assessing the need for a new capital expenditure, or even setting up a new marketing campaign.

The Project Management Body of Knowledge or PMBOK® Guide recognizes five basic steps in completing a typical project-management assignment:

1. Initiating: defining the project planning framework via a project charter and developing a statement of work, requirements, and scope definition that outlines what is included and excluded. The major deliverables, milestones, and responsibilities also need to be assessed.

2. Planning: refining the work breakdown, estimating, and assembling the project team and scheduling.

3. Executing: considering communications needs, risk management, issue management—including escalation processes, and progress reporting.

4. Controlling: addressing what needs to be done to keep the project on track to achieve a successful completion.

5. Closing: reporting and delivery considerations, reallocation of team members, and knowledge management initiatives to retain and learn from the undertaken project.

Chapter 6
Human Resources Management

Overview

In this section, we review the human resource (HR) function and examine key characteristics of leadership. Many companies, especially smaller or early-stage firms tend to minimize the importance of this functional area. Human resources is a key contributor to an organization's health and has a strong influence on a company's competitive position in the marketplace.

HR will provide the transactional and functional operations of labour relations, payroll, benefits, hiring, and firing. However, HR is a critical part of operational excellence, which is why it has it's own place in the Business Diagnostics Framework.

Hiring and retaining motivated employees, who either support or interface directly with your clients, are critical success factors. Unhealthy or unhappy workplace environments are top reasons for losing employees, which is an enormous cost for employers. You don't have to provide free massages or Ping-Pong tables, but you do have to recognize the needs of your workforce.

The HR Function

We will review the following key HR areas which have the greatest impact the sustainability of a company's workforce:

- Recruiting and retaining employees
- Training and development
- Compensation and performance
- Planning

Recruit and Retain Employees

Of critical importance is hiring right. HR needs a clear line of sight to the skills and competencies and the work style and attitude that fits with company culture. The right hire with a willing attitude can be taught skills, but a person hired as a poor fit will cause pain for the company and themselves.

Having a reputation as a fair and reasonable employer and being described as a great place to work are the best ways to attract great employees. You might wonder where to find the best employees. The following list provides multiple sources to find new employees:

- Employee referrals
- Linked In
- Online services (free and paid)
- Industry or association job boards (online)
- Educational institutions (internships, co-op programs, and career fairs)
- Competitors
- Employment agencies
- Newspaper advertisements

When selecting and evaluating prospective new employees, take time to consider what will help your company and the person. We like Patrick Lencioni's book, *The Ideal Team Player: How to Recognize and Cultivate the Three Essential Virtues*. Lencioni describes the ideal team player as hungry, humble, and smart. We prefer his description as opposed to the term 'people smart' in that people skills are as important as competencies. While you consider the best fit for your company, you need also to be aware of the following recruitment practices:

- Write down what you are looking for in the short term and long term. How will this position grow with your company? How does it fit with the rest of the firm?
- Update the job description.
- Before scheduling an interview, ask yourself what you really need to know about this person? Ask questions that tease out how they are perceived by others and discuss their ability to adapt. If fit with the team is really important, how will you ensure you are not simply hiring clones of each team member? What type of skill and thought diversity is important?
- Consider how you can check your unconscious bias when reviewing resumes.
- A formalized interview process is required though an informal meeting will help the candidate relax and better understand the role and the company.
- Go beyond the reference checklist provided by the candidate for senior positions. What are the difficult-to-master soft skills required to be successful in the role?
- Determine who has the responsibility for hiring. Does this tie in with reporting relationships?

- Take careful consideration on the interview team and discuss how will you recognize and overcome your interview and selection biases?
- Endeavour to understand the internal and external drivers for the candidate. Is it to make a difference, learn, or only to have a job? Does this matter?

Employee Retention

Retaining good existing employees is a key strategy that requires the establishment of appropriate performance-based evaluation systems and a culture that promotes workplace quality, pride, and achievement.

The link between leadership and employee retention is critical. Employees will leave for a variety of reasons though compensation typically scores low on the list. Authenticity, vision, trust, and respect are listed as the top reasons that employees leave their jobs. Those four items together are the fundamentals of leadership. Linking the vision to strategy and operations is the work of leadership. Continual authentic communication will build trust and respect. If your employees do leave for other reasons, you want to wish them well, knowing they will speak well of you, helping to build that all-important reputation as a great place to work.

Employers also need to demonstrate that employees have the ability to progress to positions of greater responsibility, if it exists. If it doesn't exist, ask your employees about what, besides monetary compensation, keeps them motivated? Very often, the opportunity for professional development becomes a key element.

You can conduct employee engagement surveys that will give a window into your culture and how you are doing as a leader. The key with employee engagement surveys is to listen and act on what you learn in an authentic manner. Any disconnect between what you say and what you do will erode trust and respect. For example, if fostering an innovation culture is important for your business, a recognizable system for employees to understand what innovation means, to put forward proposals that might improve products, services, and processes, and to know how such proposals will be evaluated is necessary.

There is a recent trend toward what is referred to as intrapreneurship as a method for employee retention. In essence, the company wants employees to act like entrepreneurs by taking risks and innovating. The difficulty with this concept is that the company needs to create a safe space for that innovation and to avoid using the term as a way for leadership to avoid setting the direction and vision for the organization.

Retaining employees is not as simple as offering more monetary compensation. A classic human resources reference book we like is *First Break all the Rules* by Marcus Buckingham & Curt Coffman. They recommend surveying employees on the following 12 questions to determine how best to retain employees.

1. Do I know what is expected of me at work?
2. Do I have the materials and equipment I need to do my work right?
3. At work, do I have the opportunity to do what I do best everyday?
4. In the last seven days, have I received recognition or praise for doing good work?

5. Does my supervisor or someone at work seem to care about me as a person?
6. Is there someone at work who encourages my development?
7. At work, do my opinions seem to count?
8. Does the mission or purpose of my company make me feel my job is important?
9. Are my co-workers committed to doing quality work?
10. Do I have a best friend at work?
11. In the last six months, has someone at work talked to me about my progress?
12. This last year, have I had the opportunity at work to learn and grow?

Training and Development

Employees generally want to be competent at their work and want opportunities to try new things.

This provides an opportunity for HR to add value through training and development. Not all jobs lead to higher level work, but that can be mitigated with the right steps. Consider the following issues:

- Orientation of new employees should include an explanation of specific job duties, performance expectations, and evaluation processes. They should also be given information on the corporate culture.

- Not every job has a promotion path or a method to make the job more rewarding. For instance, most manufacturing line jobs are monotonous. But there are cross training opportunities and techniques to keep employees engaged and proud of their work and contribution.

- Ineffective training programs can lead to trial-and-error learning and frustration.

- Not everyone will make a good manager. For example, if someone is excellent in sales, it doesn't mean they should be promoted to managing others.

- Developing technology or information technology workers for progression into marketing, sales, and project management positions in the knowledge sector involves retraining and creating new career paths. This type of retraining is best accomplished by attending external practical education programs or having them delivered in-house by training consultants or on-the-job mentors.

- Development can include items that don't seem to relate directly to business skills. Some examples include personal development that will increase confidence, interpersonal skills, or communication skills.

Compensation and Performance

Employee incentives can be both financial and nonfinancial. Finding the right balance will be an on-going challenge. Here are issues to consider:

Financial compensation must be in line with the industry and competitors. It should be monitored and reviewed on a regular basis.

Raises do not necessarily need to be linked to the evaluation process. In fact, linking the two tends to limit your options on when to provide raises and creates expectations that you may not be able to meet. Instead, consider the value of the work, and align compensation to the work.

Performance-based compensation systems or profit-sharing plans need to be carefully designed and tied to the key success factors of the organization. Remember to compensate for the behaviour you want and to keep compensation within your ability to pay. This is best accomplished by using external HR specialists, although the cost of this service may be a deterrent to smaller companies.

Comprehensive benefit packages need to be developed within your sustainable capacity to pay and with consideration to your need to retain employees with mandated benefits and extra benefits. Vacation time, medical, dental, life and disability insurance plans, and group retirement benefits can be valued and costly. It is very difficult to roll back benefits.

Employee costs such as social events, games, and celebrations can build your unique culture and a sense of place and belonging. Letting employees have a say in these activities will build trust.

Employee Equity Incentive Plans

Employees often have the opportunity to participate in a company's financial growth by way of various equity incentive plans such as stock options and profit sharing.

Stock options provide the right to purchase company common shares at a stated price during a specific period of time. Usually, options are granted with an exercise price equal to the fair market value of the stock at date of grant or hire. If the stock price rises above the exercise price, the option allows the employee to purchase the stock at a lower or exercise price.

Vesting periods are the periods of time during which the options are held by the employee but cannot be triggered. There is usually a minimum one-year waiting period that is often followed by *stepped* vesting periods over the next three to four years.

While the employee can see a potential financial gain, derived when the stock exercise price is less than the current market value, stock liquidity or the ability to sell the stock to realize the value remains a key consideration, especially if private company shares have been vested and can't be sold on an open market.

Such incentive programs have the indirect benefit of locking in or handcuffing key employees, thereby reducing the risk of their departure to competitors. Clear ground rules need to be established and communicated as to the stock disposition process when the employee departs, especially if they join a competitor, and the tax implications of the options must be clearly stated.

Profit sharing can be achieved by ownership simply providing bonuses, or the company can allocate a portion of profits to be shared among employees, which is common. An Employee Stock Ownership Plan or ESOP is a formal method for employees to buy into the company.

Performance

Goal setting should be established on an annual basis and linked to a formal performance evaluation process. Goals should be reviewed every quarter to keep employee goals aligned with the annual goals of the company.

Create a system to keep company strategic goals and targets front and centre with employees. Link goals with operations and report on progress. Ask employees what will help propel them toward the goals and what might hinder them.

Employee evaluations need to be linked to goals. Very often, evaluators, for whatever reason, tend to succumb to the halo effect and give favoured employees halos and other's pitchforks. It is often forgotten that steady performers are as important as superstars.

The goal-setting process should include:

- Job objectives and responsibilities
- Performance criteria to be used in annual review: Exceeded/achieved/ did not achieve plan
- Performance assessment should include both qualitative and quantitative factors. Criteria and goals should be SMART: specific, measurable, achievable, relevant, and time framed
- Personal development needs

Human Resources Planning

Short- and mid-term planning for the human resources function involves the assessment of workforce requirements to handle pressing operational tasks. Strategic, longer term planning involves a forward-looking analysis of HR needs to meet the company's growth requirements. Both processes involve the following common actions:

- Managing growth or market contraction issues
- Anticipating product or service migrations and changes
- Assessing the types of required employees
- Establishing future compensation, training, and staff development initiatives
- Understanding leadership, management, and employee succession planning

LEADERSHIP

It is often difficult to recognize when a leader is doing a good job, but it is very easily recognized when a leader is not performing well. In our view, key leadership skills include setting and communicating strategic vision, marshalling adequate resources, establishing the right organizational structure, and acting with integrity.

The leader sets the tone for the entire corporation, whether small or large. The clarity and continual communication of the vision and the tactics on how to achieve the vision are paramount.

In this chapter, we cover the functional elements of management leadership; however, we caution that leadership is a skill that can be developed beyond simply understanding the management to-do list.

The following leadership issues and requirements need to be considered in managing a small- or medium-sized business:

- Management capacity
- Leadership skill development
- Teams and teamwork
- Organizational structure
- Mentoring

Management Capacity

Strategy is clearly the role of leadership in any company. There are countless references and thought leaders on strategy. We see strategy as the necessary follow on to vision. Your vision is what you want to be true, and strategy is how you will get there. Strategies can be complex or simple. What will you do, stop doing, and start doing to achieve the vision? You can change business models, products, marketing, and any other of the tactical parts of your business, but a lack of vision and a strategy to get there can quickly cause a lack of cohesion and affect your business.

Strategy, leadership, and management are each linked to the others. Most business owners are also the leaders and primary managers in their businesses. Many owners and managers of growing companies *don't know what they don't know* and need support during the difficult journey of running a company. We have prepared the following questions for management, so you can assess your capabilities and make changes where required. Take a moment to reflect on these questions:

- Have you been able to identify your company's key success factors, that is, what attributes allow you to successfully compete within your respective industry sector? Can you describe them in a succinct fashion?
- Have you established close and trusting relationships with your key stakeholders (employees, customers, suppliers, shareholders, investors, and so on)? How would they describe you?
- Are you able to perform a meaningful stakeholder analysis where they can be *mapped* on the basis of power and interest?
- Are you able to understand your customer's journey through your company?
- Do you maintain a high standard of ethics and integrity? Do your people know what you stand for? Do they know what ethics and integrity look like in your organization and how to apply them in your day-to-day operations?
- Do you possess strong functional management skills in the finance, marketing, operations, HR, technology, and strategic planning areas?

- Can you assess your level of competence? Someone once said that "in calm waters, every ship has a good captain." Being competent, especially from a managerial perspective, involves a complete understanding of your business.

- Are you working in the business with your head down in the trenches, or are you working on the business and assuming a more strategic perspective?

- Do you give credit to employees where credit is due? Selflessness is an important quality.

- Have you been able to create an understandable and compelling vision for the company? Does the company have an appropriate organizational structure for your competitive environment?

- Has the vision and strategic direction been clearly communicated? If you asked an employee what the business wants to achieve in three years, what would they say?

- Are you able to instill and inspire confidence among your employees, so they will take on challenging tasks and assignments?

- Do you encourage risk and invite opposing views from your people? At the same time, have they cultivated a sense of urgency and awareness that they need to contribute more than they cost?

- Do you emphasize flexibility and the development of skill sets that allow employees to work across departmental boundaries?

- Do you recognize and see how diversity, inclusion, and gender-equity can be valuable for your business?

- Are you maintaining a broad perspective by asking?

    What if…? Why do we do this…? What will it take…? What's stopping us?

- Are you able to answer and address these two key questions?

    What is keeping you awake at night?

    Where do you see your company in three years time?

Leadership Skill Development

Are leadership and management the same thing? We do not believe so, though we do believe that the best managers are also skilled leaders. Business management is a series of functional skills based on budgeting, operations, and problem solving. Each of these complex tasks can be done well by managers, though we believe that managers who possess leadership skills and who provide vision and purpose will be more successful and, ultimately, contribute more to the organization.

Developing leadership skills will result in a more proactive and effective management team. There is an entire discipline within human resources devoted to developing leadership skills. For our purposes, we believe the following are key skills for managers.

- Leaders listen: Active listening involves looking at issues from others' perspectives and understanding and learning from them. Verne Harnish, founder of the Entrepreneurs'

Organization, calls this simply caring for people and says this is the most important aspect of leadership.

- Leaders are visible through using techniques such as Management By Walking Around (MBWA). Being visible, communicating with and listening to employees at all levels of the company seems so simple, and yet it can be difficult to master without seeming forced.
- Leaders are mentors. Developing employees for future growth through constructive feedback, coaching, and teaching will assist with succession planning and allow more delegation of authority and tasks.
- Leaders empower others by strengthening employee belief in their own effectiveness. This can be accomplished by ensuring that authority and decision making are progressively pushed to lower and lower levels. Employees are encouraged to embark on reasonable initiatives without fear of retribution.
- Leaders take time to appreciate what is working well. Cooperrider's appreciative inquiry gives attention to "the best of the past and present in order to ignite the collective imagination of what might be." Beyond typical unrelenting focus on problem solving, appreciative inquiry reviews capabilities and assets with a focus on what is right. Leaders create a team experience to uncover and discuss stories about past successes and peak work experiences. The outcome is the validation of team members' capabilities, which builds confidence and the ability to innovate.
- Leaders accept feedback and create authentic, appropriate transparency. Consider feedback options and the concept of open book management.

Feedback

Great leaders seek input, advice, and feedback from their peers, employees, and other stakeholders. The simple act of asking for feedback and accepting it graciously with curiosity will build trust. Ask questions like:

> What can I do to support you?
>
> What changes can I make to support your success?
>
> How can I improve?

The key to asking for feedback is that you need to have built trust first.

There are formal processes like 360 feedback, which is also known as 'full-circle-feedback,' that gathers observations about performance from supervisors, peers, subordinates, and, sometimes, customers. The feedback is then linked to the employee's own self-evaluation. The intent is to obtain as much frank feedback from as many perspectives as possible.

Potential benefits of this type of feedback include:

- Team development—individual members share what is working effectively.
- Improved client service—if external clients are asked to participate.

- Useful insights can be gained as to overall training needs.

Concerns with 360 review systems include:

- Anonymous reviews from staff or colleagues may use the system to settle old scores. Like anonymous comments on social media, feedback can be brutal, in which case, it is rarely helpful.
- The process can be extremely time-consuming with extensive data collection, evaluation, and dissemination required.
- The process tends to focus on negatives and problems.
- Those doing the rating often receive insufficient instruction on what helpful feedback looks like.

Open-Book Management

The concept of open-book management is about transparency. All employees receive relevant information about the company's financial performance and condition. This is often tied to profit sharing, stock ownership plans, or both. This process can help employees see the necessity for change, which is invariably driven by financial realities.

Open-book management builds trust because everyone can see what is going on and where the company is headed. A major concern with this process is the extent to which employees have full access to company financial statements, which often contain confidential information that ought not be shared with competitors. There is considerable debate with regard to salaries, vacation time, and benefits. Inevitably, over time, there will be imbalances that can cause conflict between employees.

In practicality, most companies balance openness and transparency with the need to keep some corporate confidentialities.

Teams and Teamwork

Within many organizations, employees are teaming up and partnering to solve complex issues under tight time constraints. Consider the following scenarios:

- Teams are now replacing the *boss-employee* coupling of the past.
- Teams are formed to maximize competitive advantage and will often consist of members from various department or countries around the world, operating in a virtual fashion.
- Teams can be functional (i.e., sales teams organized by geography) or cross functional (i.e. engineers, marketing, and salespeople involved in the launch of a new product).
- Effective team performance often takes time to achieve. Utilizing the team's collective intelligence can be a challenge if trust or agenda issues surface.
- Teams fail when their team members are more concerned with individual agendas instead of the common goals of the group.

One of the ways to ensure successful team outcomes is to ensure a common understanding of why the team was formed and to provide guidance. In our years of teaching, we have found that the starting place is discussing the following team formation elements and committing to a commonly understood, co-developed, and written team charter that team members agree to. We have the developed the following elements to our team charters:

1. Foundation: What are your team goals and values? If you say interactions need to be respectful, be sure to discuss what respect means to each team member and what it looks like in practice. If a team goal is fun, be sure to ask what boundaries each team member has or what the collective boundary might be.

2. Operations: Who will lead and when? What are the structure, roles, responsibilities, and accountability? When will you meet, and how will you communicate?

3. Execution: How will you execute on your goal? What are the tasks, timelines, and milestones for execution of team goals?

4. Quality: What does quality mean, and what does it look like? How will you know what success looks like?

5. Conflict: How will you handle team conflict? Are there any consequences for poor team behavior?

Organizational Structure

Smaller companies experience continuous organizational and management challenges as they grow. Many of these business owners are generalists or cannot afford qualified professional staff.

The stages in the organizational life of a typical small business can be summarized as follows:

Level one: A one-person operation, and that one person does everything.

Level two: The owner becomes a player or coach and participates extensively in all facets of the business.

Level three: The owner has hired an intervening layer of management (typically sales and production or operational managers).

Level four: The management functions are more formalized with more control processes put into place.

In earlier growth stages or in smaller operations, it is more likely that one person will assume more than one functional role. As your company grows, you will need to split out functions. In more complex organizations, there are a variety of different organization structures. Figure 18 illustrates a simple functional organization chart that could be applied to level two or three businesses.

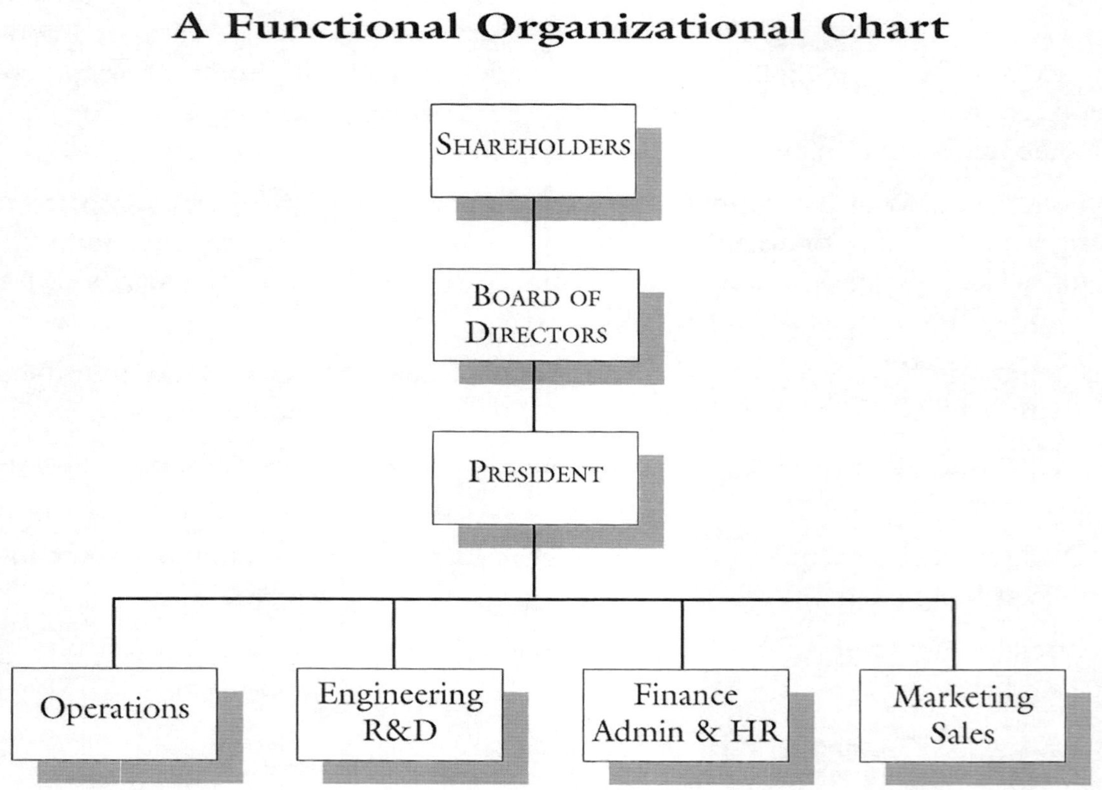

A Functional Organizational Chart

Figure 18. Functional Organization Chart

Mentoring

Owners and managers need to mentor their employees, and they, themselves, can benefit from having mentors. Running an organization—large, medium, or small—can be incredibly lonely. Often, important decisions are made, based upon gut feelings and without recourse to any objective resources that could provide a more balanced assessment of the situation.

We provide information on potential useful resources that could make the journey less lonely and provide much needed support, guidance, and experience.

A Board of Directors (and other related resources)

Establishing an effective Board of Directors include the following benefits:

- A competent and active Board of Directors is critical to the capital-raising process and company credibility. Board members will often be appointed by early-stage investors in the company.

- The Board ensures that management has developed and implemented a realistic business and strategic plan.

- Independence and objectivity are provided by outside directors versus using family members, paid professionals, or senior management.

- Carefully selected Board members can provide valuable expertise and contacts that will assist the company's growth.

An increased focus on a director's legal responsibilities and liability sometimes makes it difficult to attract talented Board members. Further, the owner may not wish to relinquish decision making to a Board. Alternatively, a Board of Advisors (or Advisory Board), consisting of a similar group of independent and qualified individuals, can be set up. Boards of Advisors typically have reduced personal liability and will not vote on corporate actions. Appointees should carefully review the terms of their engagement with their corporate lawyer.

For start-up companies, the development of an informal mentor network can be a time-saving and cost-effective strategy. Mentors can often be accessed through local Chambers of Commerce and technology associations. Retired or semi-retired legal, accounting, commercial banking, and consulting professionals or industry-specific executives and managers can be excellent sources of informal guidance and feedback.

Besides having a Board, a Board of Advisors, or finding a mentor, there are numerous business support groups—both free and paid. Furthermore, there has been a tremendous increase in the demand for executive coaching as leaders of organizations and companies realize that some form of external, objective support is required to guide them on the journey.

A key element is a *nondirective* coaching approach. The client chooses the focus of conversation, while the coach listens and contributes observations and open-ended questions. Through this coaching process, self-developed clarity leads to crafting appropriate and effective action plans. The coach serves as a method to keep the business executive accountable to their action plans.

Professional coaches undergo a rigorous certification process and are bound by a code of ethics. Coaches work in partnership with their clients and are trained to listen, observe, and customize their coaching approach to the individual's needs.

Chapter 7
The Technology Assessment

Overview

It is rare to find a business that isn't affected or can't leverage technology for product improvement, new product development, or operational efficiency. Given the importance of technology issues, an internal technology assessment is included as a final element of the Business Diagnostics Framework internal size up, even though it is included in the PEST analysis in section one.

Even if your company is not directly operating as a technology company, it is highly likely that either your suppliers or clients (or both) are either technology companies or technology enabled. This assessment process provides some insights as to their potential and their challenges; in essence, how long they might be around.

Investment and pay back considerations would normally be incorporated into such an assessment process; however, these issues are dealt with in more detail in Chapter Nine.

We wish to thank Denzil Doyle for his assistance with certain sections of this chapter. His excellent book *Making Technology Happen* has been used as a valuable reference point, with suitable permission granted.

The technology assessment consists of the following areas:

- Technology description
- Products, services, and processes
- Intellectual property issues
- Markets
- Potential risk factors
- New technology assessment

Technology Description

To understand the characteristics of a technology, consider the following questions:

- What is the technology and the opportunity? Can you describe what the value proposition is and what pain the technology solves for users? Can you summarize the concept to a stranger in a 30-second elevator pitch?

- What is the development stage? Is it a technology push or a market pull?
  - Technology push happens when enthusiastic developers and inventors push and promote their new technology before their products and markets have been clearly identified. Technology push is often described as a technology in search of a problem.
  - Market pull is when the technology clearly fits with a problem to be solved, and there is an identifiable and sufficiently large market with a need and the resources to buy the product. The development team can then set out to confirm their product premise through customer discovery, validating the product and market fit, and pull their product through an iterative technology development process—always being mindful of the market need.

These relationships are illustrated in Figure 19. To quote Denzil Doyle of *Making Technology Happen*, ask yourself the following simple question, "What is the product and how much of it can be sold?"

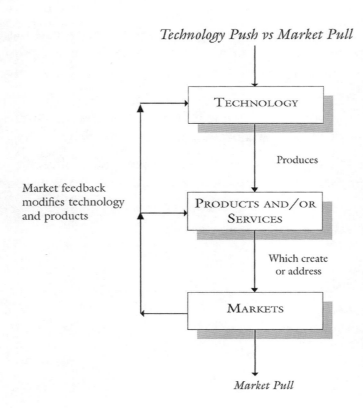

Figure 19. Technology Push Versus Market Pull

Products, Services, and Processes

With shifting client needs, trends, and rapidly changing markets, one-product technology companies are often doomed to failure. Follow-ons or product extensions will ideally consist of new additions to the product family by adding and subtracting features and functionality. Following this type of production model results in the following characteristics:

- Lower price and lower functionality
- Higher price and higher functionality
- Combinations of features and functions

Having an effective product migration strategy will lead to timely product introductions, so new products generate revenues at the same time as old ones are reaching maturity or starting to decline. In order to assess such a strategy, consider the following questions:

- What is the purpose of the product or service?
- Does it meet potential customer needs?
- What are the unique features? Cost, design, or simplicity?
- What is the estimated technological life?
- Is the product iterative, evolutionary, or revolutionary?
- At what stage is the product on the following innovation chain?
    1. Conceptual or idea stage: Concepts tend to be easy to generate and easy to kill.
    2. Research and development stage (R&D): Is the product in the technical development stage or near market or commercialization? Typically, technology is described using technology readiness levels (TRL). At TRL 1 basic principles have been observed; the levels move to TRL 9 where the system has been proven in an operating environment.
    3. Development: Engineering prototype, pilot run, client evaluations.
    4. Production: Product testing and refinements.
    5. Market development: Beta testing, setting up distribution channels.
- What type of production processes are required?
    - Capital intensive
    - Labour intensive
    - Material intensive
- What is the product migration, extension or follow-on product strategy?

Intellectual Property Issues

Safeguarding intellectual property (IP) is a complex, yet essential, task for technology companies. The status of a company's intellectual property is a key area of focus and due diligence by potential investors. The following brief review highlights the various types of IP protection:

Patents

Patent laws prevent third parties from making or selling patented products. A patent acts like a time-limited monopoly from a government to encourage innovation. In the United States, patents are granted to the first inventor to file (FITF) rather than to the first to invent.

The inventor is granted a *negative right* under the law and is able to exclude others from using and making the invention. This right is granted in exchange for making the patent information known to the public.

You will need a patent in each country where you want to enforce these rights. The terms and laws for every jurisdiction can be different and depend on the type of patent. We recommend that you check with a patent lawyer or agent.

Key questions to ask prior to implementing a patent strategy to protect your invention:

- Does the device or process have a practical benefit or utility that meets customer needs?
- Is the invention novel or new?
- Is the invention not obvious using inventive ingenuity? It must be an improvement or development that is not obvious to anyone possessing average skill in the technology field.
- Have you or anyone on your team publicly disclosed, developed, or sold products that use the invention more than one year prior to a Canadian or USA patent application?
- Do you have written records of your discovery?
- Is there an existing or potential market for the invention?
- What are the costs to manufacture and market the invention?
- Is funding in place to commercially exploit the invention?
- Do you have sufficient capital to file patents and defend your patents?

The patent registration process starts with a preliminary search, which is usually carried out in the Canadian and USA patent offices. A broader and more comprehensive infringement search can also be completed to see if the invention infringes on another patent.

Preparation and filing of the application are best done using an experienced patent lawyer or agent to guide you through this complex process. The registration process involves drafting an application that:

- Clearly distinguishes your invention from previous ones.
- Defines specific claims, which establishes the scope and quality of the patent.

If the patent is accepted, the patent holder has the legal right to exclude others from using, making, or selling the invention at the date of approval. It should be noted that up to three years could elapse between the initial application and the patent's granting, due to the considerable volume of patent applications being filed. You need to be patient and have both a development plan and the funds to support the patent process. The invention details are not revealed by the government to outsiders during the application process.

Patent Pending is a status that can be placed or affixed to a device or process after filing the patent application and prior to registration. It serves to warn others that the patent has been formally filed. Potential competitors may be deterred for fear of infringing on the forthcoming patent.

Trade Secrets and Confidentiality Agreements

A trade secret is a process, design, or compilation of specific technical data that is used by a company to ensure its competitive advantage over others who do not have access to such closely guarded information.

Trade secrets have no protection under the law, as opposed to patents or trademarks. The most significant difference between trade secrets and patents or trademarks is that the trade secret can be protected without having to disclose its closely held information.

A key tool in maintaining the trade secret is a Non- Disclosure Agreement (NDA), which can be used to stop employees from disclosing the secret. Such agreements will call for employees to confirm that they will not reveal the employer's proprietary information and that they waive any intellectual property rights associated with the project. A classic example of a trade secret is Coca Cola. The company has no patents for its formula, choosing instead to keep information closely guarded. Such agreements are essential for an organization to protect its technology by ensuring that outsiders, including suppliers and employees, have signed and are legally bound by written agreements.

Another element in protecting trade secrets is to implement access restrictions that limit or restrict access to production, laboratory research facilities, and data storage areas. Control employees' smart phones or recording devices to prevent theft of trade-secret processes or documentation with audio, photographs or video.

One drawback of a trade secret is that the product might be subject to reverse engineering.

Trademarks

Trademarks are any name, symbol, or expression that an individual or organization uses to distinguish its products or services. It can be a critical part of the brand and marketing for a company.

There are different trademark types and registration systems around the world, so consulting with a lawyer or your government trademark office is a good practice.

Benefits in registering trademarks include:

- Alerts others of the trademark's existence
- Can provide nationwide protection
- Allows the holder to commence trademark infringement proceedings if necessary

Copyright

Copyright protection provides artists and authors with the sole right to transmit, reproduce, sell, and distribute their work or to permit someone else to do so. The time limit for protection is different in different countries, though they are usually a number of years after the author's death. Registration is voluntary, but advisable. This step provides the owner with a basis to commence a copyright infringement action if required.

Check with your government's intellectual property agency. In the digital age, copyright law will continue to evolve.

Industrial Design

Industrial designs are the visual features of shape, configuration, pattern, or ornament, or any combination of these features, that are applied to a finished article. They can be registered for a defined term and have the following attributes:

- Prevent other firms from directly copying a design
- Protect the design of a functional device or object
- Provide additional intellectual property rights within some specific industries

Completion of an Intellectual Property Plan

Every technology company needs to safeguard their I.P best accomplished by creating a specific plan as follows:

- Complete an intellectual property (IP) audit to identify and inventory IP assets. The process includes a review of records management, confidentiality practices, and contracts administration.
- Analyze IP strengths and weaknesses. Decide what technologies to develop and ask yourself if IP leadership in these technologies is affordable or should you license-in outside technological processes?
- Ensure inventors are product driven. Company engineers should file patents as an ongoing and integral part of product development. They should also complete patent infringement searches as part of the predesign process.
- Develop a budget for patent costs.
- Initiate an IP training program for key employees.

Markets

Technology companies often attempt to market their products or services based on technical abilities rather than satisfying customer needs. To avoid the 'product push' trap, consider the following questions:

- Have you assessed your market potential in relation to total market size?
- What is your expected market penetration and market share?
- Have you assessed replacement versus incremental markets?
  - Replacement sales are those that involve the replacement of existing units. Buyers are normally influenced by price or increased quality.
  - Incremental sales are those made to 'early adopters and visionaries' who are influenced by product functionality and newness versus price.

- Do you understand the market and the distribution channels? Are distribution agreements mutually advantageous? Should you go to market via distribution or direct to the end-user?

- Have you considered and written a marketing plan that identifies validated target market segments and the costs to go to market?

- Have you considered licensing as a go-to market strategy? If a technology process is initiated but is not suitable for development into a discrete product or service, perhaps the process can be licensed for development elsewhere?

Some benefits of licensing:

When you discover that a product or service is unsuitable for a discrete implementation, you might be able to recoup your investment through licensing. Some of the other benefits of licensing can include:

- Licensing out your technology can be an effective way to test and develop off-shore markets.

- The licenser can exploit its technology in secondary markets without you having to make large marketing and production expenditures.

- Licensees who receive the technology typically have existing products, distribution channels, or facilities, and thus, they are able to acquire the technology more cheaply and quickly than by completing their own typically expensive R&D process.

- Licensees are less likely to become future competitors.

Potential Risk Factors

When developing a new technology, and to avoid undue external and internal risks, here are some key questions to consider:

- Is there a threat of emerging new competitors, superior technology, or both?

- How short are your product life cycles with resulting obsolescence issues?

- What is the relationship between the stage of technology development and cash flow generation?

- The negative cash flow experienced during the earlier stages of product development, along with unexpected expenditure surprises, can lead to feelings of despair in the valley of uncertainty. As operations ramp up to meet market demand, cash flow shortfalls begin to diminish, leading to increased optimism.

- The fail-fast or, as Ash Maurya likes to say, learn-fast concept has developed out of the need to continue to innovate and offer new products and product extensions. Do you have a robust product development process that uses cross-functional teams and has clearly identified go, no-go gates? Have you considered the voice of the customer in your development process?

- How mobile are key employees and management? Is there potential to lose intellectual property because it walks out of the door? Can this be counteracted by stock option incentives and/or non-compete agreements?

- Are there growth-related risks? What would the impact be on the various operational functions like finance, production and operations, human resources, marketing, and sales?

- Is there a dependence on a limited number of customers?

- Is there a dependence on a limited number of suppliers? Are there alternative sources of supply, or does the potential to outsource exist?

- How strong are your proprietary rights? Is there potential for infringement lawsuits?

- Are there currency or foreign receivable risks? Can these be hedged or insured by banking or government export programs?

- Do you have the financial resources to cover ongoing R&D costs, which are necessary for product enhancements and the development of new generation technologies?

- Do you have the ability to raise additional capital via committed investors with deep pockets?

Figure 20 illustrates the often-painful process in completing product development while experiencing severe cash flow constraints.

Technology Evolution & Cash Flow Realities

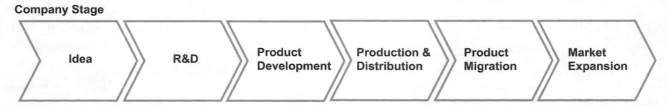

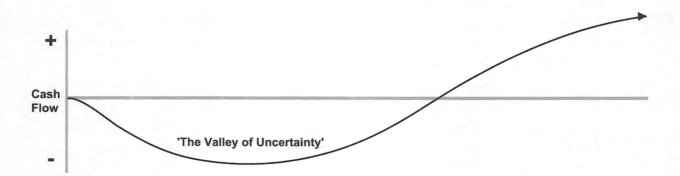

Figure 20. Technology Evolution and Cash Flow Realities

New Technology Assessments

This concluding section covers a carefully defined process that can be used to determine the potential for a new technology to succeed. This section is based on an article titled, "A Logical Approach to Understanding New Technologies" by Jonathan D. Andrews FCA and abridged with kind permission from the author.

Often a company will consider acquiring or developing a new technology to boost their growth strategies. Developing a new product for new markets can be a highly risky undertaking. Here are some key questions that you should ask before starting such a project:

1. What are the strategic benefits of this new technology to the organization?

2. When obtaining information about strategic benefits, don't limit the list to only those promoted or provided by the technology developers or vendor. The experience gained by others is also an important way to identify additional strategic benefits.

3. For business purposes, strategic benefits are a primary consideration, other factors are secondary. If there are few strategic benefits that a new technology can bring to your organization, there is little reason for an organization to pursue it any further.

4. What are the strategic planning issues that need to be considered?

5. Essential to the successful implementation of a new technology is careful planning. Inherent is the need to define strategic objectives and anticipate the kinds of risks, pitfalls, and problems that may be encountered along the way. Comments by those who have implemented new technologies have included such remarks as, "I wish we had spent more time planning and talking to customers."

6. It is clear that forward-thinking strategic and planning decisions have to be made to ensure the successful implementation of a new technology. Finding out what kind of problems can be anticipated and being prepared to address them will help to minimize the possibility of a new technology initiative becoming derailed.

7. What are the key issues that have caused a demand for this new technology?

8. This question will separate strategically beneficial, bona fide technologies from those that may be viewed as technology push solutions looking for problems.

9. If the new technology meets an existing, defined demand, there will be a resulting tangible benefit.

10. What does this new technology consist of?

11. Technologies, described as new, may be repackaged old technologies or reengineered, newer technologies from an unreceptive market. Understanding the differences is key to understanding your time to market.

12. Understanding the original technology and the environment in which it operates can help place new applications into perspective. Familiarity with a new technology at an overview level will help you appreciate how the pieces fit together. For example, sensors have their own standards and is an entire field of study, but understanding

how sensors can be integrated into an existing system will make melding technologies together easier.

13. How mature is the technology?
14. Statistics and trends found by research can provide a contextual background for a new technology. They provide insight into the popularity of a technology and can indicate how established it has become. Inevitably, adoption of an immature technology raises risk-related concerns for most organizations. As a result, it is important to review statistics and trends to gain meaningful insight into the maturity and corresponding stability and risk of the technology. It's important to be aware of which technologies are likely to be of higher risk than others.
15. Who are the developers or vendors for this technology?
16. Knowing the principal researchers, developers, or vendors and understanding the differences between their technological approach and products is key to attaining a practical, broad-based knowledge of the technology and its functionality. In higher risk situations, where the vendor is more likely to be a long-term business partner, the vendor and product functionality play a pivotal role in a successful implementation. This is particularly true in hardware technology partnerships.
17. Ask yourself how proprietary the technology is and whether that will inhibit market uptake or further technology development. Consider Chesbrough's open innovation business model. Is the vendor using open innovation to advance the technology, or are they protecting the technology and potentially limiting its advancement? How will this affect you?
18. Who is using this technology now, and what can be learned from its use?
19. There is no substitute for the real thing and being a technology fast follower can reduce risk. Gaining an insight into the implementation of the technology by at least one organization and learning about the experiences encountered can save time and money.
20. You can find early adopters by going through the vendor or by obtaining a referral from other sources, such as industry associations. In some cases, those interviewed may be quite candid in sharing the experiences they gained while adopting a new technology and, as such, will make an invaluable contribution.
21. Before developing or designing the product, many deep technology companies use online methods to survey potential users, inquiring about features and what clients will pay for. While this may seem to be counterintuitive, as it might alert your competition, the reality is that execution is what matters. Getting high-quality data that can be used quickly to bring a product to market faster can be more valuable than keeping everything a secret.
22. After you have found early adopters, keep researching to understand what other experience is needed in implementing this technology.
23. Gaining a cross-section of implementation experiences and feedback helps to build on successes and avoid the possibility of repeating the other's mistakes. You need to

understand that success is still largely a matter of perception. A technological success does not necessarily mean project or financial success.

24. The media are good sources of experiences, bearing in mind that the failures are more likely to make the headlines than quiet successes. Look for conference proceedings in the industry and see if there are technology congresses that discuss emerging fields. Look for blogs from industry influencers and watch their social networks. When using journalists or writers in a variety of media sources, it is worthwhile noting that they might be used as steppingstones in your research insofar as the people quoted will usually be willing to provide further insight when contacted directly.

Section 3
The Company Life Cycle and Related Funding Initiatives

Business Diagnostics Overview

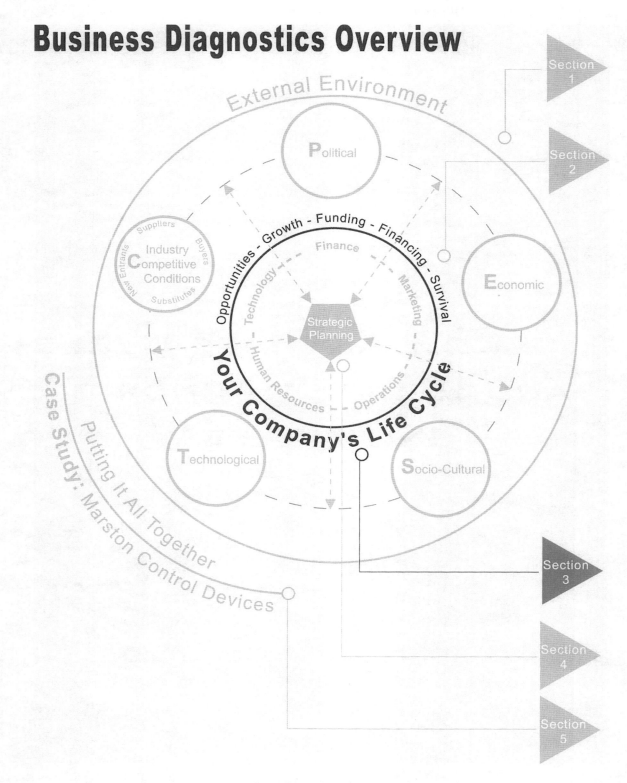

Your Company Life Cycle

Chapter 8
New Business Opportunities and Strategies

Overview

This chapter deals with the first stage of business: the new business opportunity. We consider how to determine if you are committed to the challenges that await and then review starting your own business, buying an existing business, or buying a franchise. We then discuss the elements you need to consider to be successful.

The following key areas are reviewed:

- Self-assessment
- The start-up process
- Buying an existing business
- Valuation techniques
- Buying a franchise operation
- Entering a family business
- Characteristics of successful businesses

Self Assessment

We have developed two checklists that review the elements of the proposed business venture itself along with your personal resources and characteristics. These two checklists permit an aspiring entrepreneur to assess his or her ability to succeed in their new business endeavour. The critical element is to be honest with yourself.

The Proposed Business Venture

In considering the merits of a new business venture, here are some key questions to consider:

- Do you have the necessary experience and knowledge to operate the business? If not, how will you bridge your knowledge gaps?
- Do you have any practical experience in sales, marketing, finance, or human resource management?
- How well do you understand the fundamental product or service that the business provides? Do you have industry experience or domain expertise?
- Can you reasonably expect the business to generate a profit? Or, is it a job disguised as a business or a lifestyle venture that can generate only enough to keep you employed?
- Does the business have the potential to reward you for your time, effort, hard work, and sleepless nights?
- Will there be future opportunities to expand or diversify the business?
- A series of simple but powerful questions—what is the product or service? Who will buy it, and for how much? How will you validate that your assumptions are true? How much money and time are you willing to spend to get to a yes or no decision?
- How easily could a potential competitor start a similar business?
- What will make your business different from competitors?
- How much control will suppliers of materials and labour have on your business?
- How many employees are required? What level and types of compensation are necessary?
- Do you have an experienced accountant, lawyer, and commercial banker in place?
- Will you have a co-founder or shareholder partners? How will you divide duties and resolve conflicts? Do you have a shareholder's agreement?
- Who will take over if something happens to you? Do you have a succession plan in place?

Your Personal Resources and Characteristics

The second series of questions help you to explore your own characteristics and suitability for this business venture. As you think about going into business, ask yourself this series of questions:

- Are you willing to risk your savings in this venture? Does the opportunity involve additional personal debt, and how comfortable are you with that?
- Do you have the commitment of your family? Is a secondary source of income available to support you?
- How long could your family accept a temporary drop in income?
- Do you have strong leadership and decision-making skills?

- Are you able to see what skills you lack, and do you have a plan to fill the gap?
- Are you aware of your work style and ability to adapt?
- Are you able to set priorities and keep to them?
- Do you have a strong work ethic? Are you undeterred by long hours and lost weekends?
- Are you able to make careful, rational decisions and then stick with them?
- Are you in good health and able to maintain high levels of activity?
- Do you have an established wellness routine?
- Do you have access to an informal or formal mentoring network?
- If you have a co-founder or shareholder partners, how committed are you to working out differences? Are you aware of your conflict styles?

The Start-Up Process

Starting a business from scratch is a complex and challenging exercise. There are many different definitions of a start-up, but typically the term describes the first five years since the company started operations or was incorporated. Unfortunately, most new companies or start-ups fail. The following steps offer the questions you should consider during the start-up process:

1. **Recognizing the Opportunity**
- To what extent is there a window of opportunity to exploit your idea, product, or service? What is the potential size of the market? How fast can the market grow?
- How long will it take you to enter the market and start generating revenue?
- Who is the target market and what are the definable attributes?
- Does the proposed product or service meet a tangible and, likely, urgent need? Is there a definable pain in the marketplace that you are able to address?
- Will the potential earnings be sufficient to provide an acceptable return on your capital and time? Are the earnings sustainable or will they be subject to peaks and valleys?
- Could this opportunity lead to additional avenues for market expansion or product diversification?
- Will the business generate strong profits and cash flow —avoiding over dependence on inventories and Accounts Receivable?

2. **Defining the Start-Up Business Strategy**
- How does your business model work? Who pays what to whom and when?
- Are barriers to entry in place, or can they be easily created to deter emerging competition? (Example: the early registration of trademarks or copyrights)
- Have market segments and target clients been identified, researched, and, more importantly, validated? What distribution channels are available to access these customers?

- How strong is supplier power? Are you dependent on a few suppliers who control critical inputs to your proposed product or service?

- How strong is buyer power? Will your future clients expect pricing concessions as you endeavour to launch your product or to keep them loyal?

- Have you completed a Strategic Business Plan or at a minimum, an Enterprise Review Summary to secure satisfactory sources of funding?

3. **Start-Up Resource Evaluation**

- What personnel, capabilities, and relationships do you already have? What will be required in the future?

- How will you select the right employees and supporting professionals? What types of incentives need to be offered to your employees?

- What makes the proposed venture unique? Have the necessary proprietary and value-added attributes been protected?

- What are the regulatory and legal requirements associated with running the business?

- Are there adequate financial and operational resources available to overcome unexpected obstacles and setbacks?

- Do the shareholders have access to personal funds, which could be injected as shareholder loans in the event of an emergency?

- Can you bootstrap your operation for a time? The concept of bootstrapping is using your personal finances or the operating revenues to keep the company afloat.

    1. Can you marshal resources? This means having the flexibility to get what you need by exchanging favours and asking for help. Marshalling resources is a skill that most small businesspeople do very well. They build their networks and help others when asked. Be careful to take note of any products that are exchanged in case there are tax implications. There are various ways to acquire specific resources for the new venture that do not involve significant, upfront, cash expenditures. For instance, you might consider some of the following options:

- Renting or sharing equipment

- Leasing or sharing premises

- Borrowing funds for working capital

- Subcontracting employees

- Using students or interns in appropriate roles

4. **Exit Strategies**

Part of a start-up process is thinking about how the founder's roles and responsibilities will be delegated as the company grows and how you intend to exit the company. Discussing the exit in the start-up process may seem out of place but understanding your aspirations will help you decide how to run the business. Are you looking for a long-term, sustainable commitment, or do you see yourself wanting to exit in five or ten years? The founders need to discuss their plans and formulate a suitable exit strategy.

The following list provides some common exit strategy options:

- Sale of the company to an outside party or to management and employees (Management Buy Out or MBO)
- Acquisition by a larger company, which could be a competitor, supplier, or client
- Public offering (IPO)
- Liquidation through a sale of assets, debt repayment, and distribution of proceeds to the owner(s)

Buying a Business

You can either start a business or buy a business. Buying a business can mean buying it outright or buying in and becoming a shareholder[1].

Such a step has significant financial and lifestyle implications so its important to consider the following steps when deciding whether to buy an existing business:

Why You Might Purchase a Business

- Favourable price—the company under consideration may be purchased at a price below the estimated costs of starting a new business.
- Proven track record—uncertainties will be reduced if you buy an existing business that already has a demonstrated track record.
- Established relationships— are already in place with clients, suppliers, and its workforce.
- Solid market profile—existing target market segments are already understood and developed.

Places to Look for a Business that Is for Sale

The following are some information sources that will assist you in your search process:

- Your network and industry contacts
- Online business sale and broker marketplace sites
- Newspaper and business magazine advertisements
- Trade journals
- Business brokers and certified business valuators
- Commercial realtors
- Trustees and receivers
- Local economic development and technology association offices

---

1 For more information on business transitions, see the work of our co-author Mike Thompson: http://www.ceobusinessdiagnostics.com/2018/blog/transition-pathway-review-and-selection/

- Professional advisors (accountants, lawyers, and commercial bankers)

Reasons the Business Is for Sale

There are multiple reasons for the sale of a business. You need to consider the reasons behind the sale and ask yourself how you will overcome any difficulties. The following list provides some of the reasons that a particular business has been put up for sale:

- Lack of succession plans and no apparent heirs
- Owner's retirement or ill health
- Owner has other investments or businesses that compete for his or her time
- The business expanded too fast, resulting in depleted cash resources and an inability to attract additional equity capital
- Partnership problems because of the absence of shareholder agreements
- Lost enthusiasm, reduced commitment, and fatigue in the owner and leadership team
- Specific industry sector has reached maturity, is in decline, or has had an economic shock
- Local economy is weak
- Increasing competitive pressures
- Outdated technology infrastructure and systems and no willingness by the owner to reinvest
- Litigation potential or legal actions in process
- Lease renewal or space requirement affects profitability

The Evaluation Process

Evaluating a business will look at all the factors in the Business Diagnostics Framework. The following list provides the primary factors to evaluate when buying a business and that will influence the potential selling price:

- Assess the quality and performance of existing management
- Is there a definable strategy, mission and vision?
- Review the financial history and performance via revenue, earnings, and cash generation performance.
- Where is the product or service in its life cycle?
- How do product or service prices and profit margins compare to the competition? How does the business gross profit margin compare to industry averages?
- Is there a current competitor assessment? Are there any big industry trends that create a threat or opportunity?
- Are there fundamental changes in the way business is being done in this industry or to business models?

- How is the company financed? How much debt is carried by the business? Is there pressure from creditors, the bank, or both?
- Assess the quality of assets:
  - Accounts receivable—what has been the collection track record? Inventory—are there any obsolescence issues?
  - Fixed assets—what is the estimated current market value and remaining economic life?
  - Are there any intangible assets such as brand or reputation?
  - What intellectual property assets exist? Are there patents or trademarks in place?
- What legal commitments exist? Are there any contingent liabilities, unsettled lawsuits, or any overdue rent payments or long-term supply contracts?
- What lease agreements exist? What are the maturity dates and relevant transfer clauses on purchase?
- What product risks and liabilities exist? What has been done to mitigate product risk?
- What is the product warranty? How many warranties have been extended? What is their duration? Is there any potential financial exposure?
- Is a Vendor take-back (VTB) available to assist with the funding of the purchase price?
- Can you buy the assets only and not the business with its liabilities?

Goodwill and Asset Versus Share Purchase

Before discussing valuation techniques for buying an existing business, you first need to need to consider goodwill and whether to purchase the assets or shares of a company.

Goodwill

Goodwill is the difference between the company book value and the actual purchase price. For example:

Company book value	$ 80,000
Purchase price	$140,000
Goodwill	$ 60,000

Goodwill is an intangible asset that will appear on the new company's financial statements. In essence, this purchase premium relates to a basket of intangibles that encompass copyrights, brand name, supplier connections, lease benefits, and location. The seller will take the position that these intangible factors contribute to earnings generation and, therefore, should have an ascribed value.

A buyer's reluctance to pay a goodwill premium is often mitigated by negotiating an earn out where the vendor takes back financing approximating the agreed value of goodwill. The buyer then pays back the obligation over a negotiated period of time from ongoing company earnings.

Purchase of Assets Versus Shares

In an asset purchase, it is possible to purchase assets rather than purchasing the shares of a company. Assets need to be free and clear of any encumbrances, liens, mortgages, and security agreements. For example:

The buyer sets up a new corporation and transfers all purchased assets and property leases, if appropriate, into the new corporation.

The buyer will attempt to allocate:

1. A low percentage of the purchase price for goodwill, if any, since generally, tax write-offs are not as attractive for goodwill as for fixed assets.

2. A high percentage of the purchase price for depreciable assets to maximize depreciation deductions in the future.

In a shares purchase, the buyer purchases company shares from departing shareholders and elects their own directors and officers.

- Debt can be assumed with the vendor receiving the difference between the purchase price and outstanding debt.
- Leases, contracts, and licenses typically transfer with the change of share ownership.
- Tax losses may be available for the benefit of the buyer.
- Past liabilities (direct or contingent) stay with the company and could come back to haunt the new owner.

Which is the best option? It depends on the various benefits accruing to the purchaser and vendor.

The business vendor typically wants a share sale option, so they can benefit from capital gains tax deductions that are available to qualified small business corporations, and, at the same time, they avoid any *recaptured* depreciation associated with an asset sale.

The business purchaser usually prefers the asset purchase option in order to take advantage of potential business improvement loan financing for equipment and higher depreciation charges for tax purposes. Also, any unknown problems, such as unattractive contracts, employee-related issues, or liabilities that might be associated with a share purchase, can be avoided.

VALUATION TECHNIQUES

What should you pay for a business? Valuing a business is a complex process and is not an exact science. A brief overview is presented here. It is essential to obtain professional advice from an accountant, a lawyer or chartered business valuator, or both to structure a formal purchase agreement for a business.

The following valuation approaches should be considered:

- Asset valuations
- Market valuations
- Cash flow valuations
- Earnings valuations

Asset-Based Valuation

There are three varieties of asset-based business valuations.

The modified book value adjusts the book value to reflect the difference between the historical cost and current value of the assets. Adjustments are made for any surplus appraisal value on land and buildings, while intangible asset values are heavily discounted.

- Replacement value is based on the cost to replace the firm's assets.
- Liquidation value is based on the funds available if a firm was to liquidate its assets.

A weakness to these approaches is that they all fail to recognize the firm as a *going concern* that generates sustainable revenue and earnings.

Market-Based Valuation

The market-based valuation approach is based on actual market prices of firms that have recently been sold or are trading publicly on a stock exchange. This approach tends to be more realistic and is calculated as follows:

Market-based valuation calculation:

$$\text{Price/Earnings Ratio} = \text{Market Price} \div \text{After tax earnings}$$

Weaknesses:

- Finding appropriate price to earnings multiple comparatives can be difficult. There are some online tools, but they tend to use industry aggregated information.
- Public company data is likely not appropriate given the differences in the scale of public business operations and small- and medium size enterprises.

Cash Flow Valuation

Cash flow valuation involves estimating a company's future operating cash flows and discounting back to a present value, using the investors required rate of return. Cash flows are earnings before interest, tax and depreciation, minus regular capital expenditures.

The rate of return would be computed by starting with a risk-free rate of return that is derived from the present treasury bill rate plus a risk premium, usually between 10% and 30%, depending on the size of the company and its associated risk factors such as revenues, suppliers, management, and industry strength. Risk premiums for industries can be found online at valuation firms or through a local business valuation firm. Additionally, the opportunity cost or alternate use of the invested funds needs to be considered.

Earnings-Based Valuation

With the earnings-base valuation approach, the estimated value of the firm is based on its ability to generate future, sustainable earnings.

The key question is what definition of annual earnings should be used?

There are three earnings definitions:

1. Earnings after tax—that is, the net profit before any allowance for extraordinary items.

2. EBIT—earnings before interest and taxes (EBIT). This definition measures the earning power and value of the underlying business without the effects of financing. For small- to medium-sized businesses, the most realistic valuation technique usually involves EBIT, especially if the financing (interest) effect is not shown.

3. EBITDA—earnings before interest, taxes, depreciation, and amortization, which is a more accurate measure of cash flows that are generated by a business.

An earnings-based valuation estimates stabilized earnings by considering:

- Historical earnings—use average earnings for the past five years and adjust for non-recurring revenue or expense items.
- Future earnings—are those earnings that are anticipated under present ownership.

The purchaser may derive a different, higher or lower, future earnings estimate, based on efficiencies arising from new management (higher earnings) or restructuring costs (lower earnings) that will have an impact on price negotiations.

The next step in an earnings-based valuation is to derive a capitalization rate or cap rate. The cap rate is the inverse of the multiple.

A cap rate takes the earnings and divides them by a capitalization rate. Using a price earnings rate or multiple will give the same resulting value. A cap rate of 20% is the same as a multiple of five times.

Here is an example of a cap rate and multiple:

	Cap Rate	Multiple	
Low Risk, Higher Value	20%	5x	100/20
	25%	4x	100/25
Higher Risk, Low Value	33%	3x	100/33

The cap rate and multiple selection will be somewhat subjective and are derived from a blend of quantitative and qualitative factors. These include deriving the earnings multiple and considering internal value factors:

How are Earnings Multiples derived?

- P/E ratios of comparable publicly traded companies
- Earnings multiples derived from recent company acquisitions in the same industry
- Industry rules of thumb, adjusted for a company's size and track record

Internal Value Factors

- Financial—relative strength of balance sheet, absence of intangible assets, and availability of working capital resources.
- Marketing—a broad, diversified client base, allied with significant penetration into a company's market segment. Unique products or services with the opportunity to increase future sales and earnings.
- Operations—the capacity of plant and equipment to handle future growth. Flexibility and versatility of machinery to produce new and different products.
- Surplus assets—assets that do not contribute directly to the company operations. For example, permanent term deposits or a securities portfolio would be added to the capitalized value.

Earnings-Based Valuation Example:

Company XYZ has sustainable future earnings (EBIT) per year: $155,000

- Earnings have been derived from the past five years income statements and adjusted for non-recurring revenue and expense items.
- These estimated earnings are most likely to be realized in the future under present ownership.

The agreed cap rate/multiple to be applied is: 25% or a multiple of 4 x

- Equivalent to business risk, based on review of current industry multiples as available) and company's internal value factors.
- Will need to meet the purchaser's minimum required rate of return.

There are surplus assets and term deposits of: $45,000

Valuation of Company XYZ:

Capitalized earnings	4 x $155,000 = $620,000
Plus: Surplus assets	$ 45,000
Total estimated value	$665,000

Buying a Franchise Operation

A franchise is a special type of partnership in which one company, the franchisor, grants the right to sell its products and services to another company or individual, the franchisee.

The most common type of franchise is a business format franchise. The business format is highly controlled with every aspect of the business having been blueprinted by the franchisor. Examples of a business format franchise are Tim Horton's, Burger King, and Snap-on Tools.

Another type of franchise are dealership relationship franchises. These are less restrictive franchises and involve a licensing or associate relationship. Examples include real estate, or equipment and automobile franchises like John Deere dealers.

Franchises are often viewed as a less risky alternative to business ownership. There are advantages and some disadvantages to avoid.

Advantages of Franchising

- Financial support includes these advantages:
  - Preferential financing packages that often include inventory buyback agreements between the franchisor and the franchisee's bank
  - Flexible payment terms to suppliers or product purchases from parent organization
  - Increased purchasing power
- Lower risk of business failure due to proven track record throughout the franchise network
- Additional franchising opportunities to acquire new or nearby locations.
- Brand name recognition
- Franchiser support of the franchisee includes the following:
  - Employee selection and training
  - Inventory control systems
  - Standardized suppliers and agreements
  - Lease negotiations

Franchising Hazards

- Excessive up-front franchise fees and ongoing royalty fees that are based on a fixed percentage, which can vary from 2% to 15%, of annual sales.
- Excessive advertising and promotional fees with nominal local benefit
- Growth restrictions—the franchisee is often restricted to a defined sales territory
- Encroachment—the franchisor initiates alternate distribution channels such as online sales, gas station outlets, and so on that effectively compete with the existing franchisee operation
- Differing legislative protection between states or provinces

- Mature products or services within saturated markets
- Preference to established franchise insiders which means that existing franchisees are offered prime locations before first-time franchise buyers
- Restrictions on supply-chain relationships
- Restrictions on future business sale or exit, creating high exit barriers

Key Questions to Ask a Franchisor

- As part of your due diligence process in assessing the merits of an investment in a franchise operation,
- ask the following questions:
- How long has the franchise been in business?
- How many franchise outlets are currently in operation?
- How many failures have there been over the past five years? What were the reasons for such failures?
- Is there any litigation in process?
    - Against the franchisor from outside parties?
    - Between the franchisor and franchisees?
- How many new franchises have been sold over the past five years?
- Does the franchisor have the right to buy out franchisees? How would the price be determined?
- How financially sound is the franchise? Are franchisor financial statements and bank references available?
- Does the franchisor have a borrowing relationship with a bank; if so, what are the terms and amounts of facilities?
- How many franchises are operating in the proposed market area?
- Who are the local and national competition?
- What are the up-front, royalty, and advertising fees? How do these compare to industry averages?
- What support is provided in the following areas?
    - Training?
    - Lease negotiation?
    - Financing?
    - Advertising?
    - Supplier discounts?
    - Operational systems?
- Are recent franchisee references available? Are you able to make contact with them?

Family Business Opportunities

Another route to commencing a new venture is to buy a family-owned business or enter into your own family-owned business. While all the fundamentals of business apply, family-owned businesses come with their own unique characteristics. Some issues to consider when contemplating entering into a family-owned business:

- A key benefit can be the strength of family relationships, which often help overcome serious operational setbacks.
- The founder will invariably leave a deep impact on the culture of the family firm.
- Changes in culture often occur as leadership passes from one generation to the next.
- Succession is a key issue. The planning process needs to start early in the successor's life. Tension will invariably develop between the founder and the successor as they gain experience.
- Independent research has shown that there is a lower probability that a third generation will successfully take over the business from the second generation.

There are many different supports available for family-owned businesses. In Canada, the Canadian Association of Family Enterprises (CAFE) has been established, based on the recognition that families in business often face unique challenges in the United States, the Family Firm Institute provides information and tools; globally, there are different international family business networks. Each of these groups have different goals, but generally, their value is in the knowledge sharing between generations and in providing help to build succession plans.

Characteristics of Successful Businesses

To conclude this chapter, we leave you with some observations from successful company owners who have survived the new business growth phase and shared their observations with us. In no particular order, the following list provides some of the characteristics of successful businesses:

- Founders need to have relevant hands-on knowledge and experience at the outset, rather than learning the business as they begin operations.
- Forge key alliances at an early stage with clients, suppliers, and even competitors as 'co-opetition'. Partner early and partner often.
- Ensure that close management of cash drivers such as prompt Accounts Receivable collection, inventory monitoring, and advantageous account payable settlement terms takes place.
- Hire talented people, and build a committed team. Hire for attitude; train for skill.
- Stick to what you know.
- Keep up on industry trends and threats.
- Focus, focus, focus!
- Founders need to know how to sell and stay in contact with their customers.
- Be ready to change and adapt your product and service.

- Develop a strong banking relationship. Keep in touch with your banker on a regular basis.
- Set your goals high. Think like a public company CEO, and think global from day one.
- Fully research your competition. Constantly monitor their performance and initiatives.
- Continually update your management skills.
- Build a mentoring network that provides objective advice and support.

Chapter 9
Managing Growth

Overview

As companies grow and mature, a transition from entrepreneurial management to professional management is required. Entrepreneurial management is characterized by centralized, often solo, decision-making, and an informal style, control system, and structure.

Professional management involves more delegated decision-making authority and use of formalized control systems. In this chapter, opportunities to grow the business are examined. A useful starting point is to ask, "Why grow your business?"

Why Grow?

The concept of business growth is difficult to grapple with. Does every company need to grow? Perhaps not. How you manage your business depends on what your aspirations are as a business owner. You may wish to provide an income for yourself, your employees, and, hopefully, walk away with cash when you choose to end or wrap up your business.

For many business owners, growing the top-line revenues of the business is daunting. Many businesses will become very good at what they do by optimizing their efficiency, but they are not able or don't desire to see beyond what they are to reimagine what they might be. This growth mindset is much studied and difficult to grasp. The aspirations of the owner and leadership are critical elements of whether or not a company will grow.

Discussing business growth during a pandemic is painful. We know that many businesses will not survive, causing massive disruption and difficulty for the owners, their employees, families, suppliers, and customers. However, the upheaval also represents an opportunity for others. Those businesses that are prepared with the systems and mindset to pivot are more likely to survive. This is true in pandemic times and in general. Companies that continually zoom in and out of strategy, purpose, opportunities, and threats tend to survive and thrive.

It is important to note that the type of growth you aspire to requires further qualification. Is a company seeking growth in market share? Number of clients? Revenues? Margin? Earnings? Or a combination of all these? You may wish to go back to Chapter 3 on Financial Evaluation and review typical growth indicators.

The following areas are covered in this chapter:
- Scale-up versus growth
- Growth and development strategies
- Growth dimensions
- International expansion
- The Business Growth Road Map

Scale-Up Versus Growth

To better understand the concept of business growth, it is necessary to first outline the elements of scale-up and growth. It is important to note that scale-up and growth are not mutually exclusive elements. They can, and often do, occur at the same time. Companies drop in and out of scale and growth at various times, based on their own unique development.

What Is Scale-Up?

Scaling takes place when a company evolves from creating one product and being able to produce it efficiently to increase profit. The concept is most often applied to start-up companies that have a product that matches a market and has proven revenue traction. These companies have to scale-up their production rapidly. Scaling is about optimization, stability, and efficiency.

The elements of scale-up are:
- Establishing a definable product with recognizable product or market fit as evidenced by sales
- Establishing sustainable traction across marketing and sales channels
- Building repeatable and predictable marketing, sales, and customer experience key performance indicators
- Ensuring that the use of product and delivery technology is stable and robust
- Ensuring that operations are well-understood, resourced, stable, and sustainable
- Ensuring that the business is investment ready to ensure stable finances
- Focused on people, leadership, and culture to support scale-up

Note: Typically, companies will scale-up before they grow in order to stabilize profitability.

What Is Growth?

While scaling up, efficiency, and stability are important, it is also important to focus not only on efficiency. Once a company has achieved scale-up or, at least, has a good plan to stabilize their operations and be efficient, they can start looking beyond their current optimized product and market. Once a company has the growth mindset, they can start exploring opportunities that exist beyond their optimized state.

GROWTH AND DEVELOPMENT STRATEGIES

Scale-up is about efficiency and finding value. Growth is about reaching beyond your existing products and services.

The simple formula for growth is having more clients who are buying more with more profitably and more often. Here are some questions that help to assess a company's growth potential:

- What is the profile of current prospects and clients? Will they be the same in the future?
- How do you access prospects and clients? Can different or supplemental channels be used in the future?
- Who are your direct competitors now, and will new competitors join them in the future?
- What indirect competitors exist, and are they offering a product that is a threat or an emerging disruptor? An indirect competitor offers a substitute manner of filling a client need. For example, an indirect competitor of a wallet manufacturer would be a smart phone case that can accommodate money and credit cards.
- Where are the opportunities to enhance gross and net profit margins?
- Are there partnering or alliance opportunities that will build market share, promote product migration, or build economies of scale?

Strategy comes from the Greek language and translates as *the art of generalship*. There are entire books on strategy and a mind-boggling potential of options. We have chosen five strategies, listed below, that could be considered by most companies. The key is to recognize which particular strategy provides your company with a distinct competitive advantage. To start your thinking about growth, consider these five strategies:

- Differentiation
- Business Model
- Low-cost leadership
- Focus strategies
- Integration

Differentiation

Companies can be *different* in many ways by undertaking strategies that make them distinct from their competition. A key concept is that a company needs to craft a strategy of being unique in the eyes of its customers. It has to incorporate attributes into its product or service offerings that separate it from competitor offerings and provide value to its customers.

A company can set itself apart from the competition in the following ways:

Product Iterations and Extensions

Product iteration and extensions are used to extend product life cycles and increase market share by entering new areas. They can be used by changing the product slightly, like Coke Zero; adding or subtracting features, like webservices that have basic and professional or enterprise offerings for different fees; or adding unusual combinations of features, like a fridge that also has an Internet connection. Some key questions:

- Can new features or attributes be developed that will attract potential buyers and meet their unmet needs, for example, one-stop shopping at Home Depot?
- Can the product be improved by multiple features, as Microsoft Office has done?

Here are some other ways to iterate and extend your products:

Product Packaging and Bundling

Can you iterate your product by changing how the product will be sold or by the types of bundled features and services that are offered? Can you go up or down the value chain by adding other experiences to your product?

Product Distribution

Can you change the ways you distribute your product, for instance, can you ensure accurate order completion and fast delivery like Amazon does? Or can you offer your product through a partnering opportunity as Cirque du Soleil does with Group Vidanta?"

Product Quality

Quality is often in the eye of the beholder; perception can be reality. The following checklist of quality characteristics serves to differentiate your operations from the competition:

- Durability and reliability. Example: Duracell batteries
- Safety. Example: Michelin Tires
- Consistent performance. Example: Southwest Airlines
- Prestige. Example: Cadillac and Mercedes-Benz

Service Quality

A similar list of quality characteristics can be developed for service industries:

- Awareness of client needs and wants
- Dependability
- Customer service
- Proven reputation
- Integrity and trust
- Responsiveness

BUSINESS MODEL STRATEGY

The business model can be a differentiator and disruptive to a market. The most important elements of your business model are considering what it takes to make or deliver your product, who sells what to whom, and at what cost to the end user? The concept is that by exploring your business model, you can explore new options, challenge your assumptions, and even change strategies. A key tool to help you is the Business Model Canvas. Consider which products and services have been disrupted by the following new business models:

- Sharing economy business models
- Software as a service business models
- Product as a service business models

Is there a new way to produce, present, and sell your product that will open new markets or expand your customer base?

LOW-COST LEADERSHIP

Low-cost leadership involves an intensive review of all company operations to identify and eliminate unnecessary costs and increase value, based on what the customer decides value is.

Low-cost leadership is most effective in industries where consumer-buying decisions are price sensitive.

Product simplicity can be developed by reducing cost inputs (materials, and labour), which translates to a lower unit price. Such stripped-down products and services can be observed in most industry sectors.

For example, Ryan Air and Southwest Airlines are discount airlines and Canadian Tire and Costco are warehouse stores. Each of these categories have reduced costs and can offer a stripped-down model at a lower cost for consumers.

Many online web service applications are taking a low-cost leadership approach by removing a layer of cost in the distribution and going direct to the customer. By removing a layer of distribution, they reduce costs and provide more perceived value to the client.

To optimize cost advantages, a useful approach is to examine the company's value chain, a linked set of activities and functions that add value and culminate in the delivery of a product or service to the end-user. An example is a shift to e-commerce by using online order processing as opposed to face-to-face ordering.

Implementation is the key. To assume a low-cost leadership role, the company's organizational structure, reward systems, and employee culture need to reflect the vision of a lean and effective organization. The product needs to match customer expectations.

Focus Strategies

Focus strategies are aimed at either low-cost or differentiation opportunities that concentrate on a smaller piece of the potential revenue pie. They can often offer promising revenue and gross margin opportunities.

Examples:

Offer specialty products that deliver non-standard items, for example, antique bathtubs.

Develop a niche market, which is a small, carefully defined, market segments that provide opportunities to exceed client expectations. For example, small, luxury eco-tourism resorts provide a carefully defined experience for a very specific clientele.

Concentrate on a limited geographic territory. Focus on local or regional markets that have been overlooked by larger companies, for example, local food manufacturing.

Integration

There are two types of integration—vertical and horizontal.

Vertical integration: Describes opportunities that exist to expand within a company's own (vertical) industry sector. Vertical integration has the following two trajectories:

Backward integration extends business activities *back* in the supply chain toward raw materials and sources of supply For example, e.g., a car company can invest in a steel company to ensure its source of supply.

Forward integration extends business activities *forward* in the supply chain and closer to the company's marketplace. For example, a food wholesaler establishes a retail outlet, taking care to ensure there is no direct competition with existing retail clients.

Horizontal integration: Involves the assumption of increased control over competitors in a similar market. This type of integration usually translates to a merger or takeover, which can be friendly (rescue or collaboration) or unfriendly (corporate raid). This consolidation is common in industries in which there are multiple players, and the market share is fragmented.

Can you relate each of the following strategies to the typical tactical elements of a growth strategy?

- Product iterations and extensions
- New product development

- New market segments and verticals
- New geographic markets
- Joint ventures and licensing
- Mergers and acquisitions
- Diversification

GROWTH DIMENSIONS

Having reviewed various development strategies that can assist a company to grow with a tangible game plan, it is also instructive to assess growth opportunities from a product and market standpoint. Product iterations and extensions, new product development, new market segments, and geographic markets are all viable growth options to be explored in addition to managing multiple markets and products.

The Growth Directions Matrix was originally developed by Igor Ansoff for his book *Corporate Strategy: An Analytic Approach to Business Policy for Growth and Expansion* in 1968."

The Ansoff matrix is an older tool that is just as relevant today as it was when Igor Ansoff first wrote about the concept. Simply put, the Ansoff matrix is a visual depiction of business growth alternatives: market penetration (increase share), market development (new markets, existing products), product development (new offerings or product extensions) and diversification (new products and new markets).

The tool will help you get a visual sense of what is going to work for a company, and sometimes seeing a concept on paper helps make the path clear. Ansoff doesn't explicitly differentiate between market and geographic expansion, though you should.[2]

The following four options each have different needs and cost implications. The status quo is the least risky but keeps the firm stagnant and may lead to its costly and eventual decline. Offering existing products or services in new markets or new products or services in existing markets is less risky and costly than an incursion with new product or services in new markets.

The 70/20/10 Rule

We will also point out that there is a rule of thumb when considering new options. Typically, the guideline is to keep 70% of your resources supporting what exists now, 20% considering new product adjacencies of market and product development, and 10% for diversification. This rule of thumb generally holds true unless your market has potential to be or is being rapidly disrupted. In this case, it would be wise to reconsider the number of resources devoted to diversification options.

---

2 To help you with creating a product or market growth map, we have included a template found here: http://www.ceobusinessdiagnostics.com/wp-content/uploads/2015/06/Ansoff-Matrix.pdf

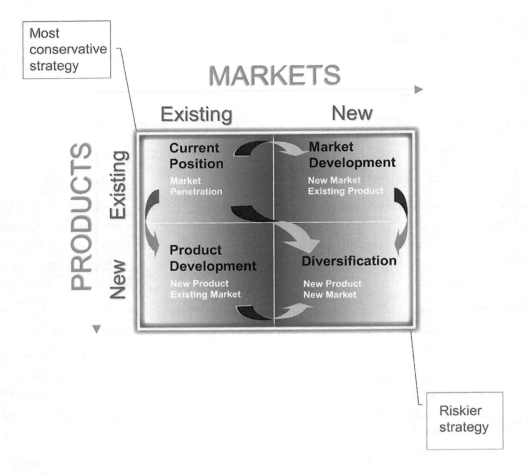

Figure 23. Ansoff Growth Directions Matrix

Consider your options, based on the four quadrants on the Ansoff Growth Directions Matrix:

Current Position: Market Penetration Strategy with Existing Products and Markets

The status quo involves maintaining steady growth and doing everything a little better, every day. Growth in this sector is achieved by adopting a market penetration strategy, striving to increase market share for existing products or services. Think of how Starbucks continually iterates their products within their current position. Here are some options within this strategy:

- Maintain or increase the market share of current products, competitive pricing strategies, advertising, marketing and drip campaigns, sales promotion, and perhaps add more resources that are dedicated to personal selling.

- Consider an aggressive existing product iteration strategy by quickly testing and piloting product iterations. Consider bundling other products and services.

- Choose to enter and dominate identified growth market segments.

- Restructure a mature market by driving out competitors; this would require an aggressive promotional campaign, supported by a pricing strategy that is designed to make the market unattractive for competitors.
- Increase usage by existing customers, for example, introduce loyalty or referral programs.

Market Development with New Market, Existing Product

A market development strategy involves finding a fresh market for existing products or services by expanding geographically either regionally or internationally, by seeking new groups of customers, or growing an existing channel and distribution partnerships, or a combination of these that can help you enter the new market.

The following list is useful when considering the move into new, potential market segments:

- How do you define the new market segment(s)?
- Are the market segments emerging or established?
- Is there good potential in adjacent, closely related, market niches that can also be targeted? That is, if you can take down one bowling pin, will others fall too?
- How will a compelling value-added differentiation be created for these new buyers?
- Are there any direct competitors or near substitutes?
- What is the expected revenue and cost structure and the break-even point for the new segment?
- What is the brand message? Is it an understandable buying proposition? Will there be a compelling tag line that conveys the features and benefits that customers will respond to?
- How easy or complex is the purchase decision and mode of payment?
- How will you build market awareness?
- What will be the most effective distribution channel?
- What are the best promotional tactics?
- Are there follow-on domestic or international expansion opportunities?
- Do potential alliance or partnering opportunities exist within these new market segments?

Product Development Strategy with New Products, Existing Markets

This strategy involves the development of entirely new products or revising additional features for existing products that are targeted at existing customers. This development can be achieved by a combination of continuous product iterations and extensions and new product launches. An example is Dyson's strategy of creating a series of high-end appliances with different uses for the existing market. While product iterations and extensions can be piloted and tested quickly, new products should undergo a robust product assessment process. There must be excellent processes for client discovery and validation that customers will buy this new product in volumes that generate the profit to justify the development cost. New product development is an entire field of study and there are certifications available[3].

The following checklist assists with the new product assessment process:

- What unmet need or want does the new product address? What problem does it solve?
- Can you validate that the new product will solve a customer pain? Can you describe the product or service quickly, so non-industry and technical people can understand what problem it solves?
- What is the product going to do? What will it look like?
- What are the purchase triggers? What will induce your customers to buy?
- Can you define the most valuable and most used features that the new product will have? Can you build a minimally viable product to test those features?
- What are the costs to take the product to market?
- What are the engineering or development costs?
- What would the go, and the no-go or project-kill criteria be at each step of the process?
- Can you define the time frame before first clients use the product or service?
- How will the new product be delivered to the end-user? What alternative distribution channels exist?
- How has the price point been justified and validated?
- What are the required product or service design and development resources?
- Have you created the testing, pilot, prototype, and market feedback process?
- If the new product is a durable goods product, what are the functionality and durability requirements?
- How will quality be demonstrated to the user?
- Will it be possible to make incremental improvements to the product or service?
- Are there any future product or service bundling opportunities?
- What are the follow up service or maintenance needs?
- Are intellectual property (I.P) rights fully protected and documented?
- How easy is it to replicate the product or service?
- Can you fulfill all the customer needs for the lifetime of the product, or is there a need to partner with other entities within the supply chain to provide a whole product solution?

---

3   We like the resources delivered by the Product Development and Management Association found at PDMA.org.

Diversification Strategy with New Product, New Markets

This strategy involves setting off in a new direction and attempting to create new products in fresh markets or leveraging promising business opportunities, regardless of whether they fit within your known market and domain knowledge. This is known as conglomerate diversification. While we discuss new products and new markets, it is important to note that diversification strategies can also apply to companies that purchase undervalued companies to turn them around. An example is the Jimmy Pattison Group, which intentionally seeks and purchases companies in functional areas though with highly diversified portfolios.

Becoming a new product, new market pioneer entails significant risks. Before undertaking this strategy, a comprehensive review and assessment of company internal resources needs to take place to ensure that capability and staying power are available to launch this new venture. Very often, companies will use a separate development team, which is located off site, so that the new product team can operate without interference from existing corporate structures and culture.

Managing Multiple Markets and Products

As a company grows, different product lines and markets will unfold. The Strategic Business Unit (SBU) concept can be used to assess and monitor a portfolio of different activities. SBUs form component parts of a company with each unit having its own products, markets, and competitors.

SBUs will either be generators or users of cash. The portfolio Growth-Share Grid, developed by the Boston Consulting Group, provides a simple portfolio analysis that is based upon market growth and relative market share. This is illustrated by Figure 24 along with a brief review of the different SBU categories.

Question Marks

- Experience low market share in high-growth markets and are sometimes referred to as *problem children*.
- Require significant cash resources to keep afloat in the hope that they can build market share over time, that is, turn them into *stars*.

Stars

- Have achieved high market share in high-growth markets. They have strong appetites for cash (to fund continuous expansion) but, on balance, they tend to be self-supporting from a cash flow standpoint.
- Watch for complacency in marketing and pricing.

Cash Cows

- Have established major market share in low-growth segments with significant cash being generated from operations.
- Products are well known and established. Their low-growth markets are mature.
- Surplus cash proceeds are often used to feed promising SBUs (question marks) elsewhere in the company.

- Watch for fast follower competition.

Dogs

- Deliver low market share in low-growth markets.
- Are often net users of cash.
- Tend to be marginal businesses that need to be divested or possibly restructured or repositioned.
- Products and business units will move around on the grid over their product life cycle. Many companies will manage their product portfolios, though typically, the analysis is not done on a regular basis. Unfortunately, companies will hold onto *dogs* for too long, often for sentimental reasons.

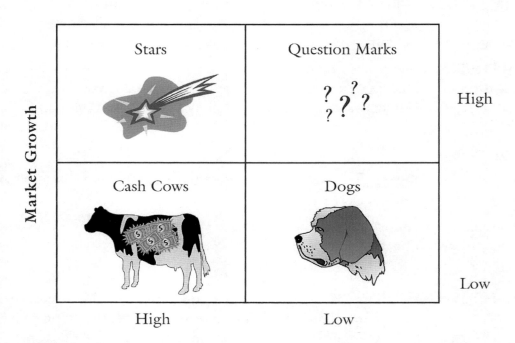

Source: Boston Consulting Group Inc. Reprinted with permission from BCG Global Services, Boston, MA 02109

Figure 24. BCG Growth-Share Grid

INTERNATIONAL EXPANSION

With global markets growing and domestic competition becoming more intense, many companies look to explore international expansion and exporting opportunities.

Benefits of such expansion initiatives include:

- Potential to expand market share
- Increase revenues and earnings
- New alliance and partnering opportunities
- Acquiring new customers and applications for existing products

Moving into the international marketplace can be a complex, time-consuming, and long- term process. A detailed analysis of international business expansion is beyond the scope of this text; however, we have summarized a few key issues that will assist the evaluation process.

First review your internal capacity, capabilities, and aspirations:

- What are your reasons for exploring international markets?
- What are your growth aspirations?
- Can you and your company accept and thrive in new cultural and social settings?
- Do you have staff that are willing to travel or have experience with international business? If not, how will you acquire the skills?
- Do you have a strong equity and working capital position to back up a long-term export venture?
- Will the international venture have a negative impact on your existing domestic business?
- Do you have sufficient employee talent and resources to open up new markets and, at the same time, look after the existing domestic market? Remember to take care of your existing markets and customers first.
- Do you have a sound relationship with your bank? Do they have a trade finance department to guide you?

If you have a geographic region in mind, critically assess the political, environmental, socio-cultural, and economic health of the target country. We recommend taking time to consider the following:

- Is there potential for political unrest or a change in regulations that could affect market entry? For instance, are there trade, market, or product regulations
- Are there any threats or opportunities identified in a PEST-C scan of the country?
- How would this country or region compare to others?
- What is the current inflation rate and trade balance?
- What are the target country's tax regimes? Does it have any product or service compliance requirements?
- Where is the country on the corruption index?
- Are you planning to target national or regional markets within the foreign country?

- Does the international expansion strategy entail a significant change in customer profile within your target offshore market?
- How will the goods or services be delivered to your new customers?
    - What are the costs and timing implications?
    - What will the shipping, duty, and insurance costs be?
    - Are there other logistics issues for getting necessary people and equipment into the country?
- Are there potential technology, distribution, or service partners that you could work with to make market entry easier or more successful? What criteria will help you select an appropriate partner?

We recommend putting your thoughts and research on paper with a market development plan, which addresses the following issues:

- How big is the international market?
    - What will be your estimated share of the target market? What was the basis of your market research?
    - How is business done in the country? Is it relationship based?
    - How closely does your expertise and competence compare to other competitors?
    - Does the competition consist of one or two gorillas or number of similar-sized firms?
    - What is your expected gross profit margin, and what are the overhead cost implications?
- What will be your entry strategy into the foreign market?
    - Will you use intermediaries such as agents, foreign distributors, or manufacturers' representatives?
    - Will you be a subcontractor, working for a host country company?
    - Will you have direct interaction as an exporter with the foreign customer?
    - Will it be necessary to establish an offshore branch office or subsidiary operation?
    - Can you forge a joint venture with another firm to penetrate a specific foreign market?
    - Can you license products, services, or technology to an offshore firm?

Export Financing

When a company decides to expand into new international markets via a defined exporting strategy, there are three key issues to consider:

- Managing payment risk
- Managing credit (receivable) risk

- Managing currency risk

Managing Payment Risk

There is a spectrum of options, ranging from secure to risky from an exporter's perspective, to manage payment. Payment needs to be clearly stated in the contracts with the exchange rates, banking, and fees understood in advance.

The most secure option for the exporter is cash in advance, which obviously eliminates all risk of nonpayment. However, in reality, few foreign buyers are willing to pay full cash, up front.

The riskiest option is the open account transaction in which the exporter has the sole responsibility in determining the ability of the purchaser to pay. The exporter must finance the transaction with its own funds, ship the goods, and then await payment.

There is a middle ground whereby a letter of credit (L/C or LoC) is established via the exporter's bank, which effectively eliminates any credit risk associated with the buyer. Financial institutes are continually changing their foreign banking instruments to facilitate trade, so check with your banker.

Managing Credit Risk

Other than generic letters of credit, there are other ways to ensure payment. The following list provides two methods:

- Export credit insurance (ECI) by which export receivables are insured by private commercial insurers, organizations like the Export Development Corporation (EDC) in Canada or the Export-Import Bank of the United States (US EXIM Bank) in the United States.
- Working with a third-party credit corporation that provides foreign buyers with a guarantee of contract completion. There may be progress payment programs (PPP) that allow exporters to obtain pre-shipment financing.

Managing Currency Risk

Foreign exchange rate risk can be reduced by having foreign currency. Another, albeit more complex, tactic is currency hedging through your bank by establishing a forward exchange contract. This contract effectively hedges the risk of adverse foreign exchange fluctuations and the value of importer's currency relative to the Canadian or American dollar.

The Business Growth Road Map

The Business Growth Road Map is based on the Business Diagnostics Framework and was developed by Terry Rachwalski and Mike Thompson during their tenure at Royal Roads University. Rachwalski supplemented the work on the Impact set element of the Road Map in partnership with Dr. Kathryn Graham and with the support and assistance of Alberta Innovates.

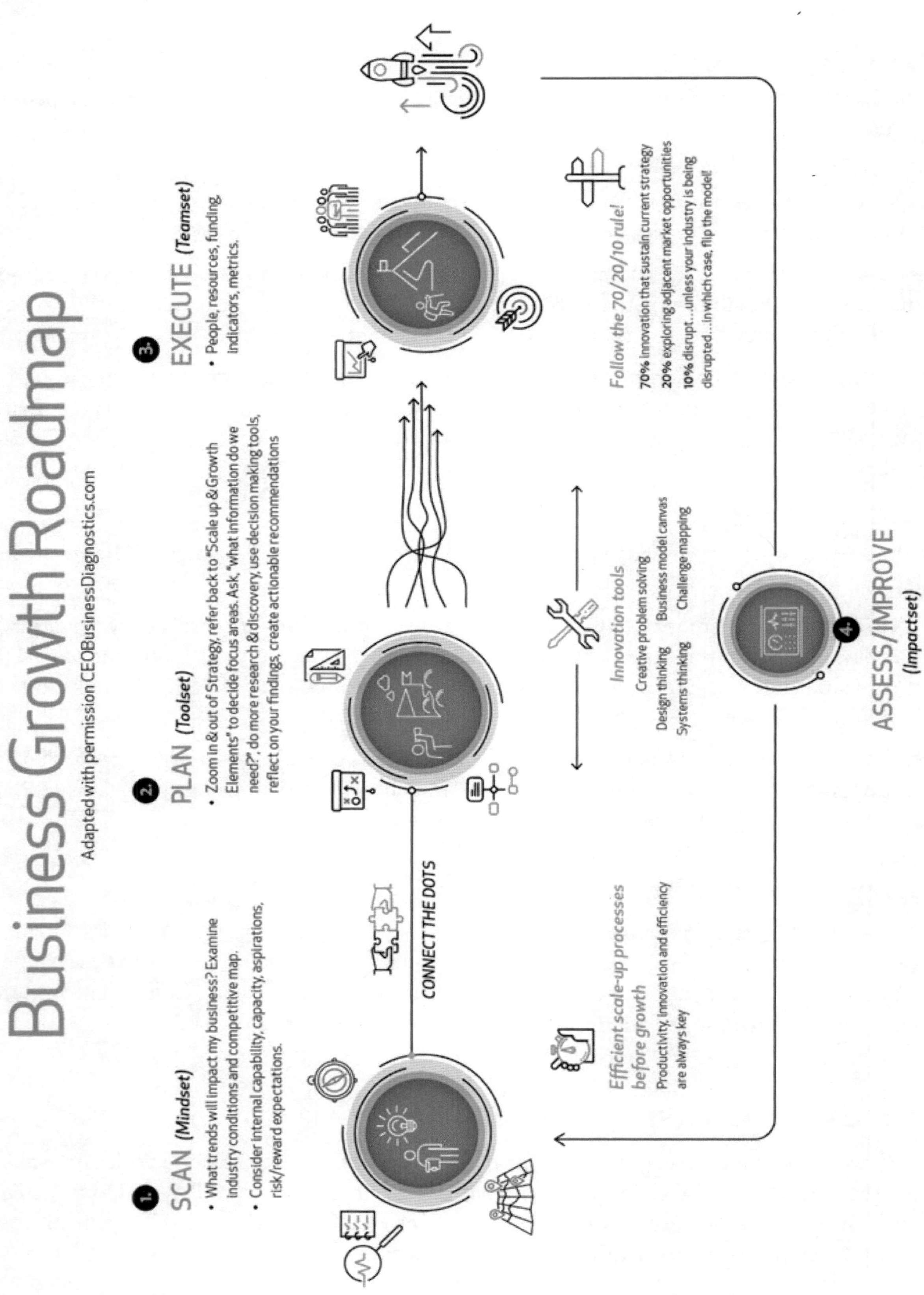

Business Growth Roadmap

Adapted with permission CEOBusinessDiagnostics.com

1. SCAN *(Mindset)*
- What trends will impact my business? Examine industry conditions and competitive map.
- Consider internal capability, capacity, aspirations, risk/reward expectations.

2. PLAN *(Toolset)*
- Zoom in & out of Strategy, refer back to "Scale up & Growth Elements" to decide focus areas. Ask, "what information do we need?", do more research & discovery, use decision making tools, reflect on your findings, create actionable recommendations

3. EXECUTE *(Teamset)*
- People, resources, funding indicators, metrics.

4. ASSESS/IMPROVE *(Impactset)*

Innovation tools
Creative problem solving
Design thinking
Systems thinking
Business model canvas
Challenge mapping

Follow the 70/20/10 rule!
70% Innovation that sustain current strategy
20% exploring adjacent market opportunities
10% disrupt...unless your industry is being disrupted...in which case, flip the model!

Efficient scale-up processes before growth
Productivity, innovation and efficiency are always key

CONNECT THE DOTS

Figure 25. Business Growth Road Map

The Business Growth Road Map was developed to help guide businesspeople through a planned growth process as they navigate an extraordinary and challenging post-pandemic business environment.

The road map has the four primary elements and is illustrated in Figure 25:

1. Scan (Mindset)
2. Plan (Tool set)
3. Execute (Team set)
4. Assess/Improve (Impact set)

Scan (Mindset)

The first part of the Business Growth Road Map requires an environmental scan. This scan starts at the outer ring of the Business Diagnostics Framework, which explores trends and threats to your business, examines the industry conditions you operate in, and reviews the competitive landscape. These concepts are covered in the first section of this book: External Size up. which encompasses Chapter 1, Business Environment and Chapter 2, Industry Conditions.

The second part of the scan includes the elements found in Section 2 of this book: Internal Size-up, which is covered in Chapters 3 through 7.

A critical element of the scan is to honestly reflect on the mindset of the company owner, his/her leadership and management. You need to assess the internal capabilities and capacity to grow and most importantly, the aspirations of the owner and their risk and reward expectations. If the owner does not wish to take on the challenges of growth, then pushing new concepts will be a difficult task[4].

Plan (Tool Set)

Planning for growth requires having the tool set at the ready to help you assess what growth path makes sense for your company, based on where you are now and what opportunities exist or are on the horizon. There are a variety of business tools to help you assess your options, many of which we cover in this book. You can zoom in and out of the Business Diagnostics Framework to continually review your industry and competitive conditions and your internal needs, capacity, capabilities, and aspirations. Based on the elements of scale-up and growth, you can decide which elements to focus on now. After you decide what to focus on, you need to review what information you have and what more you need. For example, perhaps your external scan revealed that your product would be a perfect fit for a new geographic market expansion, and you decide that expanding into this new geographic market will be your growth path. Consider all the questions you need to answer and prepare for before entering this new market. How will you decide whether to enter the market directly or via a distribution partner?

---

4   The growth mindset is a concept that has been explored by Dr. Simon Raby at Mount Royal University and we encourage you to review his work.

A note on innovation—Innovation has become a buzzword. We argue that innovation is a tool that you can use. Innovation needs to have a purpose and to solve a problem—too much innovation creates chaos; too much standardization for stability and efficiency can create stagnation. A simple tool is the 70/20/10 rule widely attributed to the book, *The Alchemy of Growth: Practical Insights for Building the Enduring Enterprise* (Baghai, Coley and White, 2000). The rule reminds us to focus 70% of efforts on your existing strategy, products and business model, spend 20% of your efforts exploring adjacent markets and devote 10% of your time exploring how your products and business might be disrupted.

In *Business Diagnostics*, we remind that this rule of thumb works relatively well as tool unless you are in a business that is about to be disrupted, in which case, it would be wise to flip the model. Think of the taxi business and the advent of ride sharing like Uber.

There are many innovation tools you can use to help your team solve problems. We use creative problem solving and design thinking, but there are many terrific systems and tools to explore.

Execute (Team Set)

In order to execute on your chosen scale-up or growth path, you need to consider what people, resources, and funding you will need to be successful. What will it cost, and how long will it take? What financing and resources need to be in place? Can you create a timeline with milestones?

Assess and Improve (Impact Set)

The final piece of the Business Growth Road Map is continual assessment and improvement, which is grounded in metrics and reporting dashboards that are used to help decide when to change course or intervene. Your impact set metrics improve your decision-making and should lead you right back to the scan and mindset with the zoom in and out of strategy philosophy.

Chapter 10
Sources of Equity Funding

Overview

Another crucial element in the development of a new business opportunity is securing sufficient funding to grow and maintain the enterprise. This chapter examines the equity investment process and how it interfaces with the business life cycle. Discussion in this chapter relates to the earlier stages of the growth curve that are characterized by greater risk, absence of positive cash flow, and the need for equity, NOT debt. Sources of debt financing, usually available only once a company has reached a more mature growth phase, will be examined in detail in Chapter 11.

Figure 26 illustrates the evolution of a technology company and the corresponding sources of funding, commencing with equity and progressing through to more conventional financing vehicles.

While the stages in the funding and business life cycle covers generic start-up companies, we will focus on technology-based operations since they typically dominate the equity-raising process in today's business environment. It is important to note that these stages are based on life cycle, not the typical seed stage rounds described by venture capitalists. There is no definitive rule about what financing will work and when. Financing will depend on the company, its profitability, and the market.

The stages of a company's development can be categorized as follows:

Seed/Early Stage. This stage typically includes idea generation and proof of concept, which is typically pre-seed funding.

Start-Up. The start-up stage encompasses product development, customer discovery, prototype testing, and some initial marketing. Usual sources of funding are family and friends, government grants, and perhaps some early angels.

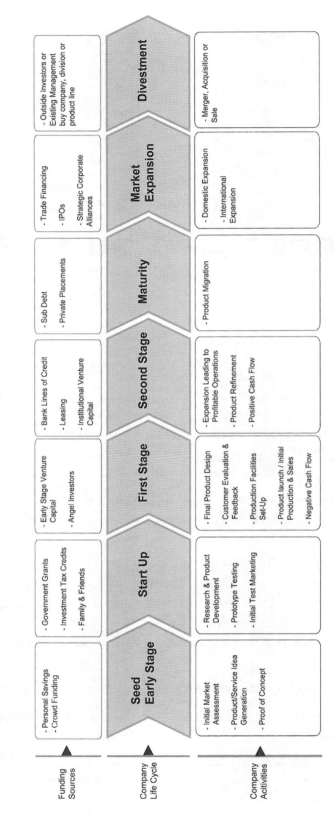

Figure 26. Funding and the Business Life Cycle

First Stage. The first stage involves the initial production and sales. The company is not yet cash flow positive. Usually, angel investors and, possibly, early-stage venture capital will be involved in a post-seed, sometimes known as a bridge, round. Venture will be a series A or B

Second Stage. The second stage involves expansion, leading to profitable operations and positive cash flow. This is typically a series B funding from venture capital funds; there might possibly be institutional investors, and debt financing is possible. There may be an initial public offering (IPO) being considered.

Maturity. In the maturity stage, product migrations are initiated, along with completion of domestic and possibly international expansions.

Market Expansion. When in the market expansion stage, additional funding can be obtained from trade financing such as strategic corporate alliances or public offering activities. Private equity may be involved.

Divestment At the divestment stage, outside investors or existing management buy the company, division, or product line, or a merger and acquisition (M&A) is completed.

THE EQUITY INVESTMENT PROCESS

The equity investment process can be broken down into six steps:

1. Identify funding requirements
2. Demonstrate investment potential
3. Complete a written investment proposal
4. Identify potential investors
5. Pitching potential investors
6. Negotiate and close the deal

Identify Funding Requirements

The most important task is to identify how much money is required to fund the venture and when the funding is needed. Too often, founders guess about how much money they need. Revenue derived from customers is the least expensive manner to fund your business. However, if you need equity, be mindful that it is the most expensive resource you will bring in, so taking the time to do financial modelling that is based on the best information you have is well worth the time it takes. Here are some key points to consider in raising outside capital:

- How much cash do you need, and when do you need it?
- Create a financial model with sensitivity analysis to demonstrate different scenarios. How many dollars will be generated internally from ongoing cash flows, and how many dollars will be required from external equity sources?

- Equity sources will include the company founders' cash and resources from outside investors. Government programs, research tax credits, and winning pitch competitions are helpful, but they shouldn't be relied on to keep your company running.

- How will the funds be allocated?
    - Working capital
    - Sales and marketing costs
    - Capital assets
    - Research and development

- When will the funds be advanced? What are key performance benchmarks or milestones?

- Will the company be able to generate a sufficient rate of return to reward the investors? Equity investors will typically look for between 25% and 40% annualized returns over a three-to-five-year time horizon.

- Remember that different investors require different levels of profit sharing, decision-making, and management. There must also be a broad exit strategy (IPO, sale of company, management buyback, M&A, and so on) envisaged for the investor.

- Be aware of the 20/60/20 rule for equity investors when reviewing the success of their investments:
    - 20% are winners
    - 60% are the *living dead*
    - 20% do not survive

Demonstrate Investment Potential

It is critical to understand the risk assessment process that an equity investor will undertake. In the first phases of a start-up, the founder is typically heavily involved in the minimally viable product, the technology development, and customer engagement. However, if this company will need outside investment to grow, the founder will quickly need to become immersed in demonstrating their investment readiness. To ensure that you are ready to answer investor's questions, be aware that the following criteria are usually considered by investors:

- What is the caliber of the management team? What are the specific management skills and attributes in place now, and what are those required for the future? What experience does the management team have from previous ventures, either successful or not?

- Will the investor be able to build a solid and enduring relationship with the founder, the target company, and its management? This is a critical first step.

- What is the company's market opportunity? Are there unique product and service features?

- Is the industry segment known, large, and attractive to the investor? Does the segment match the investor's risk comfort level?

- Is there evidence of a critical need and customer acceptance for the product or service?

- What are the terms of the investment?

- What percentage of the company is being offered? Usually, the first equity offering in an early- stage, start-up, and first stage are for under 50% of the total shares because the investor does not want to assume day-to-day operational control and associated headaches. Some early stage or angel investors may want to structure a deal that gives them effective control until certain performance milestones are reached.

- What is the estimated value of the business? How was the value derived? How many other investors are at the table?

- Sophisticated investors will be looking to add value to the company, aside from their investment of capital. This is also known as smart money that will contribute more than just cash. These investors may have business contacts, financing relationships, or knowledge of potential strategic partnerships that could assist the company in achieving its growth objectives.

- How will return on investment (ROI) requirements be met?

- What is the historical and projected operating performance and financial structure?

- Are intellectual property interests protected? What other barriers to entry are in place?

- How many shareholders are there, and what is their power? Is there a road map that details the expected dilution of shareholdings over time? To accomplish this, there will normally be a capitalization table included with the term sheet. The simpler the capitalization table, the easier it is for an investor to make a deal.

- Is there a viable exit strategy (three to five years) down the road?

- Is there a written Strategic Business Plan or Enterprise Review Summary in place? Is there a pitch deck?

- How will the investment be monitored and controlled? For examples, are any of the following in place—Board seat, financial statement reporting requirements, capital expenditure approvals, and so on.

Complete a Written Investment Proposal

We often hear stories about investments deals being done with a quick pitch and a back-of-the-napkin deal. Most investment proposals are built on the primary components of the company strategy, the elements of the business and operational plan, and will be tailored to the equity investment initiative. Focus should be on the investor's needs and requirements. We believe that writing out an investment proposal and then breaking it down into a pitch deck of 10-12 slides is the most effective method to prepare. It is important to be completely familiar with your narrative, story, and financials, so you can effectively answer questions from potential investors.

Key areas to emphasize in the written investment proposal and pitch deck:

- The problem you are solving and the market opportunity

- Why your solution is different from other proposed solutions
- Your management track record, which explains your experience and builds credibility
- The business model, market strategy, and how the problem is solved now
- Compliance with all legal and regulatory requirements
- Revenue/earnings growth projections to meet investor's ROI
- Use of proceeds
- The equity stake that is available to the investor, amount of funding, investment terms, and duration
- Anticipated exit strategies for the investor

To prepare for equity investment, you will need to have your documentation complete. Be sure to obtain feedback from outside professional advisors. A useful document to get started on this step is an Enterprise Review Summary (ERS), which is a concise three-to-four-page summary that describes the funding opportunity for the investor and which can accompany a pitch deck. This concept is covered in greater detail in Chapter 13 – Strategic Business Plans.

Typically, due diligence is done with access to an online data room that is provided, based on a signed non-disclosure agreement or a term sheet. Your data room will hold all the sensitive company information that validates your technology; shows how you have validated your customer and market; includes sales and marketing costs and metrics; shows key traction metrics for your industry; and discloses your financial data, including salaries and shareholder capitalization table, option pool, and any share sales and buy backs. Typically, the venture capital firm will advise what information they need to have available; the information they require will depend on what stage the company is in. In a well prepared and structured data room, you can anticipate the need and have the documentation available.

Identify Potential Investors

It is important to match your investors to your stage of company. Further, it is important to match the style of investing. An investment is typically for between two and ten years, so you need to be sure you are compatible with your funders. Understand that this is a two-way process. It is essential to assess the potential investors' background and capabilities. They will be completing extensive due diligence on you, the investee, and you should do due diligence on them as well. When you are looking at investors, consider the following elements:

- Consider their character, reputation, and credibility. What other companies have they invested in? What do those founders have to say about the investor?
- How compatible are you? Is there a shared personal and business vision? Do you share ethics and values?
- What is their past track record? Have there been any problem investments?
- How involved do they want to be? What does that look like?

- Judge their commitment and financial staying power. Will the investor be involved and have strong links to the next round of funding?
- Does the investor have the ability to bring other resources, such as market or competitor knowledge, to the table,? Do they understand prevailing industry and technology issues?

You can identify and do due diligence on investors via your local, regional, or national innovation and small business supports agencies, through technology and industry associations, professional services (accountants, legal advisors, bankers), mentors, and your personal network.

The following categories of equity investor can be identified, beginning with the earliest players that come to the table:

Founder's Cash

Personal cash injections from savings accounts, securities, home equity sources, and so on. Credit cards are increasingly being *maxed out* to generate the required start-up capital. This option is not for the faint of heart and certainly is not recommended as a funding source.

Friends and Family (F and F)

F and F is also known as love money, seed money, or guilt money. Dollar amounts are generally small, up to $100,000, with proceeds typically used to test concepts, discover and validate customer need, initiate product development, and market research. This type of investor will typically invest in you, the founder, as opposed to the business opportunity.

Crowdfunding

Crowdfunding can be used to gauge or create excitement in your product or venture. Typically, the site will charge a fee or require a percentage of monies raised. The founder will create bonuses or rewards for those who invest early and offer pre sales. Crowdfunding works best when there is a very clear need and a great video or animation story that is easily shared. There may be tax and regulatory implications in different jurisdictions to be aware of.

Government-Backed Programs

It is risky for companies to rely on government-backed programs and funding. Government funding certainly shouldn't find its way into forecasts until the agreement is signed. Funding rules and amounts change quickly and have varying amounts of paperwork.

In Canada, the primary source of early government-backed funding is from federal innovation programs. The most stable and well-known is the Industrial Research Assistance Program (IRAP), which provides advice and financial assistance through the National Research Council. Each province has government-backed funds, but they typically offer less than the federal programs. These programs change frequently.

In the United States, the place to start is your state innovation agency or the federal Small Business Administration. There are a variety of loan programs and research grants.

Angel Investors

Angels are generally individuals who are contacted through professional advisors or angel networks. These are typically high net-worth individuals with a particular domain expertise and varying degrees of investing sophistication and who will invest early stage amounts in the $50,000 to $750,000 range. Angels will sometimes form consortia or group funds to reduce risk and increase due diligence.

- Angels typically look for 35-45% ROI (Return on Investment) within three to five years.
- Angels will usually bring experience, contacts, and strategic advice to the table.
- They are more likely to become involved in an earlier stage company and one with global potential.
- Angels tend to invest in local companies (within a 50-km radius of their home).

Venture Capital Firms

Most venture capital (VC) firms seldom work with very early-stage start-ups. They are more likely to allow founders, angels, and governments to take early-stage risk. VCs seek out more companies that have traction, a big market, and need equity to scale-up efficiency and increase revenue to achieve positive cash flow generation. Venture capital firms are likely to have the following characteristics:

- These investors will be professionals with extensive experience and contacts, looking for annualized returns in the 30+% range.
- Investment size will range from $2 to $10 million, depending on the stage.
- The payback term will vary from five to ten years.
- These firms tend to travel in herds and will often syndicate an investment to achieve relative safety in numbers.
- They tend to invest in thematically linked areas like enterprise software as a servicer, property technology (prop tech), or financial technology (fintech).
- They tend to invest in trends and to have more than one investment in a particular hot trend.
- Scalability is important to this type of investor. A business that is able to add new clients with little extra effort and cost is said to be scalable.
- The required demonstration of customer traction will vary with investor, but most are looking for recurring revenue, a high profit margin, and an understanding of how sustainable the client revenues are over time.
- Some venture funds are based on social enterprise endeavours, which is also known as Social Enterprise investing or Impact Investing. If your product or service contributes to solving environmental or social problems, consider contacting a social enterprise fund. Also note that in the United States, there are beneficial corporations or *B* corps, which is a corporate structure available in some states.

Institutional Investors

Institutional investors are capital market funds from banks and pension funds. They provide equity to medium-sized businesses with investment requirements usually in the $10 million+ range. They will invest based on their risk profile and portfolio needs.

Private Equity Investors
- Private equity firms tend to want to gather companies in complementary industries that they know well or are looking to gather and consolidate.

Strategic Corporate Investors
- These funds consist of corporations or strategic alliances and corporate partnerships with established, successful companies that are looking to gain new product and market access or expand into new technologies. They might be called a corporate venture fund, though the return is usually strategic not just monetary.

Public Offerings

Initial Public Offerings (IPOs) involve raising additional capital through a formalized share-offering process on public exchanges. Before initiating this process, take careful note of the following considerations:

- This process usually takes place after a number of private rounds of equity investments. Timing is crucial from both the external investment climate and the company's internal cash generation performance.

- Further dilution of the founding shareholder's interests takes place, along with new accountability to other stakeholders such as public shareholders, regulators, and so on.

- A prospectus, available to public shareholders, provides a detailed description of the company and the investment opportunity. Regulators provide tight control over the process to protect the public.

- Underwriters sell the stock through the selected stock market after deciding on the issue price, based upon orders booked from retail and institutional investors.

- The process can be very expensive and requires a huge time and financial commitment. There are substantial accounting requirements prior to the IPO that must be met.

- The listing process entails costs between 6 and 8% of the issue, which will be retained by the underwriters. Intensive road shows and lengthy investor relations initiatives add to the overall cost.

- One outcome arising from an IPO is that suppliers, customers, and competition suddenly have a detailed update on your historical and projected financial performance and your strategic plans by way of the prospectus that is issued to potential investors.

- If the IPO process is successful, there will be significant gains in credibility, access to international capital markets, and the ability to offer more liquid stock options to attract top-tier employees.

- Given the complexity of the process, it is crucial to ask this question a number of times: "Is the company ready to go public?"

Pitching Potential Investors

The number of pitch and demonstration opportunities have exploded as innovation ecosystems mature. While many deals are done personally, there is merit in practicing your pitch because it helps you clarify your narrative. There is a typical cadence and flow to pitch decks. They tend to focus on the market, but creating excitement balanced with reality can be tricky. It's unlikely you will get it exactly right the first time, so use pitch nights for practice and feedback; often your local business groups offer pitch coaching. We caution early-stage entrepreneurs that pitch competitions can take up a lot of time, so be sure to weigh the risk and reward; focus on building your traction, instead of building the perfect pitch deck. The goal is investment, not winning competitions. The following list offers some tips and tactics to achieve an effective presentation:

- Practice the presentation beforehand. Then practice again. Stay within the time limit.

- Determine who from your team will be the presenter. This person should ideally be the company founder or CEO who is able to communicate his or her passion, commitment, and staying power to the potential investor audience.

- Know your audience and tailor the message accordingly. Fun pitch nights, investors, corporate strategic partners, or potential clients will each require a different presentation.

- Address the audience directly and, if you are pitching in person, establish eye contact. Ensure that the audience is paying attention to you, not your beautiful slide deck. Memorize your narrative, rather than reading it from previously prepared notes.

- Quickly arrive at the company's value proposition and uniqueness. It is critical that the audience understands and becomes excited at the opportunity facing them and are ready to reach for their wallets.

- Seasoned investors and strategic partners will *bet on the jockey, not the horse.* You need to demonstrate which key management people are now in place along with their strengths and experience. Later stage investors or potential partners usually want to see that key personnel are already hired.

- Product functionality typically does not have to be demonstrated at the presentation, but you should show any proof or screen shots that you have. That the technology works is usually understood, though it will be validated by a due-diligence process that is completed at a later date. Instead, focus on the market opportunity.

- Support the presentation with sales or marketing elements that further illustrate the market potential.

In your practice sessions, be ready for some hard-nosed questions that may be asked. The questions will be tough, and it is important to be honest without getting defensive. Investors want to know who you are and how you react. Be prepared to answer questions concerning these aspects of your understanding and commitment:

- What is your background and track record?
- What is your financial commitment?

- Describe your market niche and what strategy and business model you will use to dominate the market.
- Explain your process to understand your customer and required sales channels?
- Provide details on your management team's experience and technical capabilities.
- How will the requested investment funds be used?
- What are your revenue and earnings growth assumptions?
- What is your competitive advantage? Who are your competitors? What are their relative strengths and weaknesses?
- Do you have any intellectual property or other barriers to entry?
- What steps have you taken to protect your intellectual property and ensure exclusivity with no strings attached? Were you working for someone else when you first developed the product or technology?
- What ROI will be achieved over the life of the investment? Is there a viable exit strategy?
- How will the proceeds of this investment influence your existing business strategy?
- What are your motivations—ego or wealth creation? Ego implies a desire to stay at the helm and in control at all costs, even when the ship is sinking.
- What are your weaknesses? This is a tough question that tests your willingness to disclose information. It is critical that you outline any challenges or obstacles frankly if you are to win the confidence of the potential investors.

Negotiating and Closing the Deal

Most investors will complete an extensive due diligence review either themselves or via an independent third party. The due diligence will involve the following actions:

- Checking your references
- Validating information found in your data room
- Reviewing legal agreements and bank authorities
- Completing a facilities tour
- Obtaining credit bureau reports
- Analyzing historical financial statements
- Reviewing financial projections and assumptions
- Reviewing operation processes and plans

Consider the following key points for negotiating and closing the deal:

- The personal relationship between the investor and investee (founder) must be solid and enduring.

- The investor will issue a preliminary Term Sheet that outlines the terms of the deal. This document needs to be carefully reviewed with your accountant, lawyer, and Board.
- The investor will complete further due diligence prior to the completion of formal documentation and the shareholder agreement. This is an essential document that requires careful review with your legal advisors.
- A wide range of stakeholders has to be considered at this crucial stage, so the closing process is invariably protracted and involves more lawyers.
- Raising capital is a time-consuming and often frustrating effort. No matter when you think it should be completed, it will take longer due to unforeseen delays, especially the preparation of legal documentation and Term Sheet negotiations.
- Start early, and seek funding assistance before you need it. Never negotiate a Term Sheet when you are cash strapped.

Pre-Revenue, Start-Up Company Valuations

In the previous chapter, company valuations, based on the business as a going concern, were discussed. With pre-revenue start-up companies, if there have been no sales, stabilized earnings, or cash flow, it is more complicated to perform a realistic valuation calculation. An investor will be prepared to commit some new venture capital to a deal but will also want to attain a meaningful shareholding in the company. The following methodology describes how such an equity stake is derived:

The concept here is to project the valuation process into the future by completing some simple future value calculations. It should be noted that the same percentage ownership result can also be obtained by taking future earnings and completing a present value calculation.

Here Is an Example With Some Assumptions

1. An early-stage start-up enterprise requires $500,000 for new product and market development.
2. The investor, after assessing the venture's risk profile, determines that a 35% rate of return, compounded annually over five years, is required.
3. The company's financial projections estimate net earnings before interest and income tax (EBIT) at $800,000 achieved at the end of year five. These projections have been carefully assessed and stress tested by the investor.
4. The investor's research indicates a current industry price/earnings multiple in the eight times range.

Calculating the Start-up Valuation and Equity Stake

The future value of the company in year five, based on the price/earnings multiple and forecast EBIT, is $800,000 EBIT multiplied by the 8 times price/earning multiple = $6.4 million

The future value of the investor's $500,000 investment compounded (monthly) at 35% through to year five = $2.24 million.

The investor's equity stake is determined by dividing the future value of the investor's investment by the future value of the company = $2.24M/$6.4M = 35%

Therefore, the investor would negotiate a 35% or more stake in the company. The owner would retain 65%, having received a $500,000 equity injection to expedite product and market development.

If the company has a proven history of sales and positive earnings, potential investors would likely use a revenue multiple model that is based upon similar sale transactions that are observed in the specific industry sector.

Chapter 11
Sources of Debt Financing

Overview

In this chapter, sources of debt financing are reviewed. While there are no hard and fast rules, early-stage companies will usually be funded from equity sources (owner, seed capital, angels, and so on). Debt financing is invariably difficult to obtain and giving away equity in the early stages can prove a more expensive route over time if the company proves to be successful.

Why is debt financing difficult to obtain?

The primary reason is cash flow. A company should be able to demonstrate that it can generate sustainable cash flow from its operations in order to service the debt by paying interest and repaying any debt obligations. Many early-stage companies struggle to become cash flow positive and do not need a heavy liability of debt to burden their operations.

As a company matures and builds a solid track record of revenues, earnings, and cash flow generation, a wide array of financing vehicles become available to them. This growth can be funded by both debt and additional equity streams like venture capital rounds. The second part of this chapter provides strategic tips that will assist you in negotiating mutually beneficial opportunities with your bank.

We will walk you through:

- Types of debt financing
- Dealing with banks

Types of Debt Financing

In this section, the following sources of financing are presented:

- Commercial banks

- Government initiatives
- Other types of debt financing

Commercial Banks

Commercial banks are the primary source of debt financing for small-and medium-sized companies. The different types of loans are detailed below:

Operating Lines of Credit

Operating or revolving lines of credit can be used to finance short-term working capital needs such as Accounts Receivable collection and inventory purchases.

Operating lines of credit have the following features:

- An authorized dollar limit is established, based on a forecast of peak cash needs in any one month of the year.
- Borrowing is usually on-demand, with a floating interest rate that is established at an agreed-upon percentage over the prevailing prime rate, for example, prime + 1%.
- Operating borrowing is usually margined. That is, you can only borrow up to a specified percentage of Accounts Receivable and inventories on your books as at a specific month end, for example, 75% of Accounts Receivable under 60 days, plus 50% of inventory at estimated cost.
- Security generally consists of a General Security Agreement (GSA) that provides the bank with a specific legal charge or claim over your Accounts Receivable, inventory, and potentially, other company assets, which is known as a floating charge.

Term Loans

A term loan is typically extended for equipment purchases with the term of the loan matched to the expected life of the asset. For example, if the equipment is expected to be amortized over three years, then the term loan would be for three years.

Term loans have the following features:

- They are available on a floating or fixed-rate basis.
- The loan security will consist of a fixed, specific charge over the asset being acquired.
- Financing in the range of 60% to 70% of the equipment price is usually negotiable.

Commercial Mortgages

Commercial mortgages are designed to assist with the purchase or refinancing of commercial real estate.

Commercial mortgages have the following features:

- Usually available on a fixed-rate basis. Interest rates are locked in for one-to seven-year terms. Amortization periods are typically between 15 and 25 years, depending on the quality and location of the real estate asset.

- Financing is typically available for between 60% and 75% of current real estate appraised value.
- Loan security consists of a first mortgage over the real estate asset along with an assignment of rents and fire insurance. Personal or corporate guarantees may also be required.

Letters of Credit

Letters of credit are typically available for exporting or importing situations when the exporter wants to sell goods or services but wants the assurance of payment before commencing production and delivery. In another situation, a letter of credit might be available when the offshore importer wants to purchase goods or services but does not want to pay until shipping and title documents are received and are in good order.

Bridge Loans

A bridge loan is interim financing that is provided on a short-term basis to cover project costs pending inflow of sales proceeds or long-term financing. As an example, a real estate developer wishes to finance the construction of a townhouse development. Construction and interest costs will be financed by the bank, pending sale of the townhouse units.

Credit Cards

Credit cards can be used for short-term financing of expenses for the business.

Personal Loans

Personal loans may be available to the company owner to raise additional funds that can then be injected into the company by way of a shareholder loan.

Government Initiatives

It is important to note that government assistant programs are modified often and typically with a change in government. In previous chapters, we mentioned Canadian and American programs such as IRAP, Export Development Canada, and the U.S. Small Business Administration loans. In the United States, there are also training and information workshops through the U.S. Trade and Development Agency. There will also be regional programs offered by states and provinces, which are too numerous to list.

Most governments have loans and grants available to businesses, depending on the particular strategies of the government. Be sure to review what is available for operations, exporting, research and development, new product commercialization, productivity, and innovation.

Other Types of Debt Financing

There are a variety of new banking instruments that have evolved out of the technology industry that offer loans based on revenue sharing and a variety of instruments. Some of these instruments are explained in the following sections.

Leasing

Leasing is available from banks, equipment manufacturers, and lease financing companies for business equipment and larger ticket items, for instance, specialized manufacturing equipment. The lease is a contract and is a liability or debt. Lease terms typically run from 36 to 60 months and cover a portion of the cost of the asset being leased. It is important to obtain professional advice from your accountant to ensure that there are favourable tax consequences arising from leasing versus borrowing to purchase.

Some of the benefits of leasing include the following:

- Leasing preserves working capital (cash) for expansion purposes.
- Leasing leaves operating credit lines available for non-fixed asset-financing needs.
- Leasing provides a hedge against equipment obsolescence.

Figure 27 summarizes the buying versus leasing decision and the resultant ownership relationships.

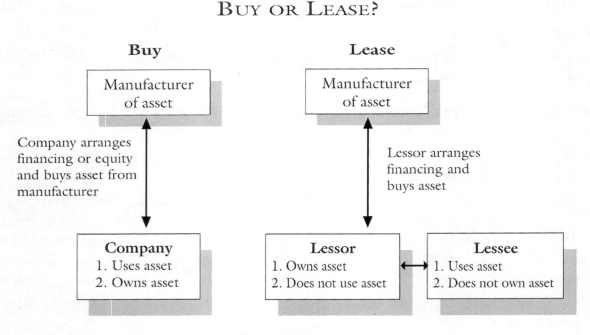

Figure 27. Buy or Lease

Floor Plan Financing

Floor plan financing is a loan provided by manufacturers that allows retailers or distributors to acquire product and inventory and make it available for sale. The floor plan loan is repaid from the product sales proceeds. This is a more common financing option for those who deal in higher priced products like vehicles in car showrooms.

Mezzanine Financing

Mezzanine financing is also known as a subordinated debt or sub debt. This form of financing falls between traditional debt and equity on the balance sheet. Sub debt is a blend of equity and conventional debt with no reliance on collateral assets, yet it requires regular monthly interest and principal payments.

Mezzanine financing has the following features:

- Relatively high interest rates (12% to 18%) provide the mezzanine lender with a reasonable return relative to the risk profile of the company.
- An equity component, usually stock warrants, is often required, enabling the lender to acquire future equity of the company. The lender usually does not want control, so the equity will be less than a controlling interest.
- The deal size may be as high as $5 to $10 million.
- The term is usually up to five years with monthly blended payments. Seasonal payments, cash sweeps, or balloon payment mechanisms can also be set up.
- The General Security Agreement (GSA) may provide a floating charge against the business assets, subordinated to the senior lender. Limited personal guarantees, along with an assignment of key person insurance, is usually required.

Benefits of mezzanine financing include the following aspects:

- It is targeted at rapid growth companies that need supplemental funding over and above traditional sources of debt and equity.
- Sub debt lenders look primarily at the company's cash flow and the enterprise value for payment and return on equity as opposed to more traditional lenders who derive comfort from the book value of assets, which have been pledged as collateral.
- Mezzanine financing may be less expensive than pure equity investments and more flexible than conventional debt.
- Board seats are not usually required for a lender to advance mezzanine financing.
- Usually, mezzanine financing results in an improved working capital position.

Sub debt can be used for any of the following purposes:

- Strategic acquisitions
- Significant marketing or operational growth expenditures
- Management buyouts
- New product development

Typical underwriting criteria for sub debt:

- Strong management must be in place with a significant ownership stake in the business.
- The company is experiencing strong revenue growth (minimum 20% per year).
- A positive cash flow (EBITDA) that is demonstrated over a minimum one-year period.
- Other sophisticated investors (venture capital firms) and lenders (banks) are also participating.

- There is a healthy relationship with the senior lender, plus adequate operating credits are in place.
- A defined exit strategy, for example, IPO, refinancing, or sale of the company, is in place).

Restructuring Loan Payments

Debt restructuring is negotiated with your lender, typically to allow interest-only payments to support a firm through slow cash flow periods. Other options would be to structure the loan to allow for balloon payments at the end of a loan term, which would lower prior principal monthly payments, or to allow for lump sum principal payments seasonally when the company has cash.

Bootstrap Financing

Bootstrapping is using whatever resources you have available to finance your company. The bootstrapping concept can be extended into bootstrap financing, which arises when a venture is launched with modest personal funds and is then bootstrapped up the growth curve by implementing creative survival strategies. Close attention to cash flow and cash resources is a key feature of this process.

Some strategies from the world of bootstrap finance:

Factoring

A factoring company purchases your Accounts Receivable, advancing 70% to 90% of a specific invoice amount. Servicing fees (2% value of the receivable) are charged along with an interest rate (Prime + 3% plus) on funds advanced prior to the collection of the invoice. This can be an alternative source of financing for companies that do not yet qualify for operating credit lines.

- Factoring does not create additional liabilities that are added to the Balance Sheet because existing Accounts Receivable are merely discounted by the factoring company.
- The accelerated receipt of cash can relieve seasonal cash flow pressures and allow companies to take advantage of trade discounts from suppliers or special product purchase opportunities. Factoring is typically used in the resource industry when upfront costs are high.

Customer, Supplier, Landlord Credit

It may be possible to negotiate with your clients that they provide advance payments in the early stages of a particular project. Trade credit terms can be negotiated with suppliers, often with long lead times to allow for seasonal impacts on the cash flow cycle. Financial assistance from your landlord, assuming that the premises are rented, may be available to complete additional leasehold improvements. Temporary deferral of monthly rent during a tight cash flow period may also be negotiable.

Other Options to Manage Cash

- Expand slowly and carefully. While first mover advantage may be lost, the slow and steady approach to expansion means less pressure on limited working capital resources.
- Minimize unnecessary capital expenditures.

- Have employees accept stock options or profit sharing in lieu of industry standard wages until the business becomes more established.
- With custom orders, negotiate a 30/60/10 payment structure from customers: 30% up front, 60% upon delivery, and a 10% holdback to cover performance issues.
- Try to acquire a *lighthouse client*: a well-known and credible industry leader who will serve as an attractive reference to other potential clients, corporate strategic partners, and investors.

Dealing with Banks

In this section, we highlight the importance in maintaining a healthy and sustained relationship with your commercial banker:

How to Build a Strong Relationship with Your Banker

There are five key steps to building a strong relationship with your banker:

1. **Find the right banker.**
2. **Demonstrate credibility and reliability.**
3. **Build a team of professional advisors.**
4. **Communicate.**
5. **Utilize other bank resources.**

Find the Right Banker

It seems trite and obvious, but you need to find a banker that is a good fit for you and your company. If you are seeking a new bank, remember that the key is to build an enduring relationship with your individual commercial banker and to ensure that person highlights your needs within their banking group.

Your banker also runs a business within a business with a portfolio of commercial clients that forms part of the bank's overall loan and deposit portfolio. Like any successful business, commercial bankers have to grow their client base, provide outstanding customer service, and deliver profitable returns to their shareholders. Getting the right fit for your business is important.

Questions to Ask a Potential Banker

- What are your qualifications and length of commercial lending experience?
- Do you have a team approach to commercial banking relationships? Who provides ongoing support to you, and to whom do you report?
- Can you provide an overview of your commercial loan portfolio? Which industries do you specialize in, and where have you had the most success?
- How important is commercial banking to your bank?

Demonstrate Credibility and Reliability

By demonstrating your credibility and reliability, your banker can come to trust your integrity, which will help as they create a case for adding your company to their lending portfolio.

- Through business plan presentations, demonstrate your intimate knowledge of company operations, major competitors, and industry opportunities and threats.
- Provide credible, accurate, and timely financial information as part of your monthly reporting and annual review process.
- Anticipate your financing needs early, for example, temporary bulges, new capital financing needs, and so on.
- Invite your banker to your place of business regularly, provide a tour, and introduce key personnel.
- Under promise and over deliver.

Build a Team of Professional Advisors

Your banker will want to know who provides you with accounting, legal, and strategic advice. The banker will likely know these professionals personally. Do not hesitate to involve your accountant in any complex or difficult loan negotiations.

Communicate

Clear communication is important in all aspects of business. With your banker, it is important to keep them informed regarding any issues, positive or negative, that might impact your business operations or industry segment.

- Report bad news or deteriorating trends early, along with a plan of action to deal with them. Avoid providing your bank with unpleasant surprises.
- If your revenues are increasing and you need a larger line of credit, keep your banker informed of your needs.
- Let the bank know whether or not they are meeting your expectations. Get issues out on the table quickly.

Utilize Other Bank Resources

Your bank is far more than a place to borrow money. Most banks offer a variety of paid and free services to support their clients. Other areas where bank support can be provided include:

- Cash management services
- Monitoring of account activities
- Trade finance, export and import assistance
- Foreign exchange information, currency conversions, and hedging strategies

- Interest rate hedging, strategies to swap floating for fixed interest rates, and establishing caps or floors to minimize future interest rate fluctuations.
- Economic updates
- Business advice and consulting services, educational sessions

The Loan Application Process

Before you start an application for a new or increased commercial loan, consider the essential questions to ask yourself. Figure 28 provides a description of these questions through the simple WARS acronym.

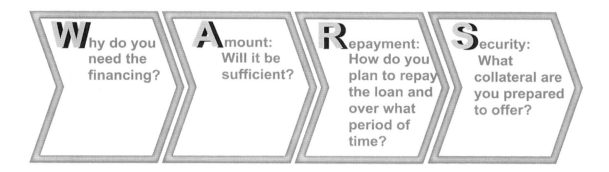

Figure 28. WARS model

You should write a short presentation to outline the financing requirement along with supporting company financial statements and/or projections, and a current personal financial statement. Even if personal guarantees are not required, the depth of pockets of company principals will often be a key component of the bank's risk assessment process. Here are some specific guidelines to consider when applying for a commercial loan:

Is This a New Operating Line or an Increased Banking Facility?

- Define the purpose. Do you want to finance your receivables, or do you require working capital requirements, or assistance in some other area?
- Indicate the required dollar amount and demonstrate the need with monthly cash flow projections.
- Explain what margin conditions you are considering, for example, 75% or eligible receivables, 50% cost of inventory.
- Outline your work in progress (WIP) as this margin may be feasible.
- Provide receivable and payable listings along with inventory breakdowns.
- Consider the prevailing interest rate.
- Consider any monthly loan administration fees that may be negotiable.

Is This a New or Increased Term Loan Or Mortgage?

- Indicate the purpose and required dollar amount.
- Detail the desired repayment, term, and amortization. The amortization term should match the economic life of the asset that is being financed.
- Consider your cash flow coverage of the payments. The cash coverage should be a minimum of 1.25 times the payment.
- Include current and credible property and equipment appraisals.
- Provide insurance details along with an environmental assessment and indemnity.
- Consider the fixed or floating interest rate compared to the rate from other lenders.
- Consider and negotiate removing any application fees.

Collateral Considerations

Consider what collateral will be required by the lender:

- General Security Agreement (GSA)
- Inventory financing
- Collateral mortgage or assignment of rents for commercial properties
- Chattel mortgage for equipment loans

Other Collateral Issues

- Personal guarantees will often be required, especially if the company does not have a track record of revenue and earnings growth and a strong balance sheet. The bank will usually need a second way out if mishaps or serious problems occur. The primary way out is the company's ongoing ability to generate sustainable cash flow, backed up by assets such as Accounts Receivable, inventory, or property that fuel the cash generation. If this process becomes seriously impaired, recourse to other avenues of repayment via personal assets and resources becomes an important second line of defense to a lender.
- Banking subrogations are encountered when shareholder loans are postponed to the bank's security interest. In effect, these equity funds may not be withdrawn or reduced without bank approval. Subrogated shareholder loans are often included in equity calculations for leverage test covenants.
- The bank may request assignment of life, disability, or key-person life insurance, especially if succession plans are not clearly defined.

How Bankers Assess Your Company Risk

Once a loan proposal has been presented to the commercial banker, the internal loan application commences. This is a complex process with internal negotiation often taking place between the frontline commercial banker that you work with and the bank's credit department. A key ingredient of a company's successful loan approval is the completion of a detailed risk assessment by the frontline bankers for the credit department review.

Company owners can greatly enhance this process by providing a comprehensive information package to their banker. It is important that company owners gain a greater understanding of this risk assessment process. It is their company going under the microscope. It is important to understand that the bank will continue to need information after you have a loan agreement.

Financial test covenants are often included in bank term sheets and offers of credit. They can best be described as financial benchmarks that need to be met on an annual basis, evidenced by the client's audited or reviewed engagement financial statements. Each test covenant will have the relevant financial ratio calculation clearly defined. Some examples of financial test covenants are:

- Working capital ratio – minimum 2:1
- Debt to equity ratio – maximum 1.5:1
- Debt service coverage – minimum 1.25x

The bank may also require financial monitoring. Operating lines of credit will involve prompt provision of monthly Accounts Receivable, Accounts Payable, and inventory listings. These are often accompanied by interim monthly or quarterly in-house financial statements, so ongoing performance can be measured against the prior year and budget forecast. Understanding that this information will be needed on an on-going basis will help you prepare for the loan application process.

A bank's risk assessment process can be segmented into the following key areas. Below we review each item with a checklist of questions and issues the bank will consider:

- Company strategy
- Market potential
- Infrastructure and operations
- Financial performance
- Management capability

Company Strategy

- What is the company's growth and development strategy? Is it based on cost/price leadership, differentiation, focus on differentiation of products or services or distinctive or niche market segments or a unique business model?
- What are the company's sustainable competitive advantages?
- What are the key success factors necessary to prosper in the particular industry segment?
- Which of the following corporate growth strategies have been implemented? When and why?
    - Product iterations or new product development
    - Expanding market segments or geographical expansion
    - Integration (vertical or horizontal)
    - Licensing

- Outsourcing
- Joint ventures or corporate alliances
- Mergers or acquisitions
- Diversification

Market Potential

- What is the market size?
- Is there an over reliance on a few large clients, or is there a well spread, balanced clientele?
- Is there reliance on a single or a few distributors?
- How stable is market demand?
- Can you assess the sustainable market acceptance of the company's products or services?
- How vulnerable is the company to competition, including digital or technological disruption?
- What are current selling terms? How long does it take to be paid?

Infrastructure and Operations

- Are there any environmental controls and regulations, present or proposed, that could impact operations?
- Review the location, characteristics, condition, and adequacy of fixed assets. Are the premises owned or leased? Is adequate insurance in place?
- If applicable, what is the length of the manufacturing cycle, and how controllable are manufacturing costs?
- Assess the price stability and availability of raw materials and other inputs.
- Review inventory mix, location, characteristics, condition, and the ability to liquidate.
- Assess the adequacy, stability, and quality of labour. Is the workforce unionized, or is there potential for union involvement?

Financial Performance

- How reliable and current is financial information? Have year-end financial statements been prepared by an accredited accounting firm?
- Are there any issues that might not appear on the balance sheet that need to be considered? Is there a large appraisal surplus in company-owned land and buildings? Are any partners wanting to retire or be bought out?
- Assess working capital adequacy and cash driver performance. Measure liquidity by inventory turnover, Accounts Payable settlement, and Accounts Receivable collection ratios. Consider monthly or annual recurring revenue contracts and customer churn.
- What is the relationship between debt and equity? What are the historical trends?

- Is there adequate equity to support expanding sales? Look for symptoms of over-trading in shares that might indicate an insufficient working capital base to support rapidly growing sales. Is there adequate cash flow to finance growth?

- What is the trend for revenue volume and mix?

- Assess revenue and gross margin performance and trends. Review control of expenses and determine the extent of fixed overhead.

- Are there any foreign exchange risks for export or import?

- Assess the company's financial planning and related controls. Are regular monthly or quarterly financial statements completed on an in-house basis, contrasting prior year, current year, and budget performance?

Management Capability

- Examine the stability of owner's control. Are the shareholders on an amicable basis, or is there potential for conflict? Is there a buy/sell agreement along with an appropriate shotgun or trigger clause in place between the two controlling entities? The shotgun clause keeps each party honest by allowing Shareholder B to counter the offer made by Shareholder A at the same price, thereby dissuading a *low-ball* offer for the other party's shareholdings.

- Do the owners have the ability to inject funds from sources outside the company?

- Do the company owners have the required hands-on skills to manage daily operations?

- Are there any related company borrowing requirements? What is the company's reliance on the borrower or the borrower's reliance upon it? A corporate family tree is always helpful in describing more complex business structures.

- Are aggressive expansion plans being contemplated? Have such expansion plans been carefully conceived, and are they in line with company working capital, equity base, and earnings capacity?

- Is there a clearly defined chain of command and succession plan along with identified personnel who can step into the shoes of existing management for business continuity?

Due Diligence Considerations

After the bank risk assessment process has taken place, the banker will be expected to perform due diligence with regard to the client, especially if the transaction involves a new relationship. Due diligence can be defined as an organized and rigorous verification of all major components of a business transaction. Many companies will keep an electronic data room that is kept up-to-date and can be quickly used when required. From your banker's perspective, the following areas could be reviewed:

Management

- What is the shareholder structure, and is there active or passive involvement by shareholders? How well does the bank know the individual shareholders?

- Are there any significant family relationship issues such as pending divorce, ill health, or other.?
- Do management biographies and historical on-the-job performance records exist?
- Has the bank met with the senior management team? Are they competent and engaged?

Financial
- Can the relevant assets from recent or planned capital expenditures be viewed?
- What is the reputation of the accounting firm and the partner who signs the year-end statements?
- What is the quality of finance support staff and reporting systems?
- Are there any contingent or unfunded liabilities like pension contributions?

Infrastructure
- How often has the banker visited to inspect the premises and operations?
- Are the facilities well cared for?
- Has there been an inventory inspection or valuation, if appropriate?

Clients and Markets
- Can the client demonstrate knowledge of key customers and competitors?
- Does the company have a good reputation or positive brand in the marketplace?
- How are the relationships with key suppliers?

Legal
- Are there any relevant past or pending litigation?
- Are there patent or copyright protection issues

Financing Commitment Letter

The following are extracts from a typical bank commitment letter. It is provided as an example of what to expect when you have successfully completed the loan application process:

Borrower
Marston Control Devices Ltd.

Banking Facility
Operating Loan Facility in the amount of $150,000, subject to the terms and conditions as outlined below.

Rate
Bank prime rate plus one percent per annum (prime+1%) floating, accrued from day to day, calculated and payable monthly, in arrears, based on a calendar year.

Prime Rate

Prime rate means the floating annual rate of interest established from time to time by the bank as the reference rate that it will use to determine rates of interest.

Margin Conditions

Availability of the operating credit is subject to a maximum of:

75% of the bank's valuation of assigned Accounts Receivable after deducting those 61 days or more past due, accounts in dispute, intercompany accounts, contra accounts, and the value of any prior ranking claims.

Plus:

50% of the bank's valuation at cost of assigned inventory that is free and clear, excluding work in process, consignment inventory, or inventory subject to any prior charge or claim. The maximum margin value of inventory will be $50,000.

Margin Reporting

Within twenty-one (21) days after the last calendar day of each month, the following information should be delivered to the bank:

> A client-certified, aged list of outstanding Accounts Receivable that identifies accounts in dispute, intercompany accounts, contra accounts, and the value of any prior ranking claims.
>
> A certified valuation of inventory, excluding any items held on a consignment basis and identifying all inventory subject to prior charges or claims in favour of other creditors.
>
> An aged list of outstanding Accounts Payable.

General Conditions

Monthly company-prepared financial statements (balance sheet and income statement) are to be provided within 30 days of month end.

Annual company-prepared financial statements (review engagement) are to be provided within 120 days of fiscal year end.

A signed personal financial statement of John Marston to be provided concurrently with annual financial statements.

Security

Prior to any funds being advanced to the borrower by the bank, the following security documents should be executed, registered, and delivered in a form and content satisfactory to the bank:

- Appropriate documentation evidencing corporate authority.
- Registered general assignment of book debts.
- Assignment of inventory.

- Registered General Security Agreement, providing the bank with a first charge over all assets.
- Assignment of all perils insurance for equipment and inventory, with first loss payable to the bank.
- An unlimited personal guarantee from John and Ann Marston.
- Subrogation via promissory note of shareholder loans $96,000.

Financial Covenants

- Capital expenditures are not to exceed $200,000 in any fiscal year without prior bank written approval.
- Total debt to equity ratio will not exceed 2:1 at any time. Equity is defined as retained earnings, subrogated shareholder loans, and share capital.
- Working capital ratio minimum of 1.25:1 is to be maintained.

Expenses

The borrower will be responsible for the following:

- All legal and other professional fees for searching, preparing, execution, and registration of all loan and security documentation.
- All other costs and out-of-pocket expenses incurred by the bank in connection with the establishment and administration of the facilities and the obtaining of applicable security.
- Please signify your acceptance of these terms by signing and returning the attached copy of this commitment letter.

Chapter 12
Survival Strategies

Overview

Studies indicate that four out of five start-up companies cease to exist after five years. This chapter is written on the premise that the more you know about *the dark side of the moon,* the greater the chance that your company will be successful.

The chapter is divided into the following sections:

- Causes of business failures
- External warning signals
- Internal warning signals
- Turnaround strategies and options

Causes of Business Failures

As consultants, business owners and executives, the Business Diagnostics authors have observed many successful companies prosper and expand. We have also seen companies come off the rails, sometimes permanently. Business failures can often be attributed to the following causes:

Managerial or Key Employee Problems

- Lack of hands-on management along with a lack of inclination to jump in and fix potentially costly operational problems.
- Shareholder disputes that are aggravated by an absence of buy and sell agreements and shotgun clauses.
- Attempting an industry consolidation play without the financial and operational resources to digest an acquisition target.
- Growth strategies without understanding of the cost and the benefit.

- Complex management and information systems are installed at great cost but lead to greater disruption and little tangible benefit.
- Lack of investment in efficiency.
- Sole operator management with no succession plans.
- Weak management communications and poor professional support.

Product or Market Difficulties

- Venturing into new (offshore) markets without sufficient market research.
- Industry consolidation, cross-border incursions, or fast-moving competition.
- Entry of disruptive business models or products.
- Poorly conceived or executed new or follow-on product launches.
- Changing customer buying patterns, wants, or needs.
- Disruptive technology changes the industry landscape.
- Economic shocks.

Financial Weakness

- Embarking on an ambitious expansion project with too much debt and not enough equity.
- Significant receivables with protracted payment terms that result in stifled cash flow.
- Business failure of a supplier who provided critical components or equipment for a new contract.

External Warning Signals

Many business failures are preceded by warning signs that were either underappreciated or ignored. Refer back to your PEST-C scan to review the following examples of external warning signals to be aware of. Be prepared to mitigate for them.

- Unexpected or unanticipated adverse legal, political, and regulatory changes.
- Cultural and social changes that dramatically alter consumer preferences or product awareness.
- Failure to anticipate accelerating pace of technological change.
- Environmental or public health shocks that disrupt business, economic, and societal fundamentals.
- Weakening of general economic conditions that is evidenced by inflationary trends, budget deficits, higher government taxes, or reduced consumer spending.
- Unexpected interest rate *spikes* that are allied with tightening bank credit availability and stricter lending guidelines.
- Intensified competition with a new method to overcome historic barriers to entry.

- Emergence of substitute products or indirect competition.
- Increasing supplier and buyer power.

Internal Warning Signals

Sometimes, there will be internal 'red flashing lights' to heed. Here are some warnings of impending business difficulty that you can watch for:

Financial

Tightened Liquidity Evidenced By:

- Delays in collecting Accounts Receivable, along with increases in bad debt expense.
- Difficulties in meeting Accounts Payable obligations.
- Bank overdrafts and locked-in (hardcore) operating credits.
- Lack of an understanding of bank margin conditions.
- Inventory buildup is out-pacing sales growth.
- Declining revenues, gross profit margins, and earnings.

Under Capitalization

- Increasing reliance on bank and supplier debt to finance operating losses.
- Over-trading trends where working capital resources are insufficient to fund aggressive revenue growth.
- Unexpected increases in fixed costs.
- Dealing with too many banks and long-term lenders.
- Weakened retained earnings due to historical operating losses that have become acceptable.
- Inability to attract additional capital. Existing shareholders are not willing or cannot invest more.

Inadequate Financial Information

- Delayed year-end financial statements.
- Absence of current monthly or quarterly financial statements.
- Poor or non-existent cash flow monitoring and analysis.
- Weak financial information control systems that have failed to keep pace with the company's growth and increasingly complex operations.

Products and Markets

Business failure is often preceded by inadequate product management or market intelligence as evidenced by some of the following warning signs:

- Inadequate current market research and failure to listen or respond to the marketplace, and customer problems that need to be solved.

- High concentration of sales to one or to a small handful of customers.
- Increasing failure to meet product sales and market penetration targets.
- Timing difficulties in launching new products.
- Overly complex distribution and selling strategies.
- Lack of ongoing product, service, and business model innovation.

Management and Key Employees

The other clear internal warning sign is a lack of clear business vision and guidance from key professional advisors and Board members. These difficulties often present as:

- High turnover rates among key employees.
- Delayed presentation of management and financial reports.
- Overly complex corporate structure with numerous subsidiaries and involved intercompany transactions.
- Obsession with tax-avoidance strategies.
- Employees with more than one boss or supervisor or an unclear matrix organizational structure.
- Delegation of tasks or responsibility without control or feedback.
- Senior management's abuse of benefits and compensation plans, including unexplained management fees without evidence of value for money.
- Personal problems (divorce, family succession issues, and disputes).
- Fraudulent activities, which could include the following:
    - Unexplained inventory shrinkage
    - Negligent financial reporting
    - Diversion of funds

Turnaround Strategies and Options

In general, a turnaround strategy can be implemented by adopting the following process with timelines that are appropriate to the depth of the problem:

1. Develop a recovery plan (from one to three months).
2. Implement the plan (three to six months).
3. Stabilize the business and return to growth (six months to a year).

It is crucial to commence the turnaround strategy on an urgent basis and craft the recovery plan as quickly as possible. The remaining implementation and stabilization steps will take more time. Companies are not turned around overnight; however, time is still a key consideration.

Before beginning the turnaround process, solvency and viability need to be considered.

Solvency

In most cases, a company is said to be insolvent if it is unable to meet its obligations as they become due, and the net realization value of its assets does not cover its liabilities.

The Altman Z-Score—Edward Altman created a Multiple Discriminant Analysis tool—combines a set of financial ratios to come up with the Altman Z-Score. While the tool was created in the 1960s, it is still relevant. Statistical techniques are used to predict a company's probability of failure using variables from a company's balance sheet and income statements.

The following five ratios are weighted to derive the Z-score:

- EBIT/Total Assets
- Net Sales /Total Assets
- Market Value of Equity / Total Liabilities
- Working Capital/Total Assets
- Retained Earnings /Total Assets

To return the company to a solvent state, some form of urgent external capital injection will need to take place.

Viability

A viable company is one that is able to carry on profitable operations now and into the medium term. If the company is not viable, it is not worth expending valuable resources in an attempt to save it.

In assessing the viability of a distressed business, some key questions must be considered:

- Is there a sufficient depth of market and market awareness for the company products or services?
- Is there an effective sales force, or is a sales methodology in place to market the product or service?
- Are reasonable gross margins being obtained?
- Does the business model still make sense?

If the company is neither solvent nor viable, formal liquidation and wind-down will take place through receivership or bankruptcy proceedings. This process is complex, expensive, and beyond the intention and scope of this book.

If a company is solvent and appears reasonable viable, you are ready to develop the recovery plan and then to implement it.

Develop the Recovery Plan

A critical first step is to complete a detailed stakeholder analysis – who are the key players that you must consider and work with if you are to survive?

These will include creditors such as the bank, suppliers, tax authorities, plus customers, employees, shareholders, and management.

A quick and effective process is to map these stakeholders according to their relative interest in the situation and their relative power. Consider the benefits and risks with each stakeholder, their degree of influence, and ability to assist with the difficulties. Each of the stakeholders can then be mapped to four key areas to be reviewed: financial resources, marketing resources, human resources, and operational resources. This process of mapping a recovery plan to stakeholder analysis is summarized in Figure 29.

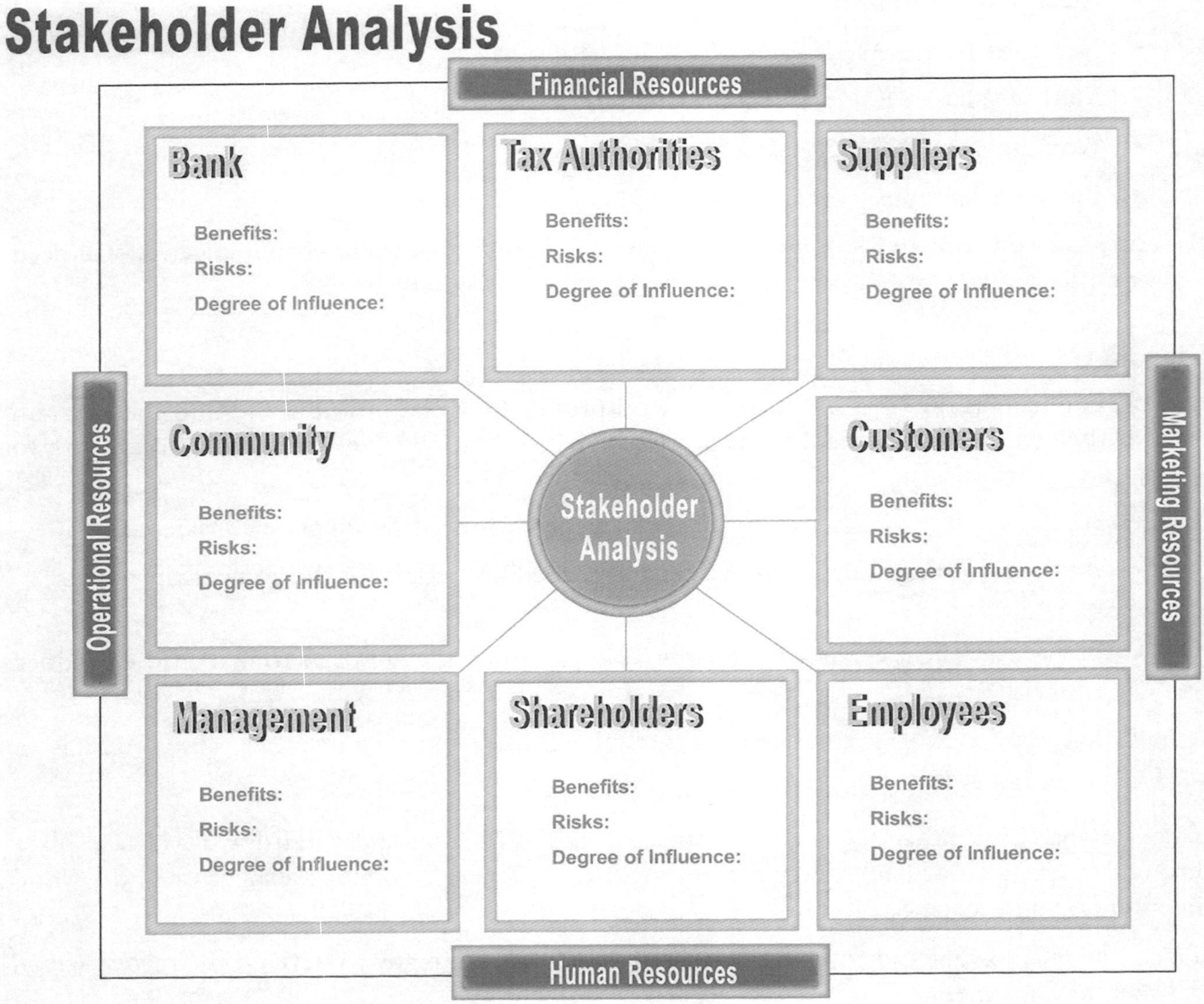

Stakeholder Analysis

Figure 29. Turnaround Stakeholder Analysis

The following areas will need to evaluated to complete the stakeholder analysis:

Financial Resources

- Perform a critical assessment of current cash resources—check for excessively high Accounts Receivable and inventories. Can they be collected or reduced to generate cash?
- Assess the potential for sale and leaseback of fixed assets. This can often be another source of cash generation.

Marketing Resources

Analyze revenue and profitability trends by market segment.

Assess the 80:20 rule—which 20% of your clients provide 80% of the revenues?

Verify product acceptance in the marketplace via quality and customer need issues, and review effectiveness of after-sales service and costs.

Review gross profit margin performance by major product lines.

Analyze the return on investment and the effectiveness of big-ticket marketing items like advertising and trade shows. What can be done with less cost and still provide value?

Operational Resources

If the business is a manufacturing operation, establish the percentage of production capacity that is currently used, and check for manufacturing or production flow issues that can affect profitability.

Check for obsolete production equipment.

Identify any procurement problems.

Human Resources

- Assess employee turnover and wage and salary costs relative to industry standards.
- Question senior management about the cause of the present downturn and how they would resolve it. What capability and commitment do they have to turn the company around?
- Can the company's organizational structure be simplified?

Implement the Recovery Plan and Stabilize the Company

After the above stakeholder map and evaluation process has been completed, the following implementation steps, by functional area, can be considered:

Financial

- Increase revenues and market penetration through cost-effective advertising, and possibly lower prices for longer term contracts or product bundling.
- Reduce surplus and redundant assets by selective sell-off.

- Restructure debt by extending amortization, negotiating interest and/or principal relief. In rare cases, debt forgiveness (usually with unsecured creditors) can be negotiated.

- Arrange equity injections through existing shareholders, possibly employees, outside investors, or government sources.

- Convince clients to provide up-front cash payments to pay for raw materials and supplies.

Operational

- Restructure the company's organization to flatten reporting relationships and to realign operations around a reduced number of product lines, market segments, or both.

- Merge with or be acquired by a compatible company. Such a step can provide financial, operational, and technical support to an ailing company.

- Initiate selective, but effective, cost-cutting measures. These could include pay concessions by employees with, hopefully, short-term pain for longer term gain, or restructure from salary to commission payment systems.

Section 4
Strategic Planning

Business Diagnostics Overview

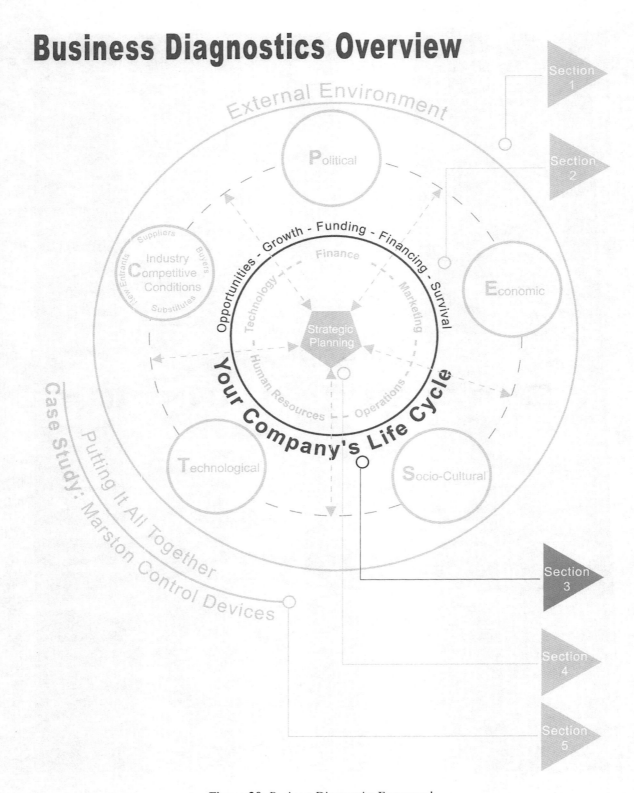

Figure 30. Business Diagnostics Framework

Chapter 13
Strategic and Business Planning

Overview

Strategy sits at the center of the Business Diagnostics Framework. The Business Diagnostics Framework starts with an external size up of the business environment and industry conditions that are reviewed in Section 1 of this book. In the middle of the framework circles is the internal review that is covered in Section 2. Section 3 covers the revolving strategies for the company life cycle and funding. We complete the cycle with the strategic planning target at the middle of the framework. The fundamental concept behind the Business Diagnostics Framework is that strategy is derived from knowledge of your external and internal environments plus the business life cycle that you are in.

Strategy and business planning are not one-time exercises. It is the job of the senior management team to zoom in and out of the Business Diagnostics Framework, continually adding information that enhances your strategy.

Most every business will have strategy retreats. We argue that spending the time to gather the data and insights for strategy planning will result in better decisions.

There are myriad business strategies covered in Chapters 8 and 10. In crafting your strategy, you have to decide what you are doing, stop doing, and start doing. These are your tactics to deliver on your strategy. This combination of strategy and tactics are written in a business plan.

Business Planning

The business planning process is essential to the success of all enterprises. Whether you use the proverbial back-of-a-napkin planning, a business model canvas, or a consultant, all businesses need to plan their business and write the plan down. You can start one with a business model canvas, although as you grow, business planning becomes a critical operational tool. Some guidelines and tips in the crafting of effective business plans, with a strategic focus, are provided in this chapter.

While numerous templates and guides exist for business plan completion, developing a comprehensive plan is difficult due to the multitude of purposes such plans encounter. Different audiences need to see a written business plan for different purposes, and you need to be able to write a plan for your own internal tactical needs. There may be other operational plans that are deeper explorations of the various sections of a business plan such as a marketing and communications or operational plans. All these plans need to be aligned to the central strategy, mission, and goals of the company.

To simplify (and demystify) the process, the following groups have been segmented into different audiences:

- External (investors, bankers, other lenders)
- Internal (senior management, employees, Boards of Directors or Advisors)

Each audience will receive a different set of plans, which are detailed in the following sections:

External Audiences

The Strategic Business Plan is common to both audiences; however, external audiences will typically receive an initial overview of an investment or banking opportunity. There are many different ways to create a short overview. We use a short and simple Enterprise Review Summary or ERS.

Figure 31. The ERS

Following completion of the Strategic Business Plan and, if an investment opportunity is being pursued, a public offering, private placement process, or both may be initiated via another set of documents—the offering memorandum and a term sheet or prospectus, or both.

Internal Audiences

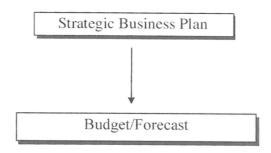

Figure 32. The Strategic Business Plan

Internal audiences will also have the opportunity to review the Strategic Business Plan, which acts as a foundation document. It is accompanied by a detailed budget and forecast with a financial model.

BUSINESS PLANS FOR EXTERNAL AUDIENCES

While clients and suppliers sometimes comprise the external audience, the focus for this presentation will be to investors, lenders, or both groups because raising external funding remains a key challenge for many start-up and growing companies.

The Enterprise Review Summary (ERS)

The Enterprise Review Summary or ERS concept is an expansion of the popular Business Opportunity Document (BOD) and can be a written extension of your business model canvas but with more emphasis on financial performance.

The ERS is a simple four- or five-page, plain-language document that describes how an investor will make money from a product, service, or process that is generated by a company. If financing is required, the form of security and repayment will be described.

In essence, the ERS is an initial hook, and it is often fine-tuned to form the Executive Summary in a formal business plan. You will note that, having followed the Business Diagnostics Framework, writing an Enterprise Review Summary is a fairly simple process because you have already gathered all the information. The ERS is the written version of a pitch deck. It typically is less flash and more substance. The following list provides the primary components of the ERS:

- Overview
- Company description
- Management
- Current business and industry environment
- Products or services, including any technology attributes
- Markets, including segmentation, competitor evaluation, and marketing and sales tactics

- Financial performance and projections
- Funding requirements and use of funds:
  - Investors – return on investment and exit point
  - Lenders – debt retirement and time frame
  - Each of these headings will be followed by a maximum of two to three paragraphs

It is important to note that the pay-back section that is addressed to lenders would be completed only if the company was in a positive cash flow position during the time of the financial documents presented.

Note: An example of an ERS is contained in the Marston Control Devices Ltd case study.

The Strategic Business Plan

In this section, the key components of a Strategic Business Plan are presented along with some supplementary information about some issues to consider within each section. The order of the topics is less important than the logical flow and relevance so the reader can follow the story of your business and intended actions. The structure can be summarized as follows:

- Executive summary
- Description of the organization
- Management structure
- Products and services
- Company external environment
- Industry analysis
- Company internal resources
- Competitor analysis
- Business strategy
- Financial feasibility and forecasts
- Marketing and sales analysis
- Human resources issues and plan
- Operations and IT/technology assessment
- Appendices

Executive Summary

The Executive Summary is a one- to three-page overview of the complete Strategic Business Plan. This section includes background, critical issues, and key recommendations. It is essential to have this section written after the other sections are completed. An Enterprise Review Summary can be fine-tuned to meet this requirement.

Description of the Organization

This section explains the type of company and provides a history if the company already exists. It also describes the proposed form of organization, including an easy-to-understand mission, vision, and objectives. When describing the organization, consider the following points:

- Is the company's overall strategy consistent with prevailing industry opportunities and threats?
- Are the company's objectives consistent with its resources—financial, marketing, operations, technology, and so on?

Management and Organizational Structure

This section will address shareholders, executives, senior management, and key employees. Information regarding the Board of Directors or advisors should also be provided. A brief stakeholder description and analysis can also be provided if one is required. When writing this section, you should include information that considers the following points:

- Do senior managers have a shareholding interest in the company? What is the percentage, vesting period, and triggers?
- Are the necessary marketing, operational, and financial skills in place or attainable in the near term?

Products and Services

Existing products and services, along with potential follow-on offerings, are detailed in this section. An assessment of the company's present competitive advantage and its unique method of solving the customer's problem along with how you have or intend to validate solutions should be completed. If there are any intellectual property (IP) strategies, include a summary of them.

Company External Environment

This section includes a PEST analysis, in which any external opportunities and threats are reviewed.

Industry Analysis

The industry sector describes current trends and market conditions. A brief Five Forces analysis should also be provided here. It's not necessary to use the Five Forces format, but the analysis helps the reader visualize the opportunities and threats.

Company Internal Resources

Include brief size ups that you would have completed using the Business Diagnostics Framework. Include your detailed strengths, weaknesses, and aspirations for the following functional areas:

- Finance
- Marketing and sales

- Human resources
- Operations and I.T./technology
- Research and development

Competitor Analysis

Primary and secondary competitors should be described along with an evaluation of their relative strengths and weaknesses. Any indirect competitors or substitutions that could pose a threat or opportunity should be considered.

Business Strategy

The organization's present strategic pathway should be described with links to the information and insights you have gathered. A review of alternative strategic directions that might be taken should also be included. If you have decided not to follow a particular strategy, explain how you came to that decision.

Financial Feasibility and Forecasts

This section provides a historical review of financial statements (for the last three to five years). Include balance sheets, income statements, cash flow, and working capital models.

A ratio analysis should be completed with suitable commentary provided.

A forecast income statement –for one to two years should be completed and accompanied by a sensitivity financial modelling analysis that considers best-, expected-, and worst-case scenarios. These are typically done by month. If possible, a forecast balance sheet should also be provided. Some institutions will want a five-year forecast, though it is recognized that these forecasts are best guesses, and the last three years are typically broken down by year not by month.

If this is a start-up operation, a break-even analysis together with an indication of funding sources and allocation of proceeds should be completed.

When you are planning the financial feasibility and forecast section, you should consider these key questions:

- Do forecast Earnings Before Tax (EBT) reveal steady growth in line with present industry norms?
- Will the break-even point be reached within two years if it is a start-up operation?
- Is forecast return on investment (ROI) less than 20%? This percentage or lower would be considered weak from an investor's point of view.
- Does forecast EBITDA provide sufficient debt service coverage from a lender's standpoint?
- Will the projected balance sheets reveal too much leverage with a high debt-to-equity ratio?

Marketing and Sales Analysis

This section details the company's customers and what type of competition will be encountered. Key features that should be included are:

- Identification of market segments
- Analysis of target markets and profile of target customers
- Methods to identify and attract customers and your targeted cost of client acquisition
- Selling approaches and how you intend to get to predictable revenue
- Type of sales force and distribution channels
- Sales and marketing metrics
- How sales and marketing will integrate with operations
- Marketing tactics, which should include the six Ps: price, product, place, promotion, people, and partners

When you plan your marketing and sales analysis section, you need to consider the following issues:

- Is there a high dependence on a limited number of clients?
- Are there limited controls of pricing and distribution channels?
- Has a detailed competition assessment been completed?
- Is there a reliance on building users before asking for payment (monetization)? If so, what is the revenue plan, and how many users can be converted to buyers?
- Are you using growth-marketing or growth-hacking techniques? What are the positives and downsides in your market?
- What metrics will you monitor? How will these metrics change over time?

Human Resources

This section addresses current recruitment and training practices in addition to a review of compensation, performance management, employee engagement, professional development, and incentive programs.

Operations and IT Assessment

The operations segment includes a review of the business process, facilities, quality, risk management, and legal issues. IT issues include e commerce requirements, computer security, and privacy and technology applications. Technology can include how you can leverage technology, but it could also mean how to use technology as a competitive advantage or what trends might be considered a threat.

Some questions to consider when you are putting together this section of the Strategic Business Plan:

- Does the company have an appropriate location in relation to clients, suppliers, and employees? Does it have access to technology resources? How will location or remote work and supply affect you?

- Do you have a dependence on a few key suppliers?
- Is there adequate capacity in relation to projected sales?
- Are there any potential environmental or safety hazards?

Offering Memorandum, Prospectus, or Term Sheet

When companies decide to raise additional equity, through either an initial public offering (IPO) or private placement, various regulatory bodies require the publication of an offering memorandum or prospectus.

This documentation details the investment opportunity to potential investors together with a comprehensive disclosure of risk factors. Detailed capital and share structure information is also provided.

A more comprehensive review of the IPO and private placement process is not the intention of this book. Additional details can be obtained from local brokerage houses or venture capital firms.

If a company intends to raise additional equity from the private markets, typically, once the investor has done an initial review, there will be a non-disclosure agreement and a term sheet that outlines the company valuation, the number of shares, and voting rights. A term sheet is the opening for negotiation, rather than a binding legal document. The term sheet is typically the trigger for an investor to complete deeper due diligence; more negotiation usually ensues before a legal agreement is executed.

BUSINESS PLANS FOR INTERNAL AUDIENCES

With a business plan for internal audiences, we recommend the same format as established for external audiences but with more focus on the organization's strategic direction at the front of the plan.

The conventional approach is to allow more space for communicating the strategic direction and vision:

- Vision statement—what we want to be
- Mission statement—what we do
- Goals identification—where are we heading with regard to revenue growth, customer satisfaction, and technical excellence).
- Objectives – are our objectives SMART—specific, measurable, achievable, realistic, and time framed

In our somewhat unconventional view, we feel that the whole vision and mission process is often just paid lip service, with no real enthusiasm to craft an appropriate strategic pathway. Worse, without a clear understanding, business planners spend days agonizing over just the right words, rather than understanding the meaning and purpose. Too often, we hear, "but they don't have a vision statement," as a criticism, rather than seeing people looking holistically at the evidence of the vision. If you ask a business person what their vision is, you might not get an actionable answer. If you lead them through a process, the vision and mission can become clear.

One technique is to engage the strategic planning participants in envisioning the future. A skilled facilitator can help a group get unstuck simply by asking, "If we are successful, what does our business look like in five years, three years, and one year?" Then, the facilitated questions can cascade down into a discussion of what business is really being engaged in. What is working well? What is the competitive advantage? These discussions can culminate with the following key questions:

- What is our core purpose?
- What problem are we trying to solve and why?
- What do we do that is different and that we are really good at?
- What principles do we follow when making this change?

We have found that this process leads to a high level of engagement among the planning participants and helps build consensus on what needs to be done. The mission and vision will become clear by asking the questions rather than jumping to the daunting 'what is your vision' question.

At the end of the internal business plan, there should be key action items and implementations steps aligned to the company goals and objectives for each of the various operations finance, marketing, operations/I.T, and human resources sections.

These are allocated to all the categories indicating who will do what, when and how. The relative cost of these initiatives and time to implement should also be determined.

Budget and Forecast

The budget is an internal document containing the quarterly balance sheets, income statement and monthly cash flow statements, together with capital expenditure forecasts and cost center breakdowns by department.

The forecast is a monthly projection detailing key financial performance areas such as sales pipeline, revenue, inventory, and cash flow. In assessing the budget and forecast documents, the following two key steps need to be followed:

1) Establish specific, measurable objectives

Some examples:

- Increase revenues by 15% on an annual basis
- Maintain gross profit margins at 45%

These objectives will usually evolve from the key action items in the finance section.

2) Set up tracking and control systems

Example:

Quarterly review: Balance sheet, capital expenditures, and operational action items

Monthly review: Profit and loss statement, cash flow statement, and so on

Six Ways to Create an Effective Strategic Business Plan

1. Focus on the Market

Strive to be market driven, meeting customer needs rather than promoting the product feature or service offering. The potential of the marketplace and resulting revenue/earnings is far more important than a focus on the company products and services.

Demonstrate the user benefit rather than promoting the product or service virtues and innovation. If the offering can provide significant cost savings to clients, for example, a pay-back period under two years, this translates to a significant user benefit.

Be customer centric by describing how you fix your customer's pain with your unique product or service.

Determine the potential client's interest in your product or service by validating that they will buy and will want to send you referrals.

Find ways to pilot new products or services in a minimally viable or basic form to potential users, and provide value to the client for their participation.

Build goodwill and loyalty; you will need it one day.

Document booking orders with supporting data that indicates the number of customers who have committed to purchase. This information allows you to provide a convincing projection of the rate of acceptance for the product or service and the pace at which it is likely to sell.

Use social media and online surveys as appropriate for customer service and to gather market insights and ideas.

2. Understand and Anticipate Investor or Lender Requirements

Both investors and lenders are key sources of external funding for an enterprise so understanding and anticipating their modus operandi is essential part of the business planning process.

Investors

Use your external business plan to speak to the intended audience. Identify your potential investors. Are they friends and family, angels, venture capitalists or strategic corporate investors? Understand the investors' primary needs and objectives which can be addressed as follows:

- Provide evidence of a strong proprietary position by having patents, copyrights, and trademarks in place.
- Detail the use and specific allocation of the investors' proceeds.
- Understand the investor's exit aspirations:
    - Exit strategy or cashing out: Investors do not expect to receive a steady flow of dividends from small, fast-growing companies. Their return will be the profit that they

gain from a successful exit, either by selling their appreciated shareholdings after the company goes public or by redeeming shareholdings after the company is sold.

- Price and relative percentage ownership: The potential value of the company is usually based on projected earnings (EBIT) or cash flow (EBITDA) five years into the future in conjunction with an appropriate earnings or cash flow multiple. The relative percentage derived shareholding will mirror the investor's required rate of return, which in turn, reflects the risk of the venture.

Examples which demonstrate the higher the risk, the higher the required returns:

A company with new products and unproven management: 40%+ annual returns are usually required.

A company with developed products and proven management: 25% to 35% annual returns are usually required.

Lenders

When writing your business plan and working with your banker, remember the WARS acronym.

- Why is financing required?
- Amount of funds required?
- Repayment: Over what timeline and from what source (ongoing earnings or sale of assets?) will repayment come from?
- Security: What company assets are available?

Does the lender have a clearly defined alternate way out, and will this alternative involve the provision of personal guarantees?

3. Emphasize Management Depth and Capability

When writing your plan, be sure to explain your management team's background in terms of depth and expertise.

- Do they have proven industry experience?
- Do they have previous start-up experience?
- Can you explain gaps in their resumes?
- Do they have a track record in successfully bringing new products or services to market?

Can your management team answer questions about the business plan? It is critical that the reader of the plan understands that the management team has been fully involved in the strategic business planning process. Business owners sometimes borrow heavily from sample business plans or delegate the complete task to outside consultants. It is critical that the key elements of the plan be prepared by the company management team, not just the founder. External resources can be engaged to fine-tune and complete the final plan documents. It's your business, so it needs to be your plan that you completely understand and can act on.

4. Clearly Define Your Customers and Competitors

Your business plan needs to demonstrate that you understand your customers, who are the key drivers of revenue growth, using the Five W approach below:

- Segmentation—Which are the most attractive segments?
- Targeting—Who is buying from you?
- Preferences—What do they buy from you?
- Timing—When and how often do they buy?
- Criteria—Why do they buy?

Demonstrate on an ongoing basis your knowledge of the competition and how you are keeping track of their strategy, latest product offerings, price discounts, and so on.

5. Prepare Realistic Financial Projections

Investors and lenders will focus on the accuracy and integrity of your financial numbers.

- Projections and revenues, gross margins, and earnings have to be carefully supported by assumptions that are reasonable and that can be defended.
- Complete best-expected and worst case scenarios. You can be sure that your numbers will be stress tested by the investors or lenders.
- Ensure there is a correlation with industry norms and benchmarks.
- Avoid spreadsheet overkill with excessive analysis and scenarios that create a numerical fog, which deters and confuses the reader.

6. Complete the Executive Summary (last) THEN Write Your Pitch Deck

This is the most important section of your business plan. People will read it first and formulate their initial impressions based on these critical pages.

If you do not get the potential investor's attention with the Executive Summary, they will likely not read the rest of the business plan. Your ERS (Enterprise Review Summary) can usually be fine-tuned to meet the information requirements of the Executive Summary. Your pitch deck is the summation of all the business planning. There will be many things that you don't know and that require assumptions, but the business planning process will prepare you to create an excellent pitch deck.

Packaging and Presentation Tips

The Strategic Business Plan provides outsiders (investors, lenders) with a first impression of your company and its management team. As with all things, knowing your audience is the first and most important piece of advice. If you are working with a venture capitalist who wants to see your pitch deck and business model canvas first, that is what you need to do. However, it is always good to be prepared for the various audiences and expectations. The following tips will assist you in presenting a professional and effective package to your audience:

Document Appearance

Professional binding and printing are important. Avoid a too lavish or glossy appearance, which might be misinterpreted as excessive spending or too much focus on flash, rather than on substance.

The cover should bear the company's name, address, and issue date. Maintain strict copy numbers (maximum 20). This allows you to keep track of the number of copies in circulation.

We suggest that the document be 25 to 30 pages maximum. A carefully prepared Executive Summary (maximum two to three pages) can be useful in convincing the reader to continue reading or to ask for the more extensive document.

Background and supporting information can be included in an additional binder that would be available as part of the due diligence process. Supporting information might be a more detailed human resources, research, marketing and advertising, or sales plan that can be made available as complementary documentation.

Wherever possible, obtain an appointment with your prospective audience and get face to face when delivering your pitch or business plan. This strategy allows you to highlight the opportunity in person. Keep the meeting brief and leave the plan for the readers to review at their leisure.

Clearly identify the person (your lawyer, accountant, or other) who provided you with the opportunity to meet your audience.

Keep your pitch deck clean without using spreadsheets or acronyms.

Always rehearse this type of presentation.

Set up presentation equipment early and test it.

Have your presentation printed and on a USB stick just in case Murphy's Law strikes.

Business Planning: Concluding Comments

The strategic business planning process can be complex and will involve a number of stakeholders, notably the senior management team. It has to be realized that the end result will not be a rigid five-year plan, deeply engraved in stone.

Rather, it will be the creation of a broad road map that will assist the navigation of many twists and turns. Keep the Business Diagnostics Framework nearby as a guide, so you can zoom in and out of the elements, keep abreast of trends and threats, keep your business profitable, and plan out your operations and strategy.

We leave you with a few thoughts from Henry Mintzberg who sets out the five Ps of strategy from his book *Strategy Bites Back*:

- Strategy is a plan—that is a consciously intended course of action initiated by an organization.
- Strategy can be a ploy—or a manoeuvre to outwit the competition.
- Strategy is a pattern—that provides consistency of behavior.
- Strategy is a position—that can properly locate an organization in its operating environment.
- Strategy is perspective—or the way the organization views the world.

Section 5
Case Study

MARSTON CONTROL DEVICES LTD-2020

Overview

In 2005, John Marston founded Marston Control Devices Ltd. (MCD) to design, manufacture, and market a specialized control component (*"Sensorpro"*), which was connected to industrial robots. The control component consists of a sealed unit that houses sophisticated micro-controllers, which send control instructions to the robot and receive feedback on positioning, velocity, and acceleration at the various robotic joints.

The *Sensorpro* units were sold to robot manufacturers for installation onto their industrial robots. The manufacturers, in turn, sold their product to large industrial automation systems companies who developed productivity manufacturing solutions for multinational companies like Flex and Honeywell.

Commentary

Marston, a computer engineer by training, had graduated from the University of Southern California (USC) with a doctorate in Robotics. After academia, he completed various assignments, including a brief involvement with the team that successfully developed the Canadian space-arm used on the United States NASA space shuttle.

Upon relocating to Ontario for family reasons, he decided to put down some roots, and he formed his own manufacturing company to develop and market innovative, new robotic control components.

Over the next four years, the company achieved steady revenue and earnings growth. But, in 2009, cash flow challenges and increasing competition culminated with MCD's bankers threatening to cancel operating credit facilities.

Although John and his wife, Ann Marston, were able to inject some additional cash into the company, it was not enough. Fortunately, Ann's brother, Mike Smith, offered to inject $50K cash in exchange for a minority interest in the company. Mike, a mechanical engineer, had joined the company in 2006 as operations manager and was enthusiastic about MCD's future. John accepted his brother-in-law's offer, and Mike became a 20% owner. The balance of the shares (80%) were owned by John and Ann.

Marston was an enigmatic individual, somewhat of a loner, and he controlled his company with an iron hand. He was involved in virtually every aspect of the business—design, production, sales, and finance.

He had left previous employers in California to start the firm because he had difficulty working as a team player, always wanting to be involved in the total project, not just a part of it. Over the years, he had begun to achieve his goals of financial independence and was slowly picking up business skills as the company expanded.

He recently made the following comments to a business associate:

"I have been successful over the past fifteen years primarily due to the high quality and unique design features of my product. As a result, Sensorpro commands a well-deserved premium price of 10-15% over the competition.

Our average unit price is US $12,000, which represents anywhere from 15%-20% of the price of an industrial robot. Since there is a limited market here in Canada—most robots are imported—90% of my market is in the United States."

Competition was continuing to increase as American robot manufacturers had adopted a backward integration strategy and were developing their own control devices. A high-profile example was Adept Technology, which had become a global leader in the manufacture, marketing, and innovation of robots and control component products, and it had been absorbed into Omron.

Despite a downturn in economic activity during 2008 recession, the Japanese were posing a threat, steadily moving into the United States domestic market.

"One Japanese competitor firm recently obtained an order for 15 control devices on which we had bid. I was surprised at their lower price point, but I still do not think they can match our unique design and performance.

I have resolved not to get into price-cutting! This is a rapidly changing industry, and who knows what I will have to do in the future. There are only about eight firms—mine, three in Japan, three in the United States, and one in Europe, which produce similar control devices. However, the number of competitors may increase substantially over the next couple of years."

Economic conditions in the fall of 2020 were still dramatically uncertain given the emergence of a sweeping global pandemic. While the USA economy had slowly recovered from the impact of the brutal 2008 recession that arose from the US subprime crisis, it was now in disarray due to unprecedented business lockdowns and supply chain issues due to the pandemic. Similar challenges were experienced with the Canadian economy, compounded by the advent of a dramatic decline in oil prices.

While interest rates were low and inflation was stable in the 2% range, unemployment rates remained high in both countries. Also, aggressive stimulus spending to kick-start their economies had resulted in significant fiscal deficits.

The robotic control device sector had been impacted by this significant downturn in economic activity. But it was expected to rebound as automation processes continued to be developed for a wide spectrum of applications, especially in the manufacturing, semiconductor, and fiber optic sectors.

"While I have enjoyed reasonable relations with my component suppliers (there are a few established electronic supply houses from which to choose), they seem to have closed ranks. Over the past few years, they have proven tough to negotiate with, evidenced by a steady succession of component price increases.

My steady sales growth over the past few years has resulted in a few loose ends—our product catalogue and website need updating, current quality control procedures need to be implemented, and we should establish a formal sales force structure. Past sales successes largely arose through my contacts in the industrial automation sector, electronics manufacturers' trade shows, and my USC alumni connections. Media interviews have been rejected to keep the competition at bay.

My production facilities are functional, although somewhat cramped. Our five-year lease comes due next month, and I'm hoping my landlord can provide us with additional production space. The Sensorpro production process is quite streamlined (job shop assembly), and, over the past few years, I've invested in state-of-the-art assembly equipment. All orders are customized, so surplus component or finished product inventories shouldn't pose a problem.

My unique design and manufacturing techniques differentiate me from my competitors. I have not bothered with highly expensive patent protection, preferring to maintain trade secrets and closely controlled software source codes. My product allows robot manufacturers to operate with more flexibility and more productivity than I ever anticipated. With continued pick and place automation, notably in the chip manufacturing industry, the North American market should experience continued expansion. The demand is there, and our product is at the forefront.

The production process requires reasonably skilled labour; however, I have been able to condense the training process into two to three weeks. Most of my assembly workers tend to be casual, given the relatively short training horizon. Thankfully, there have been no union overtures to date. When I'm not available, my brother-in-law can adequately supervise both production and training. He is really the only one I can trust to ensure the operation is running smoothly when I'm not here. Of course, I never leave for more than a week at a time."

While MCD had generated strong revenue and earnings growth over the past three years, surprisingly, Marston was experiencing continued cash flow tightness, evidenced by bank overdrafts and occasional difficulty in meeting the payroll.

"I am somewhat puzzled. My financial statements indicate that I run a profitable business with a reasonably strong balance sheet. Yet, I am always at the limit of my bank operating line and would be hard-pressed to declare any dividends to enhance my personal net worth and set aside funds for retirement."

Marston felt that he had come to the proverbial fork in the road from a business expansion standpoint. He summarized his three apparent strategic options as follows:

> *"I can stay the course, producing the same product in the same marketplace, and work diligently to improve my profitability by ongoing expense reduction. My potential to improve gross profit margins appears low, given the difficulty I continue to experience in negotiating material price reductions with my suppliers.*

My other two options are as follows:

We can expand into Europe where there is only one competitor and license our technology to a strategic partner, ideally one with close ties to European robotics manufacturers. We would stay with our existing product, but we would expand into a new market.

I understand that major robot producers founded the European Robotics Association, known as EUnited Robotics. [5] *This association consists of robot manufacturers, system integrators, and research institutes and plays a strong advocacy role with regard industry issues and R&D policy. They would be a useful starting point to seek out a potential licensing partner.*

A further option would be to diversify our product line by developing a new control device that is targeted at the medical devices industry. There is a new generation of robotic surgical devices (instruments, clamps, and limb-positioning tools) that could utilize a redefined Sensorpro technology platform. These devices are in various stages of FDA (Food and Drug Administration) approval.

This new generation of medical devices allows surgeons to view, cut, clamp, and suture from across the operating room and while sitting at consoles with joystick controllers that manipulate robotic arms above the operating table. Voice-activated robotic arms in the OR are now being used, so the potential to develop new sensor technology in this emerging industry segment is huge."

Marston became even more enthused when he related some recent online research he had completed:

"For example, the da Vinci Intuitive system is a surgical robot system that enables surgeons to perform complex surgeries in a minimally invasive way.[6]

The emerging frontier is not only completely automated surgery but micro-bot surgery—robots with reduced cost and size reduction, using technologies such as hepatic feedback, biometric integration, like eye-tracking cameras or head-tracking robotic arms that actually enhance the surgeon's skills. In effect, the surgeon will manage an information and performance system complete with robotics."

Taking a deep breath, Marston summarized his future plans:

"I feel that a combination of new market (Europe) and new products (control devices for medical robots) would be an aggressive, yet potentially rewarding move, especially as competition in our existing industry segment continues to intensify.

I have developed a preliminary budget to launch such an expansion. Initial cost estimates are in the $750,000 range, the main cost components being R&D to commercialize the medical robot control devices and marketing costs to expand into the European market.

---

5 http://www.eu-nited.net/robotics/
6 http://www.davincisurgery.com

> *Raising these funds will likely involve outside investors as the various soft development costs would not qualify for bank financing."*

Adding to the dynamics of running a family business are the Marston's two children, Henry, 27, and Sophie, 24. Both were bright, ambitious individuals. After obtaining his Master's degree in Medical Device engineering, Henry had joined a U.S. based multinational as an associate design engineer. Sophie was in the process of completing an MBA with a specialization in Family Enterprise Management, and she had plans to open her own strategy consulting practice.

Marston reflected:

> *"Ann, Mike, and I are all in our late-fifties and need to develop a defined exit strategy for ourselves. A year ago, I would have described our strategy as staying the course: producing existing products in the same marketplace and working diligently to enhance our earnings with a view to selling the company to an outside party. My expectation was to negotiate a decent earnings multiple that, when combined with our successful track record, would assure a healthy capital gain for the shareholders.*
>
> *Now, it appears that both children want to work in the company and assume second-generation ownership. The challenge is that they have different views as to the strategic direction we should take.*
>
> *Sophie feels strongly that we should stay with our existing product, but expand into a new market like the EU. In contrast, Henry is proposing that we diversify our product line into medical devices.*
>
> *So, here is my dilemma: I want the founding shareholders to enjoy the fruits of a well-deserved retirement, yet I have the opportunity to take the company to the next stage of growth, which may involve the engagement of my children as successor shareholders. I'm concerned as to whether they're ready to take on such responsibility, but they seem to have the drive and education to succeed. That said, we'd still need to reconcile their differing views on the best strategic pathway to take.*
>
> *I am also concerned at the risk around a family succession strategy—some say it is legacy; others say it is lunacy."*

Ann also shared her views about the future of the company and the family.

> *"John and I are still young enough to enjoy ourselves, to travel, and explore new opportunities. We have made significant commitments to the business, and now it feels like it's time to perhaps wind down. Henry and Sophie may have the potential to lead the company, but that won't take place overnight. The term, exit strategy, should perhaps be better defined as a transition strategy with a formalized plan to be put into place for several reasons.*
>
> *The first reason is a practical one. Much of our personal finances are intermingled with the company. With our personal guarantees forming part of the bank's collateral package, our residence is still at risk.*

Another concern is the role that Mike's son might play in the company's future and his potential to work closely together with our own two children.

I've also heard that some family businesses create formal family and ownership councils, but so far, John is against the idea. He says we already have too many meetings."

Mike Smith also took the opportunity to express his concerns:

"John and Ann are still acting like they own 100 % of this company. They keep forgetting that I should have a say in what goes on around here.

I also feel that my son, Jeff, should be given the opportunity to get involved in this business. He recently graduated from a technology design program and has always been enthusiastic about MCD's prospects. I've worked hard and have contributed to its success, and Jeff has as much right to be here as Henry and Sophie.

Maybe I should sell my stake in the company and recoup my investment while MCD is still successful. Having said that, who would be the logical buyer for my shares?"

Finally, Henry and Sophie stepped forward to air their views. Henry said:

"MCD needs to develop new products, notably in the medical devices sector. Based on my recent research, it appears that there is a new generation of robotic surgical devices that could utilize a redefined Sensorpro technology platform. We urgently need to investigate this attractive product migration opportunity.

While Sophie disagreed with her brother on some points, she agreed with others:

"I think MCD must expand into the EU (where there is still only one competitor) and license our technology to a strategic partner, ideally with close ties to European robotics manufacturers. I completed my major MBA project for the European Robotics Association (EUnited Robotics) and developed a number of connections that could serve as a useful starting point to seek out a potential licensing partner."

John Marston recognized that the company required strategic guidance, and he summarized his needs and concerns as follows:

"First, I need to get a fix on my present corporate health, especially from a financial perspective. I also need to get a feel for the current value of the company (based on my expansion plans and resultant increased earnings) and how much I would have to give up in terms of share ownership to outside investors.

Both Ann and I also realize that we have a complex situation developing with the family and our transition plans.

I wonder if we need to consider some other transition options aside from an internal sale to family members. There may be an opportunity to attract external buyers (either strategic or financial) or perhaps identify a potential merger partner?

Another option might be to continue with a strong focus on our revenue growth trajectory and build our bench strength either internally (developing Henry and Sophie) or explore an external CEO hire to replace me?

Which would be the best option and how would such a move be accomplished?"

Next Steps

1. Based on the case and accompanying financial statements/ratio analysis, use the attached worksheets to complete an External and Internal size up of MCD along with a Strategy Review to determine the company's corporate health and the most advantageous strategic direction.

2. As part of this process, assess the best approach to handle succession and exit issues, based upon the case information.

3. Using current financial statements, derive a current valuation for the company.

4. Prepare a four-to-five- page Enterprise Review Summary (ERS) that summarizes the potential investment opportunity for an outside investor.

MARSTON CONTROL DEVICES LTD
Balance Sheet
As of September 30, 2020
(thousands of dollars)

	Sept. 2018	Sept. 2019	Sept. 2020
Current Assets:			
Cash	$ 8		
Accounts receivable	76	170	392
Inventory	108	205	431
Prepaid expenses	9	14	17
Total Current Assets	201	389	840
Capital Assets:			
Equipment, furniture, fixtures	224	258	273
Less accumulated depreciation	(27)	(42)	(56)
Net Capital Assets	197	216	217
Other Assets:			
Investment in subsidiary	55	55	55
Total Assets	**453**	**660**	**1,112**
Liabilities & Owners' Equity			
Current Liabilities:			
Bank loan operating	$ 54	$ 112	$ 235
Accounts payable	24	47	276
Accrued salaries & wages	16	10	27
Income tax payable	8	21	14
Total Current Liabilities	**102**	**190**	**552**
Long-term Debt:			
Notes payable	240	240	240
Shareholder loans	27	47	79

MARSTON CONTROL DEVICES LTD
Balance Sheet
As of September 30, 2020
(thousands of dollars)

	Sept. 2018	Sept. 2019	Sept. 2020
Total Debt	369	477	871
Shareholder's Equity:			
Capital stock	140	140	140
Retained earnings	(56)	43	101
Total Owners' Equity	84	183	241
Total Liabilities & Shareholders' Equity:	453	660	1,112

Notes to Balance Sheet:

- Investment in subsidiary relates to a $55,000 cash injection (2015) into Marston Voice Recognition Systems, a start-up company that has yet to generate revenues or positive earnings.

- Bank operating credit is authorized at $150,000 secured by a General Security Agreement (GSA) and an unlimited guarantee from Mr. and Mrs. Marston. The facility is margined to 75% eligible Accounts Receivable and 50% inventory at cost to a maximum $50,000.

- Note payable $240,000 relates to funds invested into the company by Marston's parents, on a interest only basis at prime + 4% with principal payments scheduled to commence in fiscal 2020 repaid over a five-year term ($48,000 annual payments).

- Shareholder loans increased by $32,000 in fiscal 2020 through a cash injection from Marston's brother-in-law. The balance of shareholder loans was injected by Marston and his wife when the company was founded.

MARSTON CONTROL DEVICES LTD
Income Statement
For the year ending September 30, 2020
(thousands of dollars)

	Sept. 2018		Sept. 2019		Sept. 2020	
Net Sales	$ 768		$ 1,554		$ 2,862	
Cost of Goods Sold:						
Opening inventory	59		108		205	
Plus purchases	515		1,061		2,201	
Less closing inventory	108		205		431	
Total Cost of Goods Sold	466		964		1,975	
Gross Profit	302	39%	590	38%	887	31%
Operating Expenses:						
Salaries & wages	173		322		604	
Rent	18		18		18	
Utilities	14		17		23	
Advertising	5		10		12	
Travel	17		11		16	
Insurance	6		7		8	
Telephone	12		14		22	
Bad debts	3		35		46	
Inventory write down					38	
Total Operating Expenses	248		$ 434		787	
EBITDA:	**54**		**156**		**100**	
Depreciation expense	14		15		14	
EBIT:	**40**		**141**		**86**	
Interest expense	16		18		20	

MARSTON CONTROL DEVICES LTD
Income Statement
For the year ending September 30, 2020
(thousands of dollars)

	Sept. 2018		Sept. 2019		Sept. 2020	
Income before taxes (EBT):	24		123		66	
Income tax expense	8		24		8	
Net income	$ 16	2%	$ 99	6%	$ 58	2%

Notes to Income Statement:
- Annual recurring capital expenditures are $20,000 per year.
- Property lease payments have been stable at $18,000 per year; however, the lease renewal is pending with lease rates expected to increase.

MARSTON CONTROL DEVICES LTD
Statement of Cash Flow
For the year ending September 30, 2020
(thousands of dollars))

	Sept. 2020
Cash Flow from Operations:	
Net income	$ 58
Add:	
Depreciation expense	14
Change in Accounts Receivable	(222)
Change in inventory	(226)
Change in prepaid expenses	(3)
Change in Accounts Payable	229
Change in accrued expenses	17
Change in taxes payable	(7)
Net Cash Provided by Operations	**(140)**
Cash flows from investing activities:	
Purchase of capital assets	(15)
Change in other capital assets	
Net Cash Used by Investments	**(15)**
Net cash from financing activities:	
Proceeds from long-term debt	
Proceeds from shareholder loans	32
Net Cash from Financing Activities	**32**
Net Cash Provided (Used)	**(123)**

MARSTON CONTROL DEVICES LTD
Key Financial Ratios – (thousands of dollars)

	Sept. 2018	Sept. 2019	Sept. 2020
Profitability/Cash Flow			
Gross profit margin (Gross Profit ÷ Sales)	39.00%	38.00%	31.00%
Net profit margin (Net Profit ÷ Sales)	2.08%	6.37%	2.03%
Return on equity (Net Profit ÷ Equity)	19.05%	54.00%	24.07%
EBITDA - Capex	$34	$136	$80
Liquidity			
Current ratio (Current Assets ÷ Current Liabilities)	1.97	2.05	1.52
Quick ratio (Current Assets - Inventory) ÷ (Current Liabilities)	0.91	0.97	0.74
Stability			
Debt to equity (Total Debt ÷ Total Equity)	4.39	2.61	3.61
Debt service coverage (EBITDA / Annual principal and interest payments)	3.4x	8.7x	5x
Total Debt / EBITDA	6.83	3.06	8.7
Efficiency			
A/R collection (Accounts Receivable ÷ Sales x 365)	36 days	40 days	50 days
Inventory turnover (COGS ÷ Inventory)	4.3x	4.7x	4.6x
A/P settlement (Accounts Payable ÷ Purchases x 365)	17 days	16 days	46 days
Growth			
Sales	119%	102%	84%
Net profit		518%	-41%
Assets		46%	68%
Equity		118%	32%

MARSTON CONTROL DEVICES LTD
Projected Income Statement - 5 years
(thousands of dollars)

	Sept. 2021	Sept. 2022	Sept. 2023	Sept. 2024	Sept. 2025
Sales	$ 3,500	$ 5,000	$ 8,000	$ 11,000	$ 15,000
GPM	32%	35%	36%	36%	36%
Gross profit	1,120	$ 1,750	$ 2,880	$ 3,960	$ 5,400
Operating expenses	1,290	$ 1,350	$ 2,160	$ 2,970	$ 4,050
EBIT	(170)	$ 400	$ 720	$ 990	$ 1,350
Net profit	(190)	$ 325	$ 525	$ 740	$ 1,080

Notes to Projected Income Statement:

- Marston's accountants have prepared detailed monthly income statements for the first two years, followed by quarterly statements for the remaining three years.
- Detailed assumptions will have been documented to support the projections and would obviously be available for review by the investor.
- Specific comments on the major income statement items follow:

Sales:

The trend reflects the decision to expand into Europe (licensing revenues), the development of the new medical control device platform, and ongoing production into the existing industrial automation market. Detailed breakdowns by product line and geographic area are provided to the investor via separate schedules.

Gross Profit Margin:

Improvement reflects impact of the higher margin medical device product line. Again, detailed assumptions on a product line basis would be provided to the investor.

Operating Expenses:

The larger percentage of operating expenses to sales in fiscal 2021 reflects non-recurring tooling and initial market/product development costs associated with the proposed expansion. Detailed schedules with supporting assumptions are provided.

MARSTON CONTROL DEVICES LTD
Projected Balance Sheet
As of September 30, 2021
(thousands of dollars)

	Sept. 2021
Current Assets:	
Cash	(45)
Accounts receivable	570
Inventory	400
Prepaid expenses	18
Total Current Assets	**843**
Long-term Assets	
Equipment, furniture, fixtures	473
Less accumulated depreciation	(85)
Net fixed assets	388
Other Assets	
Investment in subsidiary	100
Total Assets	**1,431**
Liabilities & Shareholder's Equity	
Current Liabilities:	
Accounts payable	356
Accrued salaries & wages	55
Income tax payable	
Total Current Liabilities	**411**
Long-term debt	
Notes payable	190
Shareholder loans	29
Total Debt	**630**

MARSTON CONTROL DEVICES LTD
Projected Balance Sheet
As of September 30, 2021
(thousands of dollars)

	Sept. 2021
Shareholder's Equity:	
Capital stock	890
Retained earnings	(89)
Total Owners' Equity	$ 801
Total Liabilities & Shareholder's Equity	$ 1,431

Notes to Projected Balance Sheet

Marston's planned allocation of the $750,000 new investment proceeds is summarized as follows:

- Additional fixed assets (new manufacturing equipment) - $200,000.
- Coverage of forecast fiscal 2016 operating losses - $190,000.
- Partial repayment shareholder loans and note payable - $100,000.
- Additional injection into subsidiary for voice recognition research - $50,000.
- Reduction in bank operating credit - $ 200,000.

Due Diligence by the Potential Investor

While the capital stock figure has increased by $750,000 (from $140,000 to $890,000), Marston's stated allocation of proceeds appears to be inconsistent.

The commentary within the case study indicates that the $750,000 proceeds are to be allocated towards R&D and the European market expansion costs.

While the new manufacturing equipment ($200,000) and fiscal 2021 operating losses ($190,000) are reasonable uses of the investment proceeds, the investor has to ask if the other proposed allocations of investment proceeds are appropriate.

- Bank operating credit repayment - $200,000: is the bank applying pressure to have its exposure reduced by lowering the amount of authorized credit available to the company?

- Is it reasonable to have Marston and his family withdraw $100,000 from the company by way of reductions in shareholder loans and notes payable?

- Is it realistic for Marston to redirect a portion of the investor proceeds ($50,000) into the dormant subsidiary company?

THE BUSINESS ENVIRONMENT

	Opportunities	Threats
Political		
Economic		
Societal		
Technological		

INDUSTRY COMPETITIVE CONDITIONS

	High	Neutral	Low
Threat of new entrants			
Bargaining power of customers			
Bargaining power of suppliers			
Threat of substitutes			
Intensity of competition			

Key success factors?

FINANCIAL SIZE UP

	Strengths	Weaknesses
Profitability and cash flow		
Liquidity		
Stability		
Efficiency		
Growth		

MARKETING SIZE UP

	Strengths	Weaknesses
ANALYSIS		
Product/Services review		
Market segment assessment		
Unmet customer needs?		
MARKET POSITIONING		
Competitor evaluation		
Pricing considerations		
Product mix issues		
Placement (Distribution)		
Promotion requirements		
People needs		
Partnering opportunities?		

OPERATIONS SIZE UP

	Strengths	Weaknesses
OPERATIONAL CAPABILITY		
Process management		
Facilities management		
Inventory management		
Quality management		
Risk management		
Project management		
LEGAL ISSUES		
USE OF TECHNOLOGY		

HUMAN RESOURCES SIZE UP

	Strengths	Weaknesses
HUMAN RESOURCE FUNCTION		
Recruitment and hiring		
Training and development		
Compensation, performance and incentives		
LEADERSHIP ISSUES		
Organizational structure		
Skills development		
Teams and teamwork		
Management capabilities		
Appreciative inquiry potential		
Mentoring opportunities		

TECHNOLOGY SIZE UP

	Strengths	Weaknesses
Technology concept and product		
Intellectual property issues		
Potential risk factors		
New technology assessment?		

STRATEGY REVIEW (1)

	Positives	Negatives
PRESENT COURSE (STATUS QUO) Define:		
TRANSITION PATHWAY ASSESSMENT Status quo?		
Internal buyers?		
External buyers?		
Grow, then sell?		
Harvest and wind down?		
ALTERNATIVE DIRECTIONS? 1)		
2)		
3)		
BEST OPTION:		
Rationale:		

STRATEGY REVIEW (2)

RESOURCES TO ACHIEVE GOALS?	
Finance	
Marketing/Sales	
Human resources	
Operations	
Management	
Innovation	
Best practices to adopt?	

STRATEGY REVIEW (3)

KEY ACTION ITEMS	
Finance	
Marketing	
Operations	
Human resources	
Technology	
Implementation steps?	
Responsibility?	
Time Frame?	

APPENDIX 1
EXTERNAL/INTERNAL SIZE UP & STRATEGY REVIEW

MARSTON CONTROL DEVICES LTD

THE BUSINESS ENVIRONMENT

	Opportunities	Threats
Political	European Community open borders Potential for government R&D grants and/or export assistance? Continued internationalization of industry segments	FDA regulations re. new medical devices product line? Adverse European regulatory environment re. new licensing arrangements?
Economic	Potential for post pandemic rebound to a stable economy, strong GDP growth? Is this industry sector reasonably recession – proof?	Over hang from a brutal, once-in-a-century global pandemic Potential for increased taxation to fund massive government deficits? Adverse exchange rate movements Canada vs. USA? Canada vs. Europe?
Societal	Increased investor awareness re. growth potential in the industrial automation and medical device sectors Health-care industry experiencing cost-containment issues with associated benefits to the medical devices industry segment.	
Technological	Continued opportunities to enhance Sensorpro technology platform B2B enhancement of buyer or seller relationships (procurement efficiencies)	Technological compatibility re. European product end users Increasing pace of technological change, with need for increased R&D resources. Potential ability of clients to turn into competitors—backward integration

INDUSTRY CONDITIONS

Competitive Landscape	High	Neutral	Low
Threat of new entrants • Unique technology platform should deter potential new entrants • High capital costs to set up manufacturing operation			X
Bargaining power of customers • Robot system manufacturers have the ability to produce competing products (backward integration)	X		
Bargaining power of suppliers • Supplier cartel pricing arrangements and inability to switch to alternate sources of supply	X		
Threat of substitutes • Clients are unlikely to switch to substitutes without incurring substantial costs			X
Intensity of competition • Industry segments growing rapidly • Larger competitors will have more financial and R&D muscle	X		

Key success factors
- High quality and proven reliability of the *Sensorpro* control device
- CEO's industry connections and reputation
- Unique technology protected via trade secrets

Blue Ocean potential?
- Given the competitive nature of the robotic control component industry sector, especially the industrial automation sub-sector, it would appear there is limited opportunity to apply the criteria of Focus, Divergence, or Compelling tag-line

FINANCIAL SIZE UP

	Strengths	Weaknesses
Profitability and cash flow	Positive profit (EBIT) and cash flow (EBITDA) performance over past three years Reasonable return on equity Modest annual capital expenditure requirements	Alarming drop in gross profit margin from 38% to 31%. Reason? Weakening EBIT/EBITDA performance over past year. Can the trend be reversed?
Liquidity	Positive current ratio, although a declining trend has been observed over past fiscal year - 2.05 to 1.52. Industry average?	Softening current and quick ratios, reflecting increased inventory levels. A/R composition and age? Inventory breakdown between raw materials, W.I.P., and finished products?
Stability	Comfortable debt service coverage (5x) Shareholder loans have increased—future source of additional equity? Earnings fully invested—no dividends paid out If Notes payable and shareholder loans are postponed, Debt:Equity ratio improves to 0.99:1	High (unfavourable) total debt: EBITDA ratio—8.7 years to retire debt from present annual cash flow Investment in subsidiary—current financial statements available? Strength? Weakening debt:Equity ratio, increasing from 2.61 to 3.61:1
Efficiency	Lengthened A/P settlement—if agreed by suppliers, then OK—a source of cash	Lengthening A/R collection (36 to 50 days over past two years). Reason? While inventory turnover has been stable, inventory levels have doubled over the past year—allied with inventory write down expense, this is a significant *red flashing light*.
Growth	Significant sales growth over past three years	Weakening earnings growth (-40%) Reason? Asset and debt growth exceed growth in equity.

MARKETING SIZE UP

	Strengths	Weaknesses
MARKET ANALYSIS		No formal review of product portfolio has taken place.
Product/Services review		
Market segment assessment		A detailed segmentation analysis for existing and proposed new markets is required
Unmet customer needs?	Appears to meet USA robot manufacturer's need for flexibility and productivity	
MARKET POSITIONING		
Competitor evaluation	Potential access to new and diverse markets?	Increasing competition from Japan + potential client backward integration?
Pricing considerations	Seen as a price leader due to demonstrated quality Apparent high quality	Unlikely to maintain present premium price as competition intensifies
Product mix issues	Reasonable delivery track record	Continued vulnerability to suppliers Absence of warranties Does not have knowledge of existing competitor product lines
Placement (Distribution)	Direct delivery to robot manufacturers (no middle link to slow down the process) Sales successes through trade shows and industry contacts—relatively low cost	
Promotion requirements		Outdated sales catalogue Previous media problems
People needs		No formal sales force No sales & marketing management function
Partnering opportunities?		Potential licensee in E.U but no formal investigation done yet

OPERATIONS SIZE UP

	Strengths	Weaknesses
OPERATIONAL CAPABILITY		
Process management	Streamlined, relatively simple production process (job shop) Relatively modern equipment Custom orders, no speculative production runs	Not ISO 9000 certified
Facilities management	Local labour force, quality and reliability appear OK Reasonable access to U.S. markets	Questionable ability to expand Imminent lease expiry
Inventory management		Inventory write-downs
Quality management		Absence of formal quality assurance and quality control procedures. Unaware of Six Sigma process
Risk management		Key person insurance in place? Business loan insurance in place? Business interruption insurance in place?
Project management		No formal PM process in place
Legal issues	Corporation with limited liability and limited recourse to the shareholders	Potential minority shareholding for brother-in-law needs to be documented
Use of technology	Appears to use latest CAD/CAM processes	Manufacturing equipment obsolescence issues? Absence of proper MIS (Management Information Systems) No knowledge or apparent interest in B2B benefits re. procurement and sales.

HUMAN RESOURCES SIZE UP

	Strengths	Weaknesses
H-R FUNCTION		
Recruitment and hiring	Non-unionized workforce	Potential for employee turnover (casual versus full-time) and resultant commitment issues
Training and development		Lack of ongoing training and development programs
Compensation, performance and incentives	Relatively simple compensation programs—casual wages and hiring process	No profit-sharing plans or provision for key employee minority share options No enhanced compensation arrangements for brother-in-law (key support person)
LEADERSHIP ISSUES		
Organizational structure	Back-up management support from brother-in-law	Too flat an organizational structure—Marston is spread too thin
Skills development	Strong client credibility (NASA background)	Questionable professional support—legal and accounting
Teams and teamwork		Inflexible—iron hand, management by crisis allied with weak bank relationship Unable to delegate
Management capabilities	Hands on style—knows all aspects of the business	
Appreciative inquiry potential		Nominal—too much focus on crisis management
Mentoring opportunities		No Board of Directors or Advisors Lack of succession plan

TECHNOLOGY SIZE UP

	Strengths	Weaknesses
Technology concept and product	Existing technology platform has unique design and cost features with a proven manufacturing track record Is developing a product migration strategy—Medical Control Devices that will have higher functionality and higher price	Needs a comprehensive technology development plan for the new Medical Control Device product line
Intellectual property issues	Trade secret strategy (non-disclosure) has minimized IP costs Proposed European licensing arrangements will allow Marston to test and exploit new market with the selected licensee unlikely to become a future competitor	No patent protection No IP plan Selection process of European licensee—criteria and due diligence? Time frame to put in place? Risk of competitors attempting to re-engineer product
Potential risk factors		Limited provision for R&D expenditures to date Potential emergence of a superior technology? Need to get a fix on duration of product life cycles—existing and proposed new product lines Potential to lose key employees to competitors?
New technology assessment?		Very preliminary work started on the new medical device product–no real sense of the R&D requirements yet.

STRATEGY REVIEW (1)

	Positives	Negatives
PRESENT COURSE (STATUS QUO)		
Manufacturer of control devices for the USA industrial automation sector	Potential for government R&D grants and/or export assistance? Continued internationalization of industry segments. Additional enhancement of Sensorpro technology platform. Further leverage industry connections and reputation.	Increasing pace of technological change, with need for increased R&D resources. Potential ability of clients to turn into competitors—backward integration. Technology protected by trade secrets but vulnerable to patent infringement suits?
TRANSITION PATHWAY ASSESSMENT		
Status quo?	Allows focus on revenue growth opportunities?	Not addressing root causes of company challenges—namely managerial succession.
Internal buyers?	Family members (Henry and Sophie) apparently willing and able to assume additional responsibility	Do the second generation have the managerial capacity and capability to assume control?
External buyers?	Could be a good strategic or financial fit with an external buyer or perhaps a merger as an interim step?	Hiring a M&A specialist firm to identify potential buyers would be a long and costly process
Grow, then sell?	Build internal bench strength via second generation ownership or hire new CEO to replace Marston?	Ability of the second generation to meet growth targets or cultural fit and goal alignment of CEO hired gun?
Harvest and wind down?	Strive for 3-4 years of optimized dividends to enhance Marston family personal wealth and then commence orderly wind down if no apparent external buyers have been located.	Does not maximize MCD's enterprise value + missed opportunities for second generation ownership?

	Positives	Negatives
ALTERNATIVE DIRECTIONS?		
1) Expand industrial automation into EU via license agreement	Expand into a new market with a proven product	At this stage, no research or due diligence has been completed with regard to a potential EU partner Technological compatibility re. European product end-users?
2) Diversify into medical devices sector with new product line	Increased investor awareness re. growth potential in the medical device sector	FDA regulations re. new medical devices product line?
3) Combine both EU and medical device expansions	Enjoy the benefit of both product and market expansion revenue opportunities	Considerable research and development required. Launching a too aggressive expansion without adequate financial, managerial, and operational resources

BEST DIRECTION

Stay the course but investigate the product and market expansion options via detailed market assessment studies, which would be completed by Henry and Sophie (as part of a gradual immersion into the management ranks of the business).

Rationale

This appears to be the wisest course of action, given the limited resources available to the company at this point in time.

MCD is a successful player in the industry automation sector with exciting expansion potential that has to be carefully researched. Increased financing or additional equity, on an incremental basis, could be attracted to fund the costs associated with the assessment of the new market and or product opportunities.

STRATEGY REVIEW (2)

RESOURCES TO ACHIEVE GOALS?	
Finance	Assess need for increased bank credit and external funding to launch future product/market expansions.
Marketing/Sales	Consider need for an external consultant to complete market development plans.
Human resources	Assess the need for an outsourced CFO to tighten financial reporting and controls.
Operations	Evaluate cost of new CAD system and office network.
Management	Need to explore potential for the second generation to enter the business, on a gradual and incremental basis, in order to assess their managerial capability and capacity.
Innovation	There will be an ongoing need to invest in R&D resources, especially if the medical devices option is explored.
Best Practices to adopt?	Investigate potential for local university grad students to work on the new medical device applied research relative to product design and market segmentation (under guidance of in-coming second generation). Investigate joining TEC (Vistage) to benefit from external mentoring. Assess need for Six Sigma to enhance production quality and delivery process.

STRATEGY REVIEW (3)

Key Action Items	
Finance	Provide bank with Enterprise Review Summary to obtain additional financing and/or new equity to fund product/market expansion research and due diligence.
	Provide A/R, A/P, and inventory listings along with interim financial statements to bank in order to negotiate renewal and possible increase of operating line.
	Analyze GPM (gross profit margin) performance and isolate factors causing decline.
	Analyze inventory position—the negative decreasing turnover trend and higher year-end inventory levels are cause for concern, especially as orders are typically on a custom basis.
Marketing	Prepare a formal marketing plan that will include a segmentation of the three target markets: <ul><li>Existing Industrial</li><li>New European Industrial</li><li>New Medical Devices</li></ul> Complete assessment of competitors (existing and potential) in each segment.
Operations	Complete ISO 9000 certification and develop quality assurance/control procedures.
	Negotiate and document formal minority shareholder agreement with brother-in-law.
	Arrange key person and business interruption insurance through insurance broker.
	Engage a seasoned commercial realtor to research prevailing lease rates and other available production space that would accommodate forecast growth.
Human resources	Negotiate lease renewal with expansion option or relocate.
	Document succession plans with lawyer/accountant in conjunction with key person insurance.
	Establish a Board of Advisors with members selected for their ability to add value to the expansion plans and investment-raising initiatives.
	Consider adding senior finance and sales/marketing positions to the company once the investment round has been completed.
Technology	Establish a technology development plan for the new medical devices control system (brother-in-law to complete).
	Have lawyer complete I.P plan and research cost and logistics of patent protection for the new product line.
	Investigate potential EU licensee selection process through industry association contacts.
Implementation steps?	The priority, responsibility, and timing to implement the above action items would be allocated between John Marston and Mike Smith.

APPENDIX 2
CURRENT COMPANY VALUATION

MARSTON CONTROL DEVICES LTD

CURRENT COMPANY VALUATION - MCD

Two approaches are appropriate, based on the financial information provided:

Asset Valuation ($ '000)

Modified book value approach, based on fiscal 2020 balance sheet:

Total Assets less any intangible assets (investment in subsidiary)

$1,112 - $55 = $1,057

less:

Total debt (excluding shareholder loans)

$871 - $79 = $792

$1,057 - $792 = $265 book value

Earnings Valuation ($ '000)

Fiscal 2020 EBIT = $86 (Average for the three-year period = $ 89)

Cap rate 25% (4x multiple), based on subjective review of value factors

No apparent surplus assets (term deposits, etc.)

Estimated value	$86 x 4	= **$344 earnings-based value**
Reconciliation	Asset approach	$265
	Earnings approach	$344

Issues to consider

- A market-based valuation is not appropriate due to MCD's relatively small size and the absence of meaningful price/earnings multiples.

- A cash flow valuation would involve assumptions as to future annual cash flows and eventual company sale proceeds at some future date. These future cash flows would then be discounted back to a present value using an arbitrary discount rate. A number of these variables may be difficult to substantiate.

- The current company value appears to lie in the $325,000 + range. Marston and his accountant could argue that:

    - the subsidiary investment does indeed have a tangible value (based on R&D completed to date)

    and

    - the cap rate at 25% is unduly conservative - a 20% rate (5x multiple) would yield a higher value ($430,000 range).

- If Marston was attempting to sell the company *as is*, the final result would be driven by negotiations between buyer and seller and their respective motivations.

- The adverse financial trends observed in our size up would require detailed explanation to the potential investor. Marston would have to make a compelling case that the company does, indeed, have solid future prospects.

APPENDIX 3
ENTERPRISE REVIEW SUMMARY

MARSTON CONTROL DEVICES LTD

ENTERPRISE REVIEW SUMMARY—MCD

The Opportunity

Marston Control Devices Ltd. (MCD) was founded by John Marston in 2005 to design, manufacture, and market a specialized control component (*Sensorpro*) that is installed on a wide variety of industrial robots.

Over the past 15 years, MCD has achieved significant sales growth, notably in the USA robot component marketplace. The company has built a strong reputation for product quality and durability; at the same time, it has maintained a price leadership position despite increased foreign competition.

Having achieved an established niche in the industrial automation arena, MCD is now embarking on an aggressive diversification strategy. A European licensing partner is being identified to take the *Sensorpro* product line into the European robot component market. At the same time, a new control device product is being developed for the robotics controls sector within the medical devices industry.

The company owners (John and Ann Marston) are seeking a capital injection of $750,000 from outside investors to assist with the company's expansion and diversification strategy.

Technology

The technology platform was developed by John Marston after a successful assignment as project manager for the Canadarm NASA project.

The *Sensorpro* units are assembled via a job shop process that utilizes state-of-the-art CAD/CAM production techniques. The product's unique design and manufacturing techniques have eliminated the need for expensive patent protection, especially as software source codes are closely controlled.

Recent research and development have led to the development of a new medical robotics control component, which is now at the engineering prototype stage. Pilot production runs and user evaluations are scheduled within the next six months prior to a formal product launch into the medical devices industry.

Products

The original *Sensorpro* control device has undergone various refinements (improved durability and functionality) over the past three years and has received strong buyer acceptance in the industrial automation marketplace.

Recognizing increased competitive pressure from offshore manufacturers, the company has formulated a carefully researched product migration strategy—the development of a new control component targeted at the medical devices industry. A new generation of robotics surgical devices (instruments, clamps, and limb-positioning tools) are being developed that will utilize a redefined *Sensorpro* technology platform.

Development of this new control component will add improved functionality to the robotics arms that allow surgeons to view, cut, clamp, and suture, using remote joystick controllers away from the operating table.

Internet-initiated and voice-activated robotics arms in the operating room are now on the radar screen with huge growth potential associated with these emerging technologies.

Markets

The first generation of *Sensorpro* units have been successfully sold to robot manufacturers for installation onto their industrial robots. The manufacturers, in turn, sell their product to large industrial automation systems companies who develop productivity manufacturing solutions for multinational companies like Celestica (Canada) and Solectron and Flextronics (USA).

There are only eight firms—MCD, three in Japan, three in the United States, and one in Europe that produce similar control devices, although the number of competitors is expected to increase in the near term.

Significant sales growth has occurred in the USA as the industrial automation sector continues to develop a wide spectrum of applications, especially in the semiconductor and fiber optic market segments.

While the North American industrial automation market is expected to grow, intensifying competition has led to our decision to expand into two new markets:

- Existing *Sensorpro* product – expansion into the European market is now appropriate, given the limited competition. A strategic partner is being identified who will be provided with a license to produce the *Sensorpro* technology platform and then target selected European robotics manufacturers.

- A new control component for the medical devices industry is being developed, targeted at the new generation of medical robotics systems that are used in hospital operating rooms.

Initial customer evaluation will take place in Ontario, Canada, followed by market development across North America.

E-commerce sales and procurement opportunities will be exploited via affiliation with a major B2B service provider.

MANAGEMENT

Company operations are closely supervised by John Marston and his brother-in-law, Mike Smith. Both have degrees in Computer Engineering. Marston has 20+ years in the robotics industry and gained international recognition and prestige through his successful project management career in NASA.

Marston is actively involved in every aspect of the business, including new research and development initiatives and supervision of daily operations.

MCD is 80% owned by Marston and his wife with the 20% balance owned by Smith.

INVESTMENT AND PAYBACK

The $750,000 investment proceeds will be utilized to expedite the R&D associated with the medical control component together with marketing costs related to the European expansion program. The proceeds are required by December 31, 2020

The investor can either take equity through a share issue or secure proceeds via a convertible debenture.

Projected Income Statements - 5 years*

(thousands of dollars)

	Sept. 2021	Sept. 2022	Sept. 2023	Sept. 2024	Sept. 2025
Sales	$ 3,500	$ 5,000	$ 8,000	$ 11,000	$ 15,000
GPM	32%	35%	36%	36%	36%
Gross profit	$ 1,120	$ 1,750	$ 2,880	$ 3,960	$ 5,400
Operating expenses	$ 1,290	$ 1,350	$ 2,160	$ 2,970	$ 4,050
EBIT	$ (170)	$ 400	$ 720	$ 990	$ 1,350
Net profit	$ (190)	$ 325	$ 525	$ 740	$ 1,080

* Detailed revenue and expense projections are available for review by the investor as part of their due diligence process.

Exit Strategy

Given the forecast growth in revenues and earnings in the next five years, there will be attractive exit opportunities, either through an IPO, or a combination of dividends and share buyback. Annualized ROI in the 25-30% range is anticipated.

APPENDIX 4
PRELIMINARY ESTIMATE OF FUTURE VALUE FROM AN INVESTOR'S PERSPECTIVE

MARSTON CONTROL DEVICES LTD

The following approach is suggested, based upon the projected five-year income statements ($ thousands) that were provided in the case.

Year-five EBIT = $1,350

Industry earnings multiple assumed: five times

Assume investor's desired ROI = 30% compounded annually over five years

Calculations

MCD future value in year five	$1,350 x 5	= $6,750
Future value investor's cash injection $750 @ 30% over five years* *($750 x (1+ 30)$_5$)		= $2,785
Equity interest	$2,785	
	$6,750	= 41%

Issues to consider

- Given all the assumptions, one could be forgiven for asking, "is this voodoo science?"
- Negotiations would likely take place in the 45% (minority interest) to 55% (majority interest) range.
- Voting share allocations have to be considered as the investor would want significant voting rights.
- The investor's $750,000 cash injection could be set up on a *quasi debt* basis via a convertible debenture. This is a debt instrument that allows the holder to appoint a receiver in the event of default and convert the debenture to shares (common or preferred) at some predetermined date.
- While this *equity stake* calculation is *back of the envelope* in its relative lack of complexity, it does provide a basis for opening negotiations that would eventually be supported by more formal valuation engagements completed by valuation professionals.

Business Diagnostics Overview

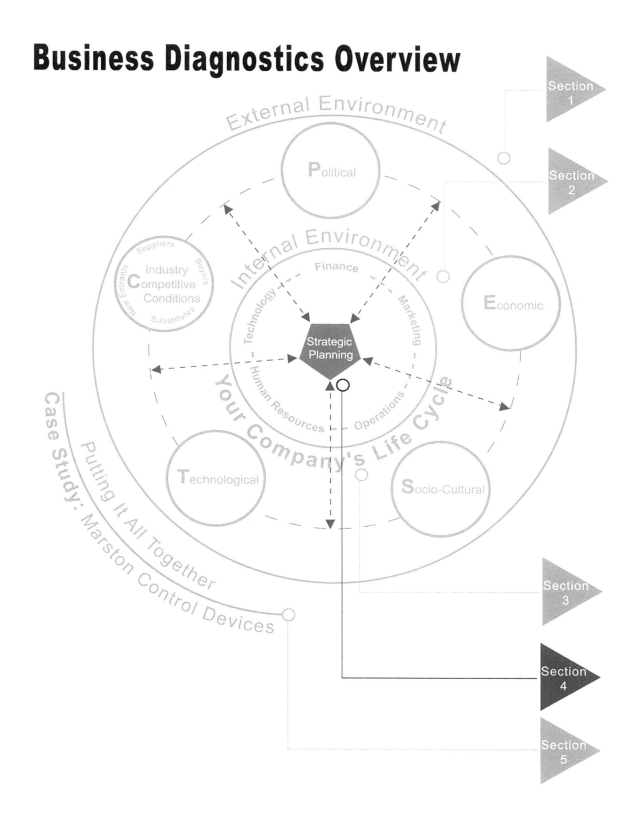

Printed in Canada